Islam

Islam

from the Prophet Muhammad to the Capture of Constantinople

Edited and translated by
BERNARD LEWIS

II: Religion and Society

New York Oxford
OXFORD UNIVERSITY PRESS
1987

Oxford University Press

Oxford New York Toronto
Delhi Bombay Calcutta Madras Karachi
Petaling Jaya Singapore Hong Kong Tokyo
Nairobi Dar es Salaam Cape Town
Melbourne Auckland

and associated companies in
Beirut Berlin Ibadan Nicosia

First published in 1974 by Harper and Row

This paperback edition published in 1987 by Oxford University Press, Inc.

Library of Congress Cataloging-in-Publication Data

Islam : from the Prophet Muhammed to the capture of
Constantinople.

Reprint. Originally published : New York : Harper &
Row, 1974. (Documentary history of Western civilization).
Includes bibliographies and indexes.
Contents: 1. Politics and war—2. Religion and
society.
1. Civilization, Islamic—Sources. I. Lewis, Bernard.
DS36.855.I77 1987 909'.097671 86-31104
ISBN-13 978-0-19-505088-2
ISBN 0-19-505088-6 (v. 2)

10 9
Printed in the United States of America

These stories may be far from history, where one usually reads that such and such a king sent such and such a general to such and such a war, and that on such and such a day they made war or peace, and that this one defeated that one, or that one this one, and then proceeded somewhere. But I write what is worthy to be recorded.

Bayhaqī, *Tārīkh*

Contents

Part II. Heresy and Revolt

Part IV. The Economy

Part V. Poets, Scholars, and Physicians

Part VI. Race, Creed, and Condition of Servitude

Preface

The following pages contain a selection, in English translation, from the original sources for the history of Islam in the Middle Ages. The excerpts have been arranged in two volumes. The first is concerned with politics and war and consists, in part, of narratives of events and, in part, of theoretical and descriptive statements on these two themes. In the second volume attention is transferred from the state to society and is focused on the religious, cultural, and social life of the medieval Muslim world. With so vast a subject, comprehensive coverage is clearly impossible. In choosing passages for translation, I have tried to give representative examples of the different periods and regions with which the work is concerned and of the different kinds of evidence on which it is based. Some stress, however, has been laid on the central lands of Islam and on the central, formative period.

It was my original intention to conform to the usual pattern and compile this book, in the main, from material already translated. I soon found myself obliged to abandon this plan. For one thing, reliance on the sources which by accident or caprice have become available in English would have produced a very unbalanced picture; for another, the existing translations vary unacceptably in quality and manner. It therefore seemed best to start afresh. All the passages in these two volumes have been newly translated by the editor, most of them for the first time into English. The majority are from Arabic; smaller numbers are from Persian and Turkish, and two are from Hebrew.

My thanks are due to Professor Claude Cahen for permission to reproduce the illustrations in volume I, pages 220-222, first published by him; to Professor S. D. Goitein for permission to use two Geniza documents edited by him and for advice on translating them; and to Professor E. Kedourie and Dr. H. M. Rabie, for reading and commenting on parts of my manuscript. I am most grateful to them for the trouble they took and the help they gave. I should also like to express my thanks to Mr. and Mrs. R. M. Burrell for reading and correcting a set of proofs.

B.L.

Introduction

The theme of this work is the history of Islam from the advent of the Prophet Muḥammad to the capture of Constantinople by Sultan Meḥmed, the Conqueror. It is concerned with a period that extends from the beginning of the seventh century to 1453; with a region that expands from Western Arabia to embrace the Middle East and North Africa, as well as parts of Asia, of tropical Africa, and southern and eastern Europe; with peoples and states which, amid many diversities, shared a common acceptance of the faith and law of Islam and professed to live by them, and, finally, with the civilization which they created.

Classical Islamic civilization is expressed in three major languages, the first of which is Arabic. It was among the Arabs of the Ḥijāz that Muḥammad was born, lived, and died, and in their language that his sacred book was written. Under his successors, the Caliphs, a great wave of Arab conquest and migration carried his faith and his book out of Arabia into the fertile crescent, eastward across Iran to the borders of India and China, and westward across Egypt and North Africa to Sicily and Spain. In the vast empire which they founded, Arabic was, for a long time, the language not only of religion, but also of government, commerce, and culture.

Most of the peoples conquered by the Arabs forgot their previous history and identity and were merged into Arabic-speaking Islam. Not all, however; the Persians, sustained both by recent memories of imperial greatness and by current awareness of their immense contribution to Islamic civilization, recovered and reasserted their separate identity. Arabic remained a scriptural and classical language in Iran, which had become a profoundly Islamic country, but from the eleventh century onward, the principal medium of expression was a new form of Persian—written in the Arabic script, full of Arabic loanwords, yet unmistakably Persian, not Arabic. The Persian cultural awakening was helped by a political revival in Iran and by the emergence of Persian dynasties and courts which used and fostered the new language. Persian became the second classical language of Islam; Persian influence was dominant in the eastern lands and powerful even in the western lands of the Islamic Caliphate.

The Persian renaissance forms a kind of overlapping interlude between the decline of the Arabs and the rise of the Turks. Medieval Islamic history begins with the irruption into the Middle East of Arab invaders from the south; it ends with the triumph of another group of newcomers, the steppe peoples from the north. The Turks, after their conversion to Islam, established an ascendancy which lasted a thousand years; they created new patterns of government and society and made Turkish the third major language of Islamic civilization.

They also brought to Islam, at a time of great weakness, the strength to survive new and terrible dangers that threatened to overwhelm it and to resist the enemies advancing from both east and west. It was Turkish rulers and armies that halted the Mongol invaders, saving Egypt and all western Islam from their rule; it was Turks again who took over the leadership of Islam in its millennial struggle with Christian Europe.

From its birth the Islamic religion was the chief contender with Christianity for the hearts of men; Islamic civilization was the nearest neighbor and deadliest rival of European Christendom. Between the two there was almost permanent conflict. Islam arose outside the Christian world, in pagan Arabia, and much of its expansion was among non-Christians. A major part, perhaps the most important part, of the victories of Islam were at Christian expense. The Arab warriors brought their religion and their dominion to the old Christian lands of the Levant and North Africa and even to Sicily, Spain, and parts of southern Italy and France, establishing an Islamic supremacy in most of the former Roman-Mediterranean world. For a while Arab Islam seemed to threaten the very existence of Christian Europe.

The advance of the Arabs in France and Italy was halted and reversed, and during the eleventh century Western Christendom launched a great counterattack which recovered Sicily and much of Spain and culminated in the arrival of the Crusaders in Syria and Palestine. Here the Crusaders encountered the new champions of Islam—the Turks—who by now governed most of the Middle East and had conquered even the great Byzantine stronghold of Anatolia. The Turks and their associates[1] held and eventually threw back the Christian invaders and began a new advance which once again

[1] Saladin, the most famous opponent of the Crusaders, was a Kurd, not a Turk. The first and last leaders of the countercrusade were all Turks, however, and even Saladin's dynasty relied largely on Turkish forces and was rapidly Turkicized.

brought Islam into Europe—this time at the eastern end and in a Turkish form. It was not until much later that the powers of Europe were able to launch a counterattack into the lands of Islam and establish European imperial domination in old Islamic territories, in Central Asia, North Africa, and finally in some of the heartlands of the Middle East.

During the centuries of confrontation and conflict, Muslims and Christians alike were more conscious of their differences than of their similarities. Yet these similarities are very great, for the two religions and the two cultures had much in common: Both shared the inheritance of the ancient civilizations of the Middle East; both had adopted the Jewish religious tradition of ethical monotheism, prophetic mission, and revelation preserved in scripture; both were disciples of Greek thought and science and heirs, in different ways, of the societies and institutions that had grown up in the Middle East and around the Mediterranean under the rule of Alexander, his successors, and the Romans. However much Christians and Muslims may have argued with one another, the very fact that they were able to do so, using a common logic and common concepts, shows the degree of kinship that existed between them. This becomes more apparent when either is compared with the remoter civilizations of Asia, in China and India. Muslims and Christians could dispute the relative merits of the Qur'ān and the Bible and the missions of Muḥammad and Christ, for both shared a common universe of discourse. Neither could have conducted a meaningful dialogue with a Hindu or a Confucian.

These inherent resemblances were confirmed and extended by their long cohabitation across the whole length of the Mediterranean world and by the mutual influences between them.

An appreciation of the affinities between Christianity and Islam, however, should not lead us to overlook the very real differences which divide them or to try and describe Islam by false analogies. Muḥammad is not the Muslim Christ, the Qur'ān is not the Muslim Bible, the mosque is not the Muslim church. One might add that Friday is not the Muslim sabbath, the ulema are not the Muslim clergy, and Sunnism is not the Muslim orthodoxy. These popular analogies, though they obviously contain a certain element of truth, nevertheless distort and conceal more than they explain.

Muḥammad, like Jesus, was the founder of a great world religion. Unlike Jesus, he achieved worldly success in his own lifetime. At first he too, like other prophets, was a humble, persecuted teacher and preacher. But instead of martyrdom he attained power. In Mecca he had been a proscribed critic of the existing order; in Medina he created his own order. As head of the *umma*, the community of his converts and adherents, he governed, dispensed justice, collected taxes, and made peace and war. In Mecca he preached; in Medina he practiced. The scope of his revelation was extended from religious and moral principles to a wide range of mundane matters; its form changed from precept to law. This change is clearly reflected in the Qur'ān.

The Qur'ān may be called the Muslim scripture; it cannot be called the Muslim Bible. For Muslims it is a single book, in the most literal sense the word of God, dictated to the Prophet by the angel Gabriel. Most historians consider it an authentic contemporary record of the teaching and activities of Muḥammad, dating from his lifetime in a recension compiled very shortly after his death. Unlike the Old and New Testaments, it is not a collection of texts assembled from works written over a long period of time; it is the work of a single author, arising from a single career.[2] The development from the earlier Meccan chapters to the later Medinan chapters illustrates very clearly the change in the Prophet's status and preoccupations.

Islam was thus involved with political power from the start. Medina was a state and, as it turned out, the nucleus of an empire with the Prophet as its first magistrate. The true and sole sovereign in the Muslim view was God, from whose mandate the Prophet derived his authority and whose will, made known by revelation, was the sole source of law. The *umma* thus expressed from its inception the fusion of politics and religion characteristic of the later Islamic states. The founder of Christianity had enjoined his followers to "render unto Caesar the things which are Caesar's, and unto God the things which are God's," and three centuries of suffering and persecution were to pass before Christianity captured the Roman empire, with the conversion of the Roman emperor Constantine, and in a sense was captured by it. Muḥammad was his own Constantine and founded his own empire. The dichotomy of *regnum* and *sacerdotium*, deeply rooted in Western Christendom, does not exist in Islam, and, indeed, such pairs of words as spiritual and temporal, lay and ecclesiastical, and religious and secular have no equivalents in the classical languages of the Muslim peoples.

[2] Most Western scholars have accepted the Qur'ān as historically authentic, in the sense of preserving what was promulgated by Muḥammad during his lifetime. Some modern scholars, however, chiefly in the Soviet Union, have argued that the text was not merely edited but actually composed under the Caliphs.

Under Muhammad's successors, the Caliphs, the community of Medina was transformed by conquest into a vast empire, and Muhammad's Arab creed became a world religion. In the experience of the first Muslims, religious truth and political power were inextricably linked: the first sanctified the second; the second confirmed and sustained the first. This experience gave rise to a firm belief in God's concern with politics and in the manifestation of God's favor by success—that is, by the victory and dominion in this world of those who obeyed His law.

In the Islamic world, therefore, there could be no conflict between Pope and Emperor, for the powers which these two represented were one and the same. The Caliph was at once head of the state, the community, and the faith. In the sense of a building, a place of daily and weekly public worship, the mosque is the equivalent of the church; but in the sense of an institution, an organized corporate body, the church has no equivalent in Islam, for the institution over which the Caliph presided was church and state at once.

For the same reason, Islam has no clergy and no orthodoxy in the Christian sense. There is no pope, no bishops or bishoprics, no hierarchy, and no councils or synods to determine and impose an approved creed and to condemn deviations from it as heterodoxy. Such authorities were never constituted in Islam, and the few attempts to do so failed utterly. The ulema are men of religious learning, not priests; they receive no ordination, have no parishes, and perform no sacraments. The nearest Islamic equivalent to orthodoxy is the *Sunna,* the custom and practice of the Prophet, his Companions, and his immediate successors, as preserved by the historic memory of the community as a whole. The basic Muslim creed is that God is one and Muḥammad is His prophet, and no one who rejects either of these propositions can be considered a Muslim. Beyond that, loyalty to Islam is expressed, first and foremost, not by correct belief but by correct behavior—that is, by acceptance of the norms and patterns of Islamic life, loyalty to the Islamic community, and obedience to the head of the Islamic state. Consequently, it is deviation from custom, withdrawal from the community, and disobedience to authority, rather than incorrect belief, which constitute the nearest Islamic equivalents of heresy. What a man believes, beyond the basic minimum, is his own concern. Authority is concerned only with his behavior, and God alone can judge a man's sincerity.

Because of this, knowledge of the past was from the start of immense, indeed, of transcendent, importance for Muslims. The mission of the Prophet was itself an event in history; its circumstances and meaning could be known to later generations of believers only through memory and record—through the work of preservation, transmission, and explanation of the first Muslim historians. The *Sunna,* too, was essentially historical. The doctrine of consensus, according to which divine guidance passed to the Muslim community as a whole after the death of the Prophet, gave a religious significance to the acts and experiences of that community, in which could be seen the revelation of God's will on earth. God, it was believed, would not allow His community to fall into sin. What the community as a whole accepted and did was right and was an expression of God's purpose. *Sunna* was defined by consensus, and past consensus was known from tradition. The study of tradition was therefore necessary for theology and holy law—that is, for salvation.

Interest in the past soon became a distinguishing characteristic of Muslim civilization. Since early times Muslim entities—states, dynasties, cities, even professions—have been conscious of their place in history; they have been interested in the deeds of those who went before them and anxious to record their own for those who came after. Almost every dynasty that ruled in Muslim lands has left annals or chronicles of some kind; in many countries, including some of high civilization, serious historical writing begins with the coming of Islam.

The earliest historical record of Islam is, of course, the Qur'ān itself. For Muslims this is a work of religion—that is, scripture, not history. However, it also provides important historical information concerning the career of the Prophet and the community which he founded. The beginnings of Islamic historical writing, in the proper sense, must be sought in the collections of *ḥadīth,* that is, traditions purporting to preserve the decisions, actions, and utterances of the Prophet. According to Muslim belief, the Prophet was the inspired bearer of God's commands, not only when he was repeating the divine text dictated to him, but also in everything that he said and did. And so in addition to the Qur'ān (the word of God), the *ḥadīths* (the word of the Prophet) came to be treated as a second source of revelation.

There was, however, an important difference between the two. The Qur'ān was edited and promulgated in a standard text not long after Muḥammad's death. Regarded as of divine authorship, it could not be increased or diminished in any way; its authenticity, textual accuracy, and authority were beyond question. *Ḥadīth,* on the other hand, was a vast and heterogeneous assemblage of individual traditions, each relating some detail of the precept and practice of the Prophet and varying greatly in provenance, content, and plausibility.

Much of it was of dubious origin. For three generations or more it was orally transmitted—and this during a period of rapid change, and of bitter conflicts and rivalries. Whether to justify an action or to promote a cause, there could be no better argument than to adduce a *ḥadīth* citing a Prophetic precedent. Even in medieval times Muslim jurists were well aware of the problems of distortion and fabrication, and of the innumerable *ḥadīths* in circulation, they chose a more limited number; these came to be accepted as authentic and constitute, after the Qur'ān, the main base of Muslim law and doctrine. Modern critical scholarship has dismissed many of these as spurious and has called most of the remainder into doubt. But, although a fabricated *ḥadīth* tells us nothing about the Prophet, it may tell us a great deal about the time, circumstances, and purpose of its fabrication.

Certain categories of *ḥadīths* are of particular interest to the historian—for example, the numerous polemic *ḥadīths* directed against one tribe, faction, or sect, in the interest of another. Some, in the form of direct prophecy of future events, are palpable fakes. Others are clever fabrications in which Muḥammad is alleged to say something about events in his own time; these are not overtly prophetic but nevertheless have a direct bearing on subsequent conflicts.

A second important group are legal traditions which state a principle or establish a precedent regarded as legally binding. Some of these may be genuine, but a large proportion represent the untheoretical response of early Islamic rulers and governors to immediate needs. Such *ḥadīths* include principles of Roman and other legal systems encountered in the conquered provinces and ad hoc decisions based on usage, political or administrative necessity, or simple common sense.

Another class of *ḥadīths,* also of great interest, consists of pronouncements, admonitory rather than prescriptive, on what were obviously matters of current controversy and concern. One such theme is racial conflict. There are traditions which condemn racial hostility or arrogance; there are also traditions which express them by condemning or extolling individual races.

Another matter of concern was inflation. There is, for example, a small group of traditions in which the Prophet is quoted as saying that "Only God can fix prices." It is obvious that the Prophet said no such thing, for such a question could hardly have arisen in western Arabia during his lifetime. It did, however, arise after his death. Muslim rulers in the Middle East, like their Roman and Byzantine predecessors, were troubled by the continuous rise in prices and attempted from time to time to halt and fix them by decree. "Only God can fix prices" is a theological statement of laissez-faire economics. This seems to have been the predominant view among the professional men of religion, since virtually all the traditions dealing with prices take this line.

One other group of traditions has a special interest—those of messianic or eschatological equality, which purport to relate the events at the end of time when the kingdom of tyranny will be overthrown and the Mahdī, the rightly guided one sent by God for the purpose, will establish the kingdom of heaven on earth. These traditions reflect the successive messianic revolts which occurred in the early formative period of Islam; they also reflect the expectations which were aroused and show what the believers hoped that the Mahdī would do.

The development of historical enquiry and exposition among Muslims was shaped by many influences, including the heroic sagas of pagan Arabia, the narrative books of the Bible, and the Iranian book of Kings. But the most important source of inspiration and example was the religious tradition. Muslim historiography grew out of *ḥadīth*. The first Caliphs obviously did not enjoy the same authority as the Prophet himself in Muslim eyes. Nevertheless, they had a certain sanctity, and the precedents established by the first heads of the Islamic community could be and were cited as authoritative in government and law. And so we find a continuation of the *ḥadīth* type of narrative in the earliest historical writings; actions and utterances attributed to the early Caliphs and their officers were handed down and attested in much the same way as the *ḥadīths*. These, too, are subject to the same suspicion of having been fabricated, or at least adjusted, to serve some interest or purpose.

The early books are simple collections of narratives, each supported by a chain of authorities purporting to go back to an eyewitness or participant. With the growing complexity and sophistication of Islamic politics and culture, more varied and more elaborate forms of historiography developed. They include universal and imperial histories, dynastic annals, regional and local chronicles, collections of biographies, and a wide range of works dealing with specific topics, groups, or periods.

There is a fundamental difference in the origins and aims of medieval Western Christian and Muslim historical writing. Latin Christian historiography began in the chaos of the barbarian invasions and was dominated by two overwhelming facts: the rise of the Church and the fall of the Roman Empire. For St. Augustine, the body politic was the work of man and was evil, a punishment or a remedy for sin. (Had not Cain founded the first city?) Echoing the Hebrew prophets, St. Augustine and his pupil Orosius saw in defeat and ruin the instruments of God's purpose: that the peoples might throng to the churches and thereby be brought to a salvation which they would otherwise never have attained.

Islamic historiography begins not with defeat, but with victory; not with the fall, but with the rise of empire. For the Muslim historian, political authority is not a human evil, or even a lesser evil, but a divine good, established to maintain and promote God's faith and law. Like the Christian, he sees God in history and believes in God's involvement in human affairs, but he sees God as helping rather than testing His people, as desiring their supremacy in this world. For the Muslim historian, therefore, the state and its affairs are not external or secondary to the true purpose of history; they are its essential theme. Even in the age of decline, when he observed that power corrupts—the equivalent Muslim dictum might be rendered as "You can't have both power and paradise"—he still believed that Muslim authority, however obtained and however exercised, was a divinely ordained necessity and that the Sunnī community, which that power was needed to maintain, was the continuing medium of God's guidance to mankind.

This conviction is reflected in a number of ways in Islamic historiography: in the careful concern for detail and accuracy, in the sharp perception and calm acceptance of the realities of power, in the ability to conceive and present events over large areas and long periods, and, finally, in the pervading belief in the rightness, and therefore the significance, of the world as it is and as it has been.

Medieval Islamic historical literature is of immense richness and variety–incomparably greater, for example, than that of medieval Europe. From this literature it is possible to construct, with considerable detail and reasonable confidence, a narrative history of events in the Islamic world. But the modern historian is no longer satisfied merely with the surface movement of events. He seeks to penetrate to the deeper levels of the historic process, to the slower, heavier movement of societies and cultures, of institutions and structures, of groups and ideas.

For this kind of history, too, the chronicles have much to offer, far more than has yet been exploited. But the historian need not confine his attention to works of consciously historical intention. In a sense the whole literature of Islam is his source, including books on religion and sects, politics and economics, philosophy and science, travel, biography, and literary works of every kind. Of particular value are the specialized works arising from the exercise of certain professions. These include the administrative literature of the bureaucracy, the geographical literature of the postal service, the juridical literature of the ulema, and, in a different sense, the eulogies and satires of the poets—the media men and public relations men of medieval Islam.

All these works, however varied in form and content, have one feature in common: they are all books, literary compositions written by an author for a reader. But for the historian, books alone are not enough. In addition, he requires documents—the contemporary and direct evidence or traces of historical events in their original form, not as transmitted and therefore necessarily transformed by the mind of a literary intermediary.

For the history of Islam between the advent of Muḥammad and the rise of the Ottoman Empire, documents are very few indeed. Record offices and archives certainly existed in medieval Islam, as is attested by numerous references in the literary sources. Unfortunately, they were destroyed and the documents they contained have disappeared. The most important groups of surviving documents are inscriptions and coins—documents written on stone and metal. These are of great value but inevitably are rather limited in scope. Some documents survive in quotation, in histories, and in collections of model letters. These may be valuable, but they are not original and must, therefore, be treated with caution.

From medieval times only two groups of documents of any significance have been discovered, both of them in Egypt. One group consists of papyri, mostly of administrative content, written between the seventh and tenth centuries; the other consists of miscellaneous papers accumulated in a repository for litter in a synagogue in old Cairo and dates mostly from the tenth to the thirteenth centuries. These are discards, not archives. Both are fortuitous groupings—unconnected documents and fragments surviving by chance, discovered by accident, and distributed haphazard, with no cohesion other than that imposed on them by curators and historians. A few documents have been found here and there in Middle Eastern and European collections, but it is not until Ottoman times that we have genuine archives which have survived as such to our own day.

The student of Islamic history enters a field where much—one might even say most—of the basic research still remains to be done. He will have at his disposal few of the tools of research that are taken for granted by his classicist or Western medievalist colleagues. Faced with the need to read sources in several oriental languages, he will find that there are no historical grammars or dictionaries for any of them, and that even the general dictionaries are few and inadequate. Most of the historical ancillary sciences are in their infancy, and there are only two or three substantial works of reference. Translation remains a hazardous enterprise, and the writing of general surveys, whether narrative or analytical, requires a measure of reliance on earlier scholarship which, all too often, reflects the findings and judgments of a time when the critical study of Islamic history was only just beginning, when few historians knew Islamic sources, and few Islamicists cared for historical method. Their evaluations, therefore, and even their simple statements of what purports to be accepted fact, need rigorous scrutiny.

In recent years, despite, and perhaps to some extent because of, such difficulties, there has been increased activity in this field. Studies of growing value and interest have been published, dealing with specific aspects of Islamic history, and there are now even a few general works of real historical quality.

Chronological Table

c.570	Birth of Muḥammad
c.612	Beginning of Muḥammad's mission
622	The Hijra of Muḥammad from Mecca to Medina
630	Muḥammad conquers Mecca
632	Death of Muḥammad; appointment of Abū Bakr as first Caliph
634	Accession of ʻUmar as Caliph
637–644	Conquest of Syria, Palestine, Iraq, Mesopotamia, Armenia, Egypt; invasion of Iran
644	Murder of ʻUmar; accession of ʻUthmān
647	First Arab raids in North Africa
650–651	Establishment of standard text of Qur'ān; most of Iran conquered
656	Murder of ʻUthmān; accession of ʻAlī; beginning of first civil war
657	Battle of Ṣiffīn
661	Murder of ʻAlī; accession of Muʻāwiya; establishment of Umayyad Caliphate
670	Foundation of Qayrawān
673–678	Arabs besiege Constantinople
680	Massacre of al-Ḥusayn, his family, and supporters at Karbalā'
683–690	Second civil war
685–687	Shiʻite revolt in Iraq
690–696	ʻAbd al-Malik strikes first Muslim gold coins and orders the introduction of Arabic in government offices
691	Foundation of the Dome of the Rock in Jerusalem
705	Foundation of great Mosque of Damascus
705–715	Arab general Qutayba captures Bukhārā and Samarqand and establishes Muslim supremacy in Central Asia
710	Completion of conquest of North Africa; first Arab landing in Spain
711–714	Arabs conquer most of Spain; cross Jaxartes and raid Kāshgar; invade Indus valley and capture Multān

719	Cordova becomes seat of Arab governor
732	Battle of Tours; Franks halt Arab advance
750	Third civil war; fall of Umayyads; accession of ʻAbbasids
751	Battle on the Talas; Arabs defeat Chinese army in Central Asia and capture Chinese paper makers; manufacture of paper at Samarqand
756	Foundation of Umayyad amirate of Cordova
c.757	Death of the author and translator Ibn al-Muqaffaʻ
762	Foundation of Baghdad
767	Death of the jurist Abū Ḥanīfa
785	Foundation of Great Mosque of Cordova
786–809	Caliphate of Hārūn al-Rashīd
789–	Rise of Idrisid amirs in Morocco; foundation of Fez
795	Death of the jurist Mālik
800	Rise of Aghlabid amirs in Tunisia; Arab merchants in Canton
820	Death of the jurist al-Shāfiʻī
821–	Rise of Tahirid amirs in Khurāsān
827	Arabs begin conquest of Sicily
831	Capture of Palermo; raids in Southern Italy
832	Foundation of "House of Wisdom" in Baghdad
836	Foundation of Sāmarrā—cantonments for Turkish slave guard
after 847	Death of the mathematician al-Khwārizmī
855	Death of the jurist Aḥmad ibn Ḥanbal
867–	Rise of Saffarid amirs in Eastern Iran
868	Death of the Arabic author al-Jāḥiẓ
868–	Rise of Tulunid amirs in Egypt
869–883	Revolt of black slaves in Iraq
875–	Rise of Samanid amirs in Transoxania, later also Khurāsān
877	Death of Ḥunayn ibn Isḥāq, translator of Greek works into Arabic
c.879	Disappearance of the twelfth Shiʻite Imam
889	Death of the author and scholar Ibn Qutayba
c.904	First Arabic treatise on agronomy
909–	Rise of the Fatimid Caliphate in Tunisia
923	Death of the Arabic historian al-Ṭabarī
925	Death of the physician al-Rāzī (Rhases)
929	ʻAbd al-Raḥmān III of Cordova adopts the title of Caliph; death of the astronomer al-Battānī

929–	Rise of Hamdanid amirs of Mesopotamia and Syria
c.935	Death of the theologian al-Ash'arī
945	Buyids in Iraq
950	Death of the philosopher al-Fārābī
960	Conversion of Qarakhanid Turks to Islam
969	Fatimids conquer Egypt and found Cairo
c.970	Seljuqs enter Islamic lands from the East
972–	Rise of (Berber) Zirid amirs in Tunisia
998–	Rise of Ghaznavid amirs in Eastern Iran
1001–1021	Mahmūd of Ghaznī conquers the Panjāb
c.1020	Death of the Persian poet Firdawsī
1031	Fall of the Caliphate of Cordova
1037	Death of Ibn Sīnā (Avicenna)
1040	Battle of Dandānqān; Seljuqs defeat Ghaznavids and establish supremacy in Iran
1052	Banū Hilāl in North Africa
1055	Seljuq Prince Tughrul enters Baghdad; consolidation of the great Seljuq Sultanate
1065–1072	Famine in Egypt
1071	Battle of Manzikert; Seljuq Turks defeat Byzantines and occupy much of Anatolia
1072–1091	Normans conquer Sicily
1075	Seljuqs capture Nicaea (Iznik) and make it their capital in Anatolia
1085	Christians take Toledo
1097	Crusaders take Iznik; Seljuqs transfer capital to Konya
1099	Crusaders capture Jerusalem
1111	Death of the theologian al-Ghazālī
1141	Battle of the Qatvān steppe; Seljuq Sultan Sanjar defeated by Qara-Khitay invaders from the East
1144	Zangī captures Edessa
1154	Nūr al-Dīn ibn Zangī takes Damascus; Idrīsī completes his geography of the world; Fatimid Caliph grants commercial privileges to Pisa
1157	Death of Sanjar; breakup of great Seljuq Sultanate
1171	End of the Fatimid Caliphate; Egypt restored to Sunnī Islam
1173	Pisa obtains commercial privileges in Alexandria
1174–1193	Reign of Saladin
1187	Saladin takes Jerusalem
1198	Death of Ibn Rushd (Averroes)

1204	Death of the Jewish physician and philosopher Maimonides
1208	Sultan of Egypt accords commercial privileges to Venice
1212	Christian victory at Las Navas de Tolosa
1215	Jenghiz Khan takes Peking
1219	Jenghiz Khan crosses Jaxartes and invades Islamic lands
1220	Mongols conquer eastern territories of the Caliphate
1229	Al-Malik al-Kāmil, ruler of Egypt, reaches agreement with Frederick II and hands over Jerusalem
1233	Death of the Arabic historian Ibn al-Athīr
1236	Christians take Cordova
1237	Rise of Hafsids in Tunisia
1240	Death of the mystic Ibn al-ʿArabī
1242–1243	Mongols invade Anatolia; defeat Seljuqs at battle of Kösedagh
1244	Muslims recapture Jerusalem
1248	Christians take Seville
1249–1250	Crusade of St. Louis to Egypt; emergence of Mamlūk Sultanate
c.1250+	Khan of the Golden Horde converted to Islam
1254	Alphonso X (the Wise) establishes a school of Latin and Arabic studies in Seville
1256–	Hülegü, grandson of Jenghiz Khan, leads Mongol army westward
1258	Mongols capture Baghdad; end of Abbasid Caliphate
1260	Mamlūks defeat Mongols at ʿAyn Jālūt
1273	Death of the poet and mystic Jalāl al-Dīn Rūmī
1289	Mamlūks capture Tripoli from the Crusaders
1291	Fall of Acre; Crusaders finally expelled from Palestine
1292	Death of the Persian poet Saʿdī
1294	Ghāzān Khan, Mongol Il-Khan of Persia, converted to Islam
c.1299–1300	Breakup of Seljuq Sultanate of Anatolia into independent principalities; emergence of Ottoman amirate in Bithynia
1303	Last Mongol invasion of Syria defeated by Mamlūks
1318	Death of the Persian historian Rashīd al-Dīn
1326	Ottomans take Brusa (Bursa)
1331	Ottomans take Iznik
1336	Death of the Il-Khan Abū Saʿīd; breakup of the Il-Khanate in Iran

1348	Construction of the Gate of Justice at the Alhambra, Granada; Black Death in Egypt
1354	Ottoman-Genoese agreement. Ottomans take Gallipoli and Ankara
1369?	Ottomans take Adrianople (Edirne)
1370–1380	Tīmūr becomes ruler of Central Asia
1371	Ottomans defeat Serbs at Chirmen, on the Maritza
1380–1387	Tīmūr conquers Iran
1382	Mamlūk Sultanate in Egypt passes to Burjī (Circassian) Mamlūks
1385	Ottomans grant commercial privileges to Genoa; capture Sofia
1387	Ottomans take Salonica
1388	Ottomans grant commercial privileges to Venice
1389	First Battle of Kossovo; Ottomans defeat Serbs
1390	Death of the Persian poet Ḥāfiẓ
1392–1398	Tīmūr invades Western Iran, Mesopotamia, the Khanate of the Golden Horde, and India; occupies Moscow and Delhi
1396	Battle of Nicopolis; Ottomans defeat Crusaders
1400–1401	Tīmūr invades Georgia, Anatolia, Syria and Iraq; captures Aleppo, Damascus and Baghdād
1400	Guns used in defence of Aleppo
1402	Battle of Ankara; Tīmūr defeats Ottomans and captures Bāyezīd I
1403–	Famine and plague in Egypt
1405	Death of Tīmūr
1406	Death of the historian Ibn Khaldūn
1422	Ottomans use guns in unsuccessful attempt to capture Constantinople
1422–1438	Reign of Mamlūk Sultan Bārsbāy; attempt to control currency and monopolize sugar, pepper, and other commodities.
c.1433+	Hajji Giray Khan founds independent Khanate in the Crimea
1444	Battle of Varna; Ottomans defeat Christian powers
1448	Second battle of Kossovo; Ottomans defeat Serbs and their allies; first recorded use by Ottomans of field guns
1453	Ottomans capture Constantinople

Bibliography of Sources

'Abd al-Ḥamīd al-Kātib. *Risāla ila'l-kuttāb*, in *Jamharat Rasā'il al-'Arab*, ed. Aḥmad Zakī Ṣafwat, ii, Cairo (Muṣṭafā al-Bābī al-Ḥalabī), 1356/1937 (variant versions in Qalqashandī, *Ṣubḥ*, i, pp. 85–89; Jahshiyārī, pp. 74–79; Ibn Khaldūn, *Muqaddima*, pp. 248–251).

'Abdallāh (Sultan of Granada). *Kitāb al-Tibyān*, ed. E. Lévi-Provençal, Les "Mémoires" du roi Zīride "Abd Allah," in *al-Andalus*, iii, 1935.

Al-Abshīhī, Shihāb al-Dīn Aḥmad. *Kitāb al-Mustaṭraf fī kull Shay' Mustaẓraf*, Cairo, 1352/1933.

Abū Da'ūd, Sulaymān ibn al-Ash'ath. *Sunan*. Cairo (Al-Tāzī), n.d.

Abu'l-Faraj, Gregorius ibn al-'Ibrī. *Ta'rīkh Mukhtaṣar al-duwal*, ed. Anṭūn Ṣālḥānī, Beirut (Catholic Press), 1890.

Abu'l Faraj al-Iṣfahānī. *Kitāb al-Aghānī*, 20 vols., Būlāq, 1285. New edition (incomplete), Cairo (Dār al-Kutub), 1345/1927–.

Abū Shāma, Shihāb al-Dīn 'Abd al-Raḥmān ibn Ismā'īl. *Kitāb al-Rawḍatayn fī akhbār al-dawlatayn*, i, ed. M. Ḥilmī M. Aḥmad, Cairo (Lajnat al-ta'līf), 1962.

Abū 'Ubayd al-Qāsim ibn Sallām. *Kitāb al-Amwāl*, ed. Muḥammad Ḥāmid al-Fiqī, Cairo ('Amira), 1353/1934.

Abū Yūsuf, Ya'qūb ibn Ibrāhīm. *Kitāb al-Kharāj*, 3rd edition, Cairo (Salafiyya), 1382/1962–1963.

Akhbār al-Ṣīn wa'l-Hind (*Relation de la Chine et de l'Inde*), ed. J. Sauvaget, Paris (Les Belles Lettres), 1948.

Anonymous Ottoman Chronicle. Tevārīh-i Āl-i Osmān (*Die altosmanischen anonymen Chroniken*), ed. F. Giese, Breslau, 1922.

Ashîkpāshāzāde. *Tevārīh-i Āl-i Osmān*, ed. 'Alī (old script), Istanbul ('Āmire), 1332/1914; ed. Nihal Atsız (new script) in *Osmanlı Tarihleri*, Istanbul (Türkiye Yayinevi), 1949.

Al-Balādhurī, Aḥmad ibn Yaḥyā. *Ansāb al-ashrāf*, ivA, ed. Max Schloessinger, revised and annotated by M. J. Kister, Jerusalem (Magnes Press), 1971.

——— *Ansāb al-ashrāf*, v, ed. S. D. F. Goitein, Jerusalem (University Press), 1936.

——— *Futūḥ al-Buldān,* ed. M. J. de Goeje, Leiden (Brill), 1866.

Bayhaqī, Abu'l-Fażl. *Tārīkh-i Bayhaqī,* ed. Ghanī and Fayyaż, Tehran (Bank Melli), 1324 (Persian solar)/1945.

Al-Bukhārī, Abū 'Abdallāh Muḥammad ibn Ismā'īl, *Al-Ṣaḥīh,* ed. L. Krehl, Leiden (Brill), 1868.

Buzurg ibn Shahriyār. *Kitāb 'Ajā'ib al-Hind,* ed. P. A. Van der Lith, Leiden (Brill), 1883–1886.

Al-Dīnawarī, Abū Ḥanīfa Aḥmad ibn Da'ūd, *Al-Akhbār al-ṭiwāl,* ed. 'Abd al-Mun'im 'Amir, Cairo (Ministry of Culture), 1960.

Geniza. Documents from S. D. Goitein, 'Te'ūda min hannamel ha'afriqani 'Aydhāb', in *Tarbitz,* xxi, 1950; idem, 'Pidyon shevuya be-Nabulus . . . ' in *Tarbitz,* xxxi, 1961–1962.

Al-Ghazālī, Abū Ḥāmid Muḥammad ibn Muḥammad, *Fayṣal al-tafriqa bayn al-Islām wa'l-zandaqa,* ed. Sulaymān Dunyā, Cairo (Iḥyā al-Kutub al-'Arabiyya), 1381/1961.

Al-Hamadānī, Badī' al-Zamān, *Maqāmāt,* ed. Shaykh Muḥammad 'Abduh, 4th edition, Beirut (Catholic Press), 1957.

Hilāl Al-Sābi', *Kitāb al-Wuzarā',* ed. H. F. Amedroz, Leiden (Brill), 1904.

Al-Ḥusaynī, Ṣadr al-Dīn Abu'l-Ḥasan 'Alī ibn Nāṣir ibn 'Alī, *Akhbār al-Dawla al-Saljūqiyya,* ed. Muḥammad Iqbal, Lahore (Univ. of the Panjab), 1933.

Ibn 'Abd al-Ḥakam, *Futūḥ Miṣr wa-akhbāruhā (The History of the Conquest of Egypt, North Africa and Spain),* ed. C. C. Torrey, New Haven (Yale University Press), 1922.

Ibn 'Abd Rabbihi, Aḥmad ibn Muḥammad. *Al-'Iqd al-Farīd,* 8 vols., ed. Muḥammad Sa'īd al-'Iryān, Cairo (Al-Maktaba al-Tijāriyya al-Kubrā), 1372/1953.

Ibn 'Abdūn, Muḥammad ibn Aḥmad. *Risāla fi'l-Qaḍā' wa'l-ḥisba,* ed. E. Lévi-Provençal, in *Documents arabes inédits sur la vie sociale et économique en occident musulman au moyen age,* Cairo (Institut Français d'Archéologie Orientale), 1955.

Ibn Abī Uṣaybi'a. *'Uyūn al-anbā' fī ṭabaqāt al-aṭibbā',* Cairo (Wahbiyya), 1299/1882.

Ibn al-'Adīm, Kamāl al-Dīn. *Bughyat al-Ṭalab fī ta'rīkh Ḥalab,* excerpts ed. B. Lewis, "Three biographies from Kamāl ad-Dīn," in *Mélanges Fuad Köprülü,* Istanbul (Yalçin), 1953, pp. 322–326.

Ibn al-Athīr, 'Izz al-Dīn Abu'l-Ḥasan 'Alī ibn Abi'l-Karm Muḥammad. *Al-Kāmil fi'l-ta'rīkh,* ed. C. J. Thornberg, Leiden (Brill), 1851–1876.

——— *Usd al-ghāba,* Cairo, 1285–1287/1869–1871.

Ibn Baṣṣāl, Muḥammad ibn Ibrāhīm. *Kitāb-al-Filāḥa,* edd. J. M. Millás

Vallicrosa and Muḥammad ʿAzīmān, Tetuan (Institute Muley el-Hasan), 1955.

Ibn Baṭṭa, Abū ʿAbdallāh ʿUbaydallāh ibn Muḥammad. *Kitāb al-Sharḥ wa'l-ibāna ʿalā uṣūl al-sunna wa'l-diyāna* (*La profession de foi d'Ibn Baṭṭa*), ed. M. Laoust, Damascus (Institut Français de Damas), 1958.

Ibn Baṭṭūṭa. *Riḥla* (Voyages), ed. C. Defremery and B. R. Sanguinetti, 4 vols, Paris, 1854. Reprinted Paris (Anthropos), 1969.

Ibn Buṭlān, Abu'l-Ḥasan al-Mukhtār ibn al-Ḥasan. *Risāla fī Shirā al-raqīq,* ed. ʿAbd al-Salām Hārūn, Cairo (Lajnat al-Ta'līf), 1373/1954.

Ibn al-Faqīh, Abū Bakr Aḥmad ibn Ibrāhīm al-Hamadhānī. *Mukhtaṣar Kitāb al-Buldān,* ed. M. J. de Goeje, Leiden (Brill), 1885.

Ibn al-Furāt, Nāṣir al-Dīn Muḥammad ibn ʿAbd al-Raḥmān. *Al-Ta'rīkh al-Wāḍiḥ,* excerpt edited by G. Levi Della Vida, "L'Invasione dei Tartari in Siria nel 1260 nei ricordi di un testimone oculare," *Orientalia,* iv, 1935.

Ibn Ḥawqal, Abu'l-Qāsim. *Ṣūrat al-Arḍ* (*Opus geographicum*), ed. J. H. Kramers, Leiden (Brill), 1939.

Ibn Hishām, Abū Muḥammad ʿAbd al-Malik. *Al-Sīra al-Nabawiyya,* edd. Muṣṭafā al-Saqqā, Ibrāhīm al-Abyārī and ʿAbd al-Ḥafīẓ Shalabī, 2nd impression, Cairo (Muṣṭafā al-Bābī al-Ḥalabī), 1375/1955.

Ibn ʿIdhārī al-Marrukushī. *Kitāb al-Bayān al-Mughrib,* ed. G. S. Colin and E. Lévi-Provençal, i, Leiden (Brill), 1948.

Ibn Jamāʿa, Badr al-Dīn Muḥammad ibn Ibrāhīm. *Taḥrīr al-aḥkām fī tadbīr ahl al-Islām,* ed. Hans Kofler in *Islamica,* vi, 1934.

Ibn Kathīr, ʿImād al-Dīn ibn Abi'l-Fidā'. *Al-Bidāya wa'l-nihāya,* Cairo (Saʿāda), 1351/1932–1358/1939.

Ibn Khaldūn, ʿAbd al-Raḥman ibn Muḥammad. *Al-Muqaddima,* Beirut, 1900.

——— *Kitāb al-ʿIbar wa-dīwān al-mubtada' wa'l-khabar,* Būlāq, 1284/1867.

Ibn al-Khaṭīb, Muḥammad Lisān al-Dīn. *Al-Iḥāṭa fī ta'rīkh Gharnāṭa,* Cairo (Al-Mawsūʿāt), 1319/1901–1902.

Ibn Māja, Muḥammad ibn Yazīd. *Sunan,* 2 vols., ed. Muḥammad Fu'ād ʿAbd al-Bāqī, Cairo (Ḥalabī), 1372/1952.

Ibn al-Qifṭī, Jamāl al-Dīn Abu'l-Ḥasan ʿAlī ibn Yūsuf. *Ta'rīkh al-ḥukamā',* ed. J. Lippert, Leipzig (Dietrich'sche Verlagsbuchhandlung), 1903.

Ibn Qutayba, Abū Muḥammad 'Abdallāh ibn Muslim. *Kitāb al-Ma'ārif*, ed. Tharwat 'Ukāsha, 2nd edition, Cairo (Ma'ārif), 1388/1969.

——— *Kitāb al-Shi'r wa'l-shu'arā'*, ed. M. J. de Goeje, Leiden (Brill), 1904.

——— *'Uyūn al-akhbār*, 4 vols., ed. Aḥmad Zaki al-'Adawī, Cairo (*Dār al-Kutub*), 1343–8/1925–1930.

Ibn al-Qūṭiyya, Abū Bakr ibn 'Umar. *Ta'rīkh iftitāḥ al-Andalus* (*Historia de la conquista de España*), ed. J. Ribera, Madrid (Real Academia de la Historia), 1868–1926.

Ibn Rusteh, Abū 'Alī Aḥmad ibn 'Umar. *Kitāb al-A'lāq al-Nafīsa*, ed. M. J. de Goeje, 2nd edition, Leiden (Brill), 1892.

Ibn Tashköprüzāde, Aḥmad ibn Muṣliḥ al-Dīn. *Al-Shaqā'iq al-nu'māniyya fī 'ulamā' al-dawla al-'Uthmāniyya*, printed in the margin of Ibn Khallikān, *Wafayāt al-a'yān*, Būlāq, 1299/1882.

Ibn Taymiyya, Taqī al-Dīn Aḥmad. *Al-Siyāsa al-shar'iyya*, ed. Muḥammad 'Abdallah al-Sammān, Cairo (Anṣār al-Sunna), 1381/1961.

Ibn al-'Umarī, Shihāb al-Dīn. *Al-Ta'rīf bi'l-Muṣṭalaḥ al-sharīf*, Cairo (Al-Āṣima), 1312/1894–1895.

Ibn al-Zubayr, al-Qāḍī al-Rashīd ibn al-Zubayr. *Kitāb al-Dhakhā'ir wa'l-tuḥaf*, ed. Ṣalāḥ al-Dīn al-Munajjid, Kuwait (Government Press), 1959.

Al-Idrīsī, Abū 'Abdallāh Muḥammad ibn Muḥammad. *Opus Geographicum*, ed. A. Bombaci, U. Rizzitano, R. Rubinacci, L. Veccia Vaglieri, part i, Naples-Rome (Istituto Universitario Orientale di Napoli, Istituto Italiano per il Medio ed estremo Oriente), 1970.

Isaac Israeli. *Sefer Musar Rōfīm*, ed. David Kaufmann in *Magazin für die Wissenschaft des Judenthums*, Berlin, 1884.

Isḥāq ibn al-Ḥusayn. *Kitāb Akām al-Marjān fī dhikr al-madā'in al-mashhūra fī kull makān*, ed. Angela Codazzi in *Rendiconti della Reale Accademia dei Lincei, classa di scienze morali etc.* sixth series, vol. V, Rome, 1929.

Al-Iṣṭakhrī, Abū Isḥāq Ibrāhīm ibn Muḥammad. *Al-Masālik wa'l-mamālik*, ed. M. J. de Goeje, Leiden (Brill), 1870.

Al-Jāḥiẓ, 'Amr ibn Baḥr, *Rasā'il*, ed. Ḥasan al-Sandūbī, Cairo (Al-Maktaba al-Tijāriyya al-Kubrā), 1352/1933.

———*Al-Bukhalā'*, Damascus (Al-Nashr al-'Arabī), 1357/1938.

———*Al-Bayān wa'l-tabyīn*, ed. 'Abd al-Salām Muḥammad Hārūn, 4 vols., Cairo (Al-Khānjī), 1380/1940.

———*Rasā'il*, 2 vols., ed. 'Abd al-Salām Hārūn, Cairo (Al-Khānjī) 1965.

———(attributed to). *Al-Tabaṣṣur bi'l-tijāra*, ed. Ḥasan Ḥusnī 'Abd al-Wahhāb, Cairo (Raḥmāniyya), 1354/1935.

Al-Jahshiyārī, Abū 'Abdallāh Muḥammad ibn 'Abdūs. *Kitāb al-Wuzarā' wa'l-kuttāb*, edd. Muṣṭafā al-Saqqā', Ibrāhīm al-Abyārī, and 'Abd al-Ḥafīẓ Shalabī, Cairo (Ḥalabī), 1357/1938.

Al-Kāshgharī, Maḥmūd ibn al-Ḥusayn. *Kitāb Dīwān lughāt al-Turk*, Istanbul ('Amire), 1333/1914.

Ka'ti, Maḥmūd Ka'ti ibn al-Ḥājj al-Mutawakkil. *Ta'rīkh al-Fattāsh*, ed. O. Houdas and M. Delafosse, Paris (Ernest Leroux), 1913–1914.

Al-Khushanī, Muḥammad ibn al-Ḥārith. *Kitāb al-Quḍāt bi-Qurtuba (Historia de los jueces de Cordoba)*, ed. J. Ribera, Madrid (Maestre), 1914.

Kračkovsky, I. Y. *Izbranniye Sočineniya*, i, Moscow-Leningrad (Akad. Nauk), 1955.

Al-Maqdisī, Muṭahhar ibn Ṭāhir. *Kitāb al-Bad' wa'l-ta'rīkh*, ed. Clement Huart, 3 vols., Paris (Ernest Leroux), 1899–1903.

Al-Maqrīzī, Taqī al-Dīn Aḥmad ibn 'Alī. *Kitāb al-Sulūk li-ma'rifat duwal al-mulūk*, ed. M. M. Ziyāda and others, in course of publication, Cairo (Lajnat al-ta'līf), 1934–.

———*Kitāb al-Mawā'iz wa'l-i'tibār fī dhikr al-Khiṭaṭ wa'l-āthār*, 2 vols., Būlāq, 1270/1853.

Al-Mas'ūdī, Abu'l-Ḥasan 'Alī ibn al-Ḥusayn. *Murūj al-dhahab*, ed. C. Barbier de Meynard and Pavet de Courteille, Paris (Société Asiatique), 1861–1877; new edition by C. Pellat, in progress, Beirut (Université Libanaise), 1966–.

———*Kitāb al-Tanbīh wa'l-ishrāf*, ed. 'Abdallāh Ismā'īl al-Ṣāwī, Cairo (Ṣāwī), 1357/1938.

Al-Māwardī, Abu'l-Ḥasan 'Alī ibn Muḥammad. *Al-Aḥkām al-Sulṭāniyya* Cairo (Maḥmūdiyya), n.d.

Mihyār al-Daylamī. *Dīwān*, Cairo (Dār al-Kutub), 1344/1925.

Moses Ben Maimon (Maimonides). *Qōveṣ teshūvōt ha-Rambam ve-igrōtav*, ed. A. Lichtenberg, iii, Leipzig, 1858.

Al-Mubarrad, Muḥammad ibn Yazīd. *Al-Kāmil*, ed. W. Wright, Leipzig (Brockhaus), 1874.

Al-Muqaddasī, Shams al-Dīn Abū 'Abdallāh Muḥammad ibn Aḥmad. *Aḥsan al-taqāsīm fī ma'rifat al-aqālīm (Descriptio Imperii Moslemici)*, ed. M. J. de Goeje, 2nd edition, Leiden (Brill), 1906.

Al-Muttaqī, 'Alā al-Dīn 'Alī ibn Ḥusām al-Dīn. *Kanz al-'ummāl*, 8 parts, Hyderabad (Dā'irat al-Ma'ārif), 1312/1894–1895.

Nāṣir-i Khusraw. *Safar-nāma*, Berlin (Kaviani), 1340/1921.

Al-Nawawī, Yaḥyā ibn Sharaf. *Manthūrāt*, excerpt ed. I. Goldziher, *Revue des Etudes juives*, xxviii, 1894.

Niẓām al-Dīn Shāmī. *Ẓafar-nāma*, ed. F. Tauer, Prague (Oriental Institute), 1937.

Niẓām al-Mulk. *Siyāsat-nāma*, ed. C. Schefer, Paris (Ernest Leroux), 1891.

Qāḍī Nu'mān ibn Muḥammad. *Sharḥ al-akhbār* in W. Ivanow, *Ismaili tradition concerning the rise of the Fatimids*, London (Oxford University Press), 1942.

Al-Nuwayrī, Shihāb al-Dīn Aḥmad ibn 'Abd al-Wahhāb. *Nihāyat al-arab*, iv, Cairo (Dār al-Kutub), 1343/1925. Unpublished volume Ms. Bibliothèque Nationale, Paris, Fonds arabe, 1576.

Papyri, Documents from

C. H. Becker. *Papyri Schott-Reinhardt*, I, Heidelberg (Carl Winter), 1906.

———'Arabische Papyri . . .', in *Zeitschrift für Assyriologie*, xx, 1906. A. Grohmann, 'Arabische Papyri. .', in *Archiv Orientální*, x, 1938; xi, 1939; xii, 1941; xiv, 1943.

———'Arabische Papyri . . .', in *Der Islam*, xxii, 1935.

Qāḍī Khān, al-Ḥasan ibn Manṣūr. *Fatāwī*, Cairo, 1865.

Al-Qalqashandī, Abu'l-'Abbās Aḥmad. *Ṣubḥ al-a'shā*, 14 vols., Cairo (Dār al-Kutub), 1331/1913–1337/1918.

Al-Qazwīnī, Zakariyyā ibn Muḥammad, *Āthār al-bilād wa-akhbār al-'ibād*, Beirut (Ṣādir), 1380/1960.

Al-Qudūrī, Aḥmad ibn Muḥammad. *Al-Mukhtaṣar; Le Statut personnel en droit musulman hanefite*, ed. G. H. Bousquet and L. Bercher, Paris-Tunis (Sirey), 1952.

Qur'ān. Cited by chapter (*Sūra*) and verse, according to two systems of numbering.

Rashīd al-Dīn. *Jāmi' al-tawārīkh*, iii, ed. Abdul-Kerim Ali-oglu Ali-zade, Baku (Azerbaijan Academy of Sciences), 1937.

Al-Rāwandī, Muḥammad ibn 'Alī. *Rāḥat al-ṣudūr*, ed. Muḥammad Iqbal, London (Luzac), 1921.

RCEA. Répertoire chronologique d'épigraphie arabe, 15 vols., Cairo (Institut Français d'Archéologie Orientale), 1931–1956.

Safara siyāsiyya min Gharnāṭa ila'l-Qāhira fi'l-qarn al-tāsi' al-hijrī (844), ed. 'Abd al-'Azīz al-Ahwānī in *Majallat Kulliyyat al-Adab*, Cairo, xv, 1954.

Al-Shāfi'ī, al-Imām Abū 'Abdallāh Muḥammad ibn Idrīs. *Kitāb al-Umm*, Bulaq (Amīriyya), 1321–2/1903–1904.

Al-Shaybānī, Muḥammad ibn al-Ḥasan. *Kitāb al-Siyar*, in Sarakhsī,

Sharḥ al-Siyar al-Kabīr, 2 vols., Hyderabad (Dā'irat al-Ma'ārif), 1335/1917.

Al-Ṣūlī, Abū Bakr Muḥammad ibn Yaḥyā. *Akhbār al-Rāḍī wa'l-Muttaqī*, ed. J. Heyworth Dunne, London (Luzac), 1935.

Sûret-i Defter-i Sancak-i Arvanid, ed. Halil Inalcik; Ankara (Türk Tarih Kurumu), 1954.

Al-Suyūṭī, Jalāl al-Dīn. *Ḥusn al-Muḥāḍara fī akhbār Miṣr wa'l-Qāhira*, Cairo, 1321/1902.

Al-Ṭabarī, Abū Ja'far Muḥammad ibn Jarīr. *Ta'rīkh al-Rusul wa'l-mulūk*, ed. M. J. de Goeje and others, Leiden (Brill), 1879–1901.

Al-Tanūkhī, Abū 'Alī, *Al-Faraj ba'd al-Shidda*, Cairo (Al-Khānjī), 1375/1955.

Al-Ṭarsūsī, Marḍī ibn 'Alī. *Tabṣirat arbāb al-albāb fī kayfiyyat al-najāt fi'l-ḥurūb*, ed. C. Cahen, 'Un traité d'armurerie composé pour Saladin', in *Bulletin d'Etudes Orientales*, xii, 1947–1948.

Al-Turṭūshī, Muḥammad ibn Walīd, called Ibn Abī Randaqa. *Sirāj al-mulūk*, Cairo, 1289/1872.

'Ubayd-i Zākānī. *Kulliyyāt*, ed. 'Abbās Iqbāl, Tehran (Zuvvar), 1343 Persian solar/1964.

Yaḥyā al-Antākī. *Annales*, ed. L. Cheikho, B. Carra de Vaux, and H. Zayyat, in *Corpus Scriptorum Christianorum Orientalium, Scriptores Arabici*, 3rd series, vol. vii, Paris (Poussielgue), 1909.

Al-Ya'qūbī, Aḥmad ibn Abī Ya'qūb. *Kitāb al-Buldān*, ed. M. J. de Goeje, 2nd edition, Leiden (Brill), 1892.

Yāqūt. *Irshād al-Arīb, or Dictionary of learned men*, ed. D. S. Margoliouth, London (Luzac), 1923.

1 Religion

1

Scripture and Worship

The first of these excerpts, from a collection of traditions, explains why and how an authorized text of the Qur'ān was established. The second describes an incident after the Arab conquest of Jerusalem and reflects any early disagreement. These are followed by a historical account of one of the most famous mosques in Islam and a few representative inscriptions from mosques and madrasas.

1. How the Qur'ān Was Assembled (Mid-Seventh Century)

Zayd ibn Thābit said: Abū Bakr sent for me at the time of the battle of al-Yamāma, and 'Umar ibn al-Khaṭṭāb was with him. Abū Bakr said: 'Umar has come to me and said, "Death raged at the battle of al-Yamāma and took many of the reciters of the Qur'ān. I fear lest death in battle overtake the reciters of the Qur'ān in the provinces and a large part of the Qur'ān be lost. I think you should give orders to collect the Qur'ān."

"What?" I asked 'Umar, "Will you do something which the Prophet of God himself did not do?"

"By God," replied 'Umar, "it would be a good deed."

'Umar did not cease to urge me until God opened my heart to this and I thought as 'Umar did.

Zayd continued: Abū Bakr said to me, "You are a young man, intelligent, and we see no fault in you, and you have already written down the revelation for the Prophet of God, may God bless and save him. Therefore go and seek the Qur'ān and assemble it."

By God, if he had ordered me to move a mountain it would not have been harder for me than his order to collect the Qur'ān. "What?" I asked, "Will you do something which the Prophet of God himself, may God bless and save him, did not do?"

"By God," replied Abū Bakr, "it would be a good deed."

And he did not cease to urge me until God opened my heart to this as he had opened the hearts of Abū Bakr and 'Umar.

Then I sought out and collected the parts of the Qur'ān, whether written on palm leaves or flat stones or in the hearts of men. Thus I found the end of the Sūra of Repentance, which I had been unable to find anywhere else, with Abu'l-Khuzayma al-Anṣārī. These were the verses: "There came to you a Prophet from among yourselves. It grieves him that you sin. . . ." to the end [Sūra ix, 129–130].

The leaves were with Abū Bakr until his death, then with 'Umar as long as he lived, and then with Ḥafṣa, the daughter of 'Umar.

Anas ibn Mālik said: Ḥudhayfa ibn al-Yamān went with 'Uthmān when he was preparing the army of Syria to conquer Armenia and Ādharbayjān, together with the army of Iraq. Ḥudhayfa was shocked by the differences in their reading of the Qur'ān, and said to 'Uthmān, "O Commander of the Faithful, catch this community before they differ about their book as do the Jews and Christians."

'Uthmān sent to Ḥafṣa to say, "Send us the leaves. We shall copy them in codices and return them to you."

Ḥafṣa sent them to 'Uthmān, who ordered Zayd ibn Thābit, 'Abdallāh ibn al-Zubayr, Sa'īd ibn al-'Aṣ, and 'Abd al-Raḥmān ibn al-Ḥārith ibn Hishām to copy them into codices. 'Uthmān said to the three of them who were of the tribe of Quraysh, "If you differ from Zayd ibn Thābit on anything in the Qur'ān, write it according to the language of Quraysh, for it is in their language that the Qur'ān was revealed."

They did this, and when they had copied the leaves into codices, 'Uthmān returned the leaves to Ḥafṣa. He sent copies of the codex which they made in all direction and gave orders to burn every leaf or codex which differed from it.

Al-Bukhārī, *Ṣaḥīḥ,* III, pp. 392–394.

2. ʿUmar in Jerusalem (636)

On the authority of Rajā ibn Ḥīwa, on the authority of an eyewitness: When ʿUmar came from al-Jābiya to Aelia[1] . . . he said, "Bring me Kaʿb!" and he was brought to him, and ʿUmar asked him, "Where do you think we should put the place of prayer?"

"By the rock,"[2] answered Ka'b.

"By God, Kaʿb," said ʿUmar, "you are following after Judaism.[3] I saw you take off your sandals."

"I wanted to feel the touch of it with my bare feet." said Kaʿb.

"I saw you," said ʿUmar. "But no. We shall make the forepart the *qibla*, as the Prophet of God, may God bless and save him, made the forepart of our mosques their *qibla*. Go along! We were not commanded concerning the rock, but we were commanded concerning the Kaʿba!"

So ʿUmar made the forepart the *qibla*. Then ʿUmar went up from the place where he had prayed to the heap of garbage in which the Romans had hidden the temple in the time of the children of Israel. And when this place came into their hands, they uncovered part of it and left the remainder.

ʿUmar said, "O people, do as I do." And he knelt by the heap and knelt on a fold of his cloak.

Al-Ṭabarī, i, pp. 2408–2409.

3. The Mosque of al-Azhar (970–1415)

This was the first mosque founded in Cairo. The man who built it was the qā'id Jawhar, the scribe, the Sicilian, the freedman of the Imam Abū Tamīm Maʿadd, the Caliph, the Commander of the Faithful, al-Muʿizz li-Dīn Allāh,[1] when he laid

[1] The late Roman name for Jerusalem.

[2] The temple rock.

[3] Kaʿb was a converted Jew, see vol. I p. 6. He is held responsible for introducing a number of Jewish beliefs and practices into Islam.

[1] The fourth Fatimid Caliph, the Conqueror of Egypt.

out the plan of Cairo. The building of this mosque began on Saturday, 24 Jumādā I 359 [April 4, 970] and was completed on 9 Ramaḍān 361 [June 24, 972]. The communal prayer was held in it. All around the dome in the first hall [*riwāq*], to the right of the prayer niche and the pulpit, the following text was written:

> In the name of God, the Merciful and the Compassionate. This is one of the buildings the construction of which was ordered by the servant and the favored of God Abū Tamīm Maʿadd, the Imam, al-Muʿizz li-Dīn Allāh, Commander of the Faithful, may God bless him, his ancestors, and his noble descendants, by the hand of his slave Jawhar, the scribe, the Sicilian, in the year 360.

The first Friday that the communal prayer was performed there was on 7 Ramaḍān 361 [June 22, 972]. Later, al-ʿAzīz billāh Abū Manṣūr Nizār, the son of al-Muʿizz li-Din Allāh added something to it. Then, in the year 378 [988], the vizier Abu'l-Faraj Yaʿqūb ibn Killis asked the Caliph al-ʿAzīz billāh to assign stipends to a number of jurists. He granted to each one of them a sufficient salary in money and ordered them to buy a house and reconstruct it. It was established next to the Azhar mosque, and every Friday they came to the mosque and formed circles to whom they lectured after the communal prayer and until the afternoon prayer. They also received a gift from the vizier every year. They were thirty-five of them. On the day of the breaking of the fast al-ʿAzīz granted them robes of honor and gave them mules to ride.

It is said that in this mosque there is a talisman such that no sparrow or other bird, pigeon, wood pigeon, or the like, will nest or hatch there. It consists of the likenesses of three birds; each likeness is on the top of a column. Two of them are in the forepart of the mosque, in the fifth hall: one is on a column in the western part; the other is on one of the two columns on the left when one faces the pulpit of the muezzins. The third likeness is in the courtyard, on the southern columns toward the east.

Then al-Ḥākim bi-Amr Allāh[2] had further work done there. He constituted tenement houses in old Cairo as *waqf* in favor of the

[2] See vol. I p. 46ff.

Azhar mosque, the mosque in al-Maqs, the al-Ḥākim mosque, and the House of Wisdom in Cairo and incorporated this in a document, as follows:

> This is a document, the provisions and details of which the chief *qāḍī* Mālik ibn Saʿīd ibn Mālik al Fāriqī caused to be attested by the legal witnesses present at a judicial hearing held by him in Fusṭāṭ of Egypt in the month of Ramaḍān of the year 400 [April–May 1010]. He called upon them to attest it, in his capacity as qāḍī of the servant and the favored of God, al-Manṣūr Abū ʿAlī, the Imam al-Ḥākim bi-Amr Allāh, Commander of the Faithful, the son of al-ʿAzīz billāh, may God bless them both, with authority over Cairo, Fusṭāṭ, Alexandria, the two holy places,[3] may God preserve them, the provinces [*jund*] of Syria, Raqqa, and Raḥba, the regions of the Maghrib, and their dependencies, and all that which God has enabled and will enable the Commander of the Faithful to conquer, of the lands of the East and of the West. This was in the presence of a man who stated that he had certain knowledge both of the places owned in their entirety and those jointly owned in shares, all of which shall be named and delimited in this document, and of the fact that they were the property [*mulk*] of al-Ḥākim until he constituted them as *waqf* in favor of the Azhar mosque in Cairo, the God-guarded, of the mosque in Rāshida, and of the mosque in al-Maqs, which were both established and founded by his order, and of the House of Wisdom in Cairo, the God-guarded, which he had already constituted as a *waqf*, with all the books which it contains, prior to the date of the present document. Some of these buildings are assigned jointly and without division to the Azhar mosque, the Rāshida mosque, and the House of Wisdom in Cairo, the God-guarded; some are assigned to the Maqs mosque, in accordance with conditions which will be stated below.
>
> The benefaction in favor of the Azhar mosque in Cairo, the God-guarded, the Rāshida mosque, and the House of Wisdom in Cairo, the God-guarded, consists of the whole of the building known as the mint [*Dār al-Ḍarb*], the whole of the commercial building [*qayṣariyya*] known as the wool *qayṣariyya*, and the whole of the building known as the new pottery building, all situated in Fusṭāṭ of Egypt.

[3] Mecca and Medina.

The benefaction in favor of the Maqs mosque consists of the whole of four shops with living quarters above them and two storehouses, all situated in Fusṭāṭ of Egypt in the district of the Banner [*al-Rāya*], to the west of the house formerly known as the pottery building. These two buildings, known by the name of the pottery building, are situated in the place known as the Rat Bath [*Ḥammām al-Fārr*]. This includes all the jointly held shares of the four adjoining shops situated in Fusṭāṭ of Egypt, also in the Banner district in the place known as the Rat Bath, these shops being known as "the shares of al-Qaysī."

These sites, within their limits, are constituted *waqf* in their entirety, including their land, buildings, ground floors, upper floors, rooms, latrines, shops, courtyards, approaches, passages, water conduits, and all rights pertaining thereto, both inside and outside.

He has made of all this a charitable foundation and an inviolable *waqf*, consecrated absolutely and in perpetuity, which it is unlawful to sell or give or make into private property [*tamlīk*] and which shall remain subject to the conditions laid down and in accordance with the rules prescribed in this document. The passing of the years shall not weaken these rules, nor the vicissitudes of events transform them. They shall not be subject to exception or to reinterpretation, nor shall there be any need to seek a judicial ruling [*fatwā*] to renew their consecration. The stipulations shall remain valid through all changes in circumstances, until God shall inherit the earth and the heavens [Qur'ān, xix, 41].

Whoever is responsible for the management and control of the *waqf* in every period shall make lettings in a God-fearing way so as to ensure the best advantage by making the offer known among those desirous of renting such premises.

He shall, in the first instance, use the income for the upkeep of the properties as required and the maintenance of the assets in good repair, but without prejudice to the beneficiaries for which the *waqf* was established.

The surplus shall be divided into sixty parts.

Among these, there shall be assigned to the said Azhar mosque in Cairo, the God-guarded, by this attestation, a fifth, an eighth, a half of a sixth, and a half of a ninth, to be expended for the maintenance and requirements of the mosque; that is, in solid gold coin of al-Mu'izz, 1067 dinars plus half a dinar and one-eighth of a dinar. Of this sum the following amounts shall be allocated:

For the preacher [*khaṭīb*] of this mosque, 84 dinars.

For the price of 1000 cubits of Abadan matting, to be held in reserve, so that the supply of matting shall not be cut off in case of need; and for the price of 13,000 cubits of plaited matting to cover the floor of the said mosque every year when needed, 108 dinars.

For the price of 3 quintals of glass lamps with their wicks, 12¾ dinars.

For the price of Indian aloes to perfume the mosque during the month of Ramaḍān and on Fridays, and for the price of camphor and musk and the wages of the attendant in charge of them, 15 dinars.

For half a quintal of candles, measure of the pepper merchants, 7 dinars.

For the sweeping of the said mosque, the removal of dirt, the stitching of the mats, the price of the thread, and the wages for the stitching, 5 dinars.

For the price of wicks for the lamps, 25 pounds, weight of the pepper merchants, 1 dinar.

For the price of charcoal to burn the perfume, 1 quintal, measure of the pepper merchants, half a dinar.

For the purchase of 2 *ardabbs* of salt for the lamps, a quarter of a dinar.

For whatever is needed to maintain the copperwork, the chains, the chandeliers, and the cupolas on the terrace of the mosque, 24 dinars.

For the price of cords of palm fiber, 4 ropes, and 6 leather buckets, half a dinar.

For the price of 2 quintals of rags for wiping the lamps, half a dinar.

For the price of 10 baskets for the servants and 10 pounds of hemp cords to hang the lamps; for the price of 200 brooms to sweep the said mosque, 1¼ dinars.

For the price of large earthenware jars, to be placed at the side of the cistern and filled with water, and the cost of moving them, 3 dinars.

For the price of oil to be burned in the said mosque, the ration for the year, 1,200 pounds, with the cost of transport, 37½ dinars.

For the stipends of those who lead the prayer, that is to say the Imams, 3 in number, also of 4 caretakers and 15 muezzins, 556½ dinars, that is, for each imam, 2 dinars and two-thirds and one-eighth for every month of the year; for each muezzin and caretaker, 2 dinars a month, and for the superintendent of the said mosque, 24 dinars a year.

For sweeping the cistern of the said mosque, removing the mud and dirt taken out of it, 1 dinar.

For repairs as needed in the said mosque, its terraces, its floors, its walls, and so forth, the sum estimated for each year, 60 dinars.

For the price of 180½ loads of straw, as fodder for the two oxen of the cistern in the said mosque, 8 dinars and a half and a third of a dinar.

For a storehouse in Cairo in which the straw is kept, 4 dinars.

For the price of two feddans of clover to pasture the said two oxen every year, 7 dinars.

For the wages of the fodderer and the water carrier, for the cords, the pails, and the like, 15½ dinars.

For the salary of the man in charge of the basin for ritual ablution, if there is one in the said mosque, 12 dinars.

That is the end of what is said about the Azhar mosque. The document then goes on to deal with the Rāshida mosque, the House of Wisdom, and the Maqs mosque. It then mentions the silver chandeliers, three in number, and thirty-nine silver lamps, of which there were two chandeliers and twenty-seven lamps for the Azhar mosque, and one chandelier and twelve lamps for the Rāshida mosque. The document stipulates that they shall be hung during the month of Ramaḍān and then returned to the place where they are usually kept. It contains numerous stipulations concerning the *waqfs,* among them that if a surplus accumulates, it shall be used to buy a property, that if a building deteriorates and falls into a disrepair and its income does not suffice for its upkeep, it shall be sold and the proceeds used for improvement, and many other similar provisions. In this document he [al-Ḥākim] also constituted as *waqf* a certain number of buildings and *qayṣariyyas* in Fusṭāṭ, which it would be pointless to mention since they are in ruins.

Ibn ʿAbd al-Ẓāhir says of this document: I saw a copy of it

which came into the hands of the chief qāḍī, Taqī al-Dīn ibn Razzīn.

In the heart of this mosque, in the prayer niche [*miḥrāb*], there was a silver band, as in the prayer niche of the mosque of ʿAmr ibn al-ʿĀṣ in Fusṭāṭ. It was removed[4] by Ṣalāḥ al-Dīn Yūsuf ibn Ayyūb [Saladin] on 11 Rabīʿ I 569 [October 20, 1173], for that was the year in which the Fatimid Caliphate came to an end. Its weight reached 5,000 pure silver dirhams. He also removed the bands from the other mosques.

Later the Caliph al-Mustanṣir[5] restored this mosque, as did also al-Ḥāfiẓ li-Dīn Allāh[6] The latter built a beautiful enclosure [*maqṣūra*] near the western door in the forepart of the mosque, inside the covered part. It was known as Fāṭima's *maqṣūra* because Fāṭima the Resplendent [al-Zahrā], may God be pleased with her, was seen there in a dream. The mosque was again restored during the reign of al-Malik al-Ẓāhir Baybars al-Bunduqdārī.[7]

The qāḍī Muḥyi'l-Dīn Ibn ʿAbd al-Ẓāhir says, in his biography of Baybars, "On Friday, 18 Rabīʿ I 665 [December 17, 1266] the communal prayer was held in the Azhar mosque in Cairo. The reason was that the amir ʿIzz al-Dīn Aydemir al-Ḥillī had lived next door to this mosque for a number of years, observing (may God be pleased with him) the rules for those who are neighbors of mosques. Believing that according to his conduct as a neighbor in this world, so tomorrow he would be rewarded in the next world, he ordered an inspection of the affairs of this mosque and restored to it various things which had been filched from it and which were in the possession of certain persons. He examined the affairs of the mosque in all aspects and earned great merit. The matter was much discussed. The amir ʿIzz al-Dīn donated a large sum of his own money for this mosque; he also spent a sum of money on behalf of the Sultan. He began to restore it. He repaired those pillars and walls which were weakened, whitewashed it, restored the ceiling, and paved, carpeted, and covered the floors,

4 The silver band contained Shiʿite formula, unacceptable to a Sunnī ruler.
5 Reigned 1036–1094.
6 Reigned 1130–1149.
7 Reigned 1260–1277.

and once again it became a sanctuary [*ḥaram*] in the midst of the city. He built a fine, new *maqṣūra* and left many pious works for which God will reward him. The amir Bilik, the treasurer, also made a large *maqṣūra* to which he appointed a number of jurists to teach jurisprudence according to the school of the Imam al-Shāfi'ī, may God have mercy on him. He also appointed to this *maqṣūra* a traditionist to teach the traditions of the Prophet, and he established for these purposes *waqfs* with large incomes. He also appointed seven men to recite the Qur'ān and appointed a professor. May God reward him for all this.

When the restoration of the mosque was completed, the celebration of the communal prayer there was discussed. Proclamation to this effect was made by criers in the city. As preacher [*khaṭīb*] he appointed the jurist Zayn al-Dīn, and the communal prayer was held there on the date mentioned. Present were the Atābek Fāris al-Dīn, the Ṣāḥib Bahā' al-Dīn 'Alī ibn Ḥannā, his son the Ṣāḥib Fakhr al-Dīn Muḥammad, a number of amirs and high officers, and various classes of people. It was a well-attended Friday service. When the prayer was over, the amir 'Izz al-Dīn al-Ḥillī, the Atābek, and the Ṣāḥib sat down. The Qur'ān was recited and prayers were offered for the Sultan. Then the amir 'Izz al-Dīn stood up and went home, accompanied by the amirs, to whom he offered all that the soul could crave and the eye enjoy. Then they parted. The question of whether it was lawful to hold the communal prayer in this mosque was discussed, and the opinions of jurists were cited and a legal opinion on the subject written, the ulema concurring in writing that it was lawful to hold the communal prayer in this mosque and to celebrate it. Several jurists gave their opinion in writing to this effect, and the communal prayer was held there and continued. This gave easement and comfort to the people, as the Azhar mosque is near to the quarters which are far from the mosque of al-Ḥākim.

He said: When the mosque was built the ceiling was low. Later it was added to and raised by a cubit. They continued to recite the bidding-prayer [*khuṭba*] in this mosque until the mosque of al-Ḥākim was built, whereupon the bidding-prayer was transferred to it. The Caliph used to recite the bidding-prayer there, then in the Azhar mosque, then in the Ibn Ṭūlūn mosque, then in the mosque of Fusṭāṭ. The bidding-prayer ceased in the Azhar mosque when Sultan Ṣalāḥ al-Dīn Yūsuf ibn Ayyūb seized power. He had appointed as chief qāḍī Ṣadr al-Dīn 'Abd al-Malik ibn Dirbās who acted in accordance with the rules of his school of jurisprudence, that is to say, that it is not lawful to hold two bidding-prayers in the Friday service in the one city, for such is the doctrine of the Imam al-Shāfi'ī. The bidding-prayer was therefore abolished in the Azhar mosque and maintained in the mosque of al-Ḥākim, since the latter is larger. Thus for a hundred years no communal prayer was held in the Azhar mosque, from the time when Sultan Ṣalāḥ al-Dīn Yūsuf ibn Ayyūb gained power until the bidding-prayer was restored in the reign of al-Malik al-Ẓāhir Baybars, as stated above.

When the earthquake occurred in Egypt in Dhu'l-Ḥijja 702 [July–August 1303], the Azhar mosque, the mosque of al-Ḥākim, the mosque of Fusṭāṭ, and others collapsed. The amirs shared the cost of rebuilding the mosques. The amir Rukn al-Dīn Baybars, the Taster [*Chāshnagīr*] undertook the rebuilding of the mosque of al-Ḥākim; the amir Salār, the Azhar mosque; and the amir Sayf al-Dīn Begtimur, the polostick-bearer, the mosque of al-Ṣāliḥ. They repaired the buildings and restored what was ruined.

The building of the Azhar mosque was restored again by the qāḍī Najm al-Dīn Muḥammad ibn Ḥusayn ibn 'Alī al-Is'irdī, the *Muḥtasib* of Cairo, in the year 725 [1325].

Then the building was restored in the year 761 [1359–1360] when the *Ṭawāshī*[8] amir Sa'd al-Dīn Bashīr, the Master of the wardrobe of the Sultan al-Malik al-Nāṣir Ḥasan[9] went to live in the house of the amir Fakhr al-Dīn Abān al-Ẓāḥidī al-Ṣāliḥī al-Najmī in the quarter of the needle makers near the Azhar mosque. He had demolished this house and rebuilt it. His house is still known there to this day as the house of Bashīr, the Master of the wardrobe. Being a near neighbor of the Azhar mosque, he wanted to leave in it a monument of his piety. He therefore sought

[8] A word of Turkish origin, meaning servant or attendant. It was variously used to denote a military rank, membership of a special corps known as the *ṭawāshiyya*, and euphemistically, a eunuch.

[9] Reigned 1347–1351 and 1354–1361.

leave of the Sultan al-Malik al-Nāṣir Ḥasan ibn Muḥammad ibn Qalāwūn to restore the mosque, and as he enjoyed the special favor of the Sultan, he was permitted to do this. A number of *maqṣūras* had been built in the mosque and filled with boxes and chests, so that there was no room. He took away the chests and boxes, removed the *maqṣūras,* and repaired the walls and ceilings so that the mosque became as new. He whitewashed the whole mosque, paved it, stopped people from using it as a passageway, placed a copy of the Qur'ān there, and appointed a reciter to read it. Opposite the southern gate he established a booth, where drinking water was distributed free every day, and above it he built a school where Muslim orphans were taught to recite the book of Almighty God. He arranged to have food cooked every day for the poor who lived in the mosque, and he installed copper cauldrons there for this purpose. In the mosque, he provided for the teaching of jurisprudence according to the Ḥanafī school; the professor, when giving his lectures, was seated by the greater prayer niche. For these purposes he established great *waqfs* which remain to this day; also the muezzins of the mosque still pray for Sultan Ḥasan at every Friday service and after each of the five daily prayers, even to this time in which we are.

In the year 784 [1382] the *Ṭawāshī* amir Bahādur, the commander of the Sultan's mamlūks, took over the supervision of the Azhar mosque. He procured a decree from the Sultan al-Malik al-Ẓāhir Barqūq,[10] according to which when any sojourner [*mujāwir*] in the Azhar mosque died without legal heirs and left property, it was given to the other sojourners in this mosque. This decree was engraved on the stone by the great north gate.

In the year 800 [1397] the minaret of the mosque, which was low, collapsed, and a higher one was built. The cost, which was met by the Sultan's own money, was 15,000 pure silver dirhams. It was completed in Rabīʿ II of the same year [December 1397–January 1398]. On the eve of the first Friday of that month they hung lamps on the minaret and lit them, so that it was illuminated from top to bottom. The Qur'ān reciters and the preachers gathered in the mosque where they read the entire Qur'ān and

[10] Reigned 1382–1399.

prayed for the Sultan. This minaret lasted until Shawwāl 817 [December 1414–January 1415], when it collapsed because of a tilt which had appeared in it. In its place a stone minaret was erected by the north gate of the mosque. The gate itself was demolished and rebuilt in stone, and the minaret was mounted on its arch. The stones for this were taken from the *madrasa* of al-Malik al-Ashraf Khalīl which had been opposite the Citadel and had been demolished by al-Malik al-Nāṣir Faraj ibn Barqūq.[11] The rebuilding was undertaken by the amir Tāj al-Dīn al-Tāj al-Shawbakī, who was chief of police and *Muḥtasib* of Cairo. It was completed in Jumādā II 818 [August 1415]. But after a short time the minaret began to lean and was about to fall. It was demolished in Ṣafar 827 [January 1424] and rebuilt. In Shawwāl of the same year [September] they began to rebuild the cistern, which is in the middle of the mosque. They found in this place the remnants of a water fountain and also the remains of corpses. The construction was completed in Rabīʿ I [828?; February 1425]. Above the cistern they erected a high structure with a cupola for the free distribution of drinking water. They also planted four trees in the courtyard, but they did not thrive and died. When this mosque was built, it had no place for ritual ablutions. Later one was built on the site subsequently occupied by the Aqbughāwiyya *madrasa;* the latter was erected by the amir Aqbughā ʿAbd al-Wāḥid. As to the place of ablution which is in the mosque today, it was built by the amir Badr al-Dīn Jangal ibn al-Bābā; later, after the year 810 [1407–1408], the place of ablution of the Aqbughāwiyya *madrasa* was added to it.

In 818 [1415] the amir Sūdūn, the qāḍī, and the chief chamberlain [*ḥājib al-ḥujjāb*] took over the supervision of this mosque. During his term of office there were events the like of which had never occurred before. Now there had always been in this mosque, since it was built, poor people who lived there permanently. Their number at this time had reached 750, including Persians, people from Zaylaʿ, from the Egyptian countryside, and from North Africa, each group with its own arcade [*riwāq*] known by its name. Thus the mosque was always busy with the recitation,

11 Reigned 1399–1405 and 1406–1412.

study, and dictation of the Qur'ān; with people devoting themselves to various sciences, such as jurisprudence, tradition, exegesis, and grammar; with groups around preachers and circles for the invocation of God's name [*dhikr*], so that a man who entered this mosque would find an intimacy with God, a delight, a refreshment of the soul which he would find in no other mosque. It had become the practice for men of property to bring all kinds of alms to this mosque—gold, silver, or copper coins—so as to serve God by helping those who lived there. From time to time people brought them various kinds of food, bread, and sweets, especially on religious holidays. In Jumādā I [July] of this year, the amir gave orders to eject all those who lived in the mosque, to prevent them from living there, and to remove all their possessions, boxes, chests, and lecterns. He acted in the belief that this would earn a reward from God. But in fact it was a great sin and caused much harm, for a great calamity befell these poor people, who were scattered and had nowhere to go. They went to the villages and suffered hardship in place of their previous security, and the mosque was deprived of most of those Qur'ānic recitations, the pursuit of knowledge, and the invocation of God's name which had been there. Nor did this content him, for he added to his misdeeds and spread it abroad that people were sleeping in the mosque and perpetrating abominations. It was, indeed, the custom for many people to stay overnight in the mosque—merchants, jurists, soldiers, and others. Some sought a blessing by their stay; some had no place to shelter; some came there for relaxation, especially during summer nights and the nights of Ramaḍān, when the courtyard and most of the arcades were full. On the evening of Sunday, 11 Jumādā II [August 18, 1415], in the summer, the amir Sūdūn arrived suddenly after the last prayer of the evening, seized a number of people, and had them flogged in the mosque. He was accompanied by his henchmen, his slaves, common rabble, and a crowd of looters. All kinds of calamity befell the people in the mosque. They were robbed, their bedding and their turbans taken from them, their belts searched, and the gold and silver attached to them stolen. The amir made a black cloth for the pulpit and two embroidered flags, the cost of which reached 15,000 dirhams, according to what I was told. But God did not wait long to punish the amir Sūdūn. The Sultan arrested him in the month of Ramaḍān [November] and imprisoned him in Damascus.

Al-Maqrīzī, *Khiṭaṭ*, ii, pp. 273–277.

4. Inscriptions on Mosques and Schools (1191–1339)

Inscription on a Madrasa in Damascus (*1191*)

In the name of God, the Merciful and the Compassionate. This college [*madrasa*] was constituted as a pious foundation [*waqf*] for the disciples of the Imam Abū ʿAbdallāh Muḥammad ibn Idrīs al-Shāfiʿī by the amir Asad al-Dīn Öküz in the year 586 [1190]. Its construction was completed during the years of al-Malik al-Nāṣir Ṣalāḥ al-Dunyā wa'l-Dīn, the savior of Jerusalem from the hands of the polytheists, Abu'l-Muẓaffar Yūsuf ibn Ayyūb, the reviver of the Empire of the Commander of the Faithful. The shop, which is to the east of it, was constituted a pious foundation for its benefit, as was one-third of the mill at Lawwān, in the year 587 [1191].

RCEA, ix, p. 176, no. 3449.

Inscription on a School in Jerusalem (*1199*)

In the name of God, the Merciful and Compassionate. May God have mercy on all who invoke His mercy on the humble one who built this blessed place and made it a primary school for the children of Muslims in general to learn the Qur'ān. He consecrated to its maintenance [*waqf*] the house known as the House of Abū Niʿāma, under the vault facing the gate of the Aqṣā Mosque, may God cause it to flourish. Its rent shall be spent for the schoolmaster, and the house shall be in his hands to pay for the teaching of orphans and the poor. The remainder shall be spent on the school and the house, the lighting of the lamp under the vault, water for the children to wash their tablets and to drink, on the condition that the schoolmaster shall be a pious and godly man. This is a *waqf* in perpetuity, forever, which shall not be altered or changed. "Whoever changes this after having heard it will be punished" [Qur'ān, ii, 181]. May God make his endeavor worthy of thanks and his offenses of pardon. May He illuminate the resting place of Ṣalāḥ al-Dīn, God have mercy on him and may He keep his children in glory and power. This was written in the course of the year 595 [1199].

RCEA, ix, pp. 220–221, no. 3514.

Inscription on a Marble Tablet, in the Mosque of Sīdī Bū Madyan in Tlemcen (1339)

In the name of God, the Merciful and the Compassionate: May God bless our Lord and our Master Muḥammad and his family and save them. Praise be to God the Lord of the Worlds, and a good end for the pious [Qur'ān, vii, 128].

The building of this blessed mosque, with the college [*madrasa*] attached to it on the western side, was ordered by our master the very just Sultan, the amir of the Muslims, the fighter in the Holy War [*mujāhid*] for the sake of the Lord of the Worlds, Abu'l-Ḥasan, the son of our master, the amir of the Muslims, the fighter in the Holy War for the sake of the Lord of the Worlds Abū Sa'īd, the son of our master the amir of the Muslims, the fighter in the Holy War for the sake of the Lord of the Worlds Abū Yūsuf ibn 'Abd al-Ḥaqq, may God support his rule and perpetuate his memory by good works. He showed his sincerity toward God by his pious works, both private and public, and he consecrated the said college for the benefit of students of the noble science and for its teaching. He consecrated the following, from his royal bounty, to the said mosque and the said college, may God enable them to profit from it:

> The whole of the garden of al-Quṣayr, situated in upper al-'Ubbād, bought from the two children of 'Abd al-Wāḥid al-Quṣayr.
>
> The whole of the garden of al-'Alūj, bought from 'Alī al-Marānī; the whole of the garden known by the name of Ibn Ḥuwayta, situated in Zuwāgha, bought from the heirs of al-Ḥājj Muḥammad ibn Ḥuwayta.
>
> The whole of the large garden and the house adjoining it on the western side known by the name of Dāwūd ibn 'Alī,

bought from his heirs, situated in the lowest part of a lower al-'Ubbād.

The whole of the two pieces of land also inherited from him and bought from his son 'Alī, the one known by the name of Ibn Abī Isḥāq and the other by the name of Ibn Ṣāḥib al-Ṣalāt, both those parts which are planted as well as those which are not.

The whole of the garden known as the garden of al-Bādisī, also inherited from him, bought from Yaḥyā the son of the said Dāwūd, situated in the lowest part of lower al-'Ubbād.

The whole of the garden called Ibn Qar'ūsh, near the said garden of al-Bādisī, also inherited from him and bought from the son of 'Abd al-Wāḥid and 'Isā.

The whole of four orchards of which the highest is known by the name of Ibn Makkiyya, the second, of Muḥammad ibn al-Sarrāj, the third, of Faraj al-Madlisī, and the fourth, of Ibn al-Qudā Qā'isa, also inherited from him and bought from all the heirs.

The whole of his two houses which are to the north of the mosque of lower al-'Ubbād, bought from them likewise.

A half-share of the garden of al-Zuhrī, with the whole of two mills built nearby, in the direction of al-Warīṭ.

The whole of two mills also built at Qal'at Banī Mu'allā, outside the Kashūṭ gate of Tlemcen, may God guard it.

The whole of the bathhouse known as the bathhouse of al-'Āliya, which is inside the said city in the neighborhood of the iron gate, with its two adjoining shops to the right as one goes out by the southern gate, the small house adjoining it on the inner side and the upper chamber above the vestibule.

A half-share of the old bathhouse inside the city of al-Manṣūra, may God protect it.

A piece of plough-land, of the size of 20 yokes, at Tīman Yubīn in Zīdūr in the territory of Tlemcen, to provide foodstuffs for the convent of al-Ubbād, may God cause it to flourish, for the poor and for pilgrims, resident and transient.

Another piece of land of 10 yokes in the said place for those who lodge in the said college at the rate of 15 *ṣā'* per student per month.

The whole of the garden of Sa'īd ibn al-Kammād, bought from his heirs, situated above Upper al-'Ubbād below the Naṣrānī canal.

The whole of the garden of al-Qā'id Mahdī, bought from his heirs, situated at Zuwāgha the God-guarded.

The whole of the garden of al-Tafrīsī, situated below the road leading to al-Warīt, bought from his heirs.

The whole of a piece of garden land, from the heirs of the said al-Tafrīsī, situated to the west of the convent, bought from his heirs.

The rest of the square adjoining the said mosque, being the remainder of the garden on which the mosque was built, bought from the heirs of Muḥammad ibn ʻAbd al-Wāḥid, from the heirs of his father, his mother, and of their maternal aunt Maymūna, so that the heirs retain no claim or right of any kind.

RCEA, xv, p. 103–107, no. 5764.

2
Belief

These two excerpts illustrate some of the consequences of differences of belief and usage among Muslims. The first, from a chronicle, describes an incident in Baghdad resulting from the activities of the puritanical Ḥanbalī school; the second, from a theological work, discusses the dividing line between correct and incorrect belief and rejects the attempt to impose a strictly defined orthodoxy.

5. Puritans in Baghdad (935)

In the year 323 [935] the Ḥanbalīs became active and their power became great. They began to raid the houses of the commanders and of the common people, and if they found wine, they poured it away, and if they found a singing girl, they beat her and broke her instruments. They interfered in buying and selling and with men going with women and boys. When they saw this, they asked the man who his companion was, and if he failed to satisfy them, they beat him and carried him to the chief of police and swore a charge of immorality against him. They raised tumult in Baghdad.

Badr al-Kharshanī, who was the chief of police, rode on 10 Jumādā II [May 17] and made proclamation on both sides of Baghdad against the companions of Abū Muḥammad al-Barbahārī, the Ḥanbalīs, that no two of them should meet, that they should not argue concerning their doctrine, and that their Imams should not pray without beginning with the formula "In the name of God, the Merciful and the Compassionate" in the morning and evening prayers. This was of no avail, and their misdeeds and sedition increased. They sought the help of the blind men who took shelter in the mosques, and when followers of the Shāfiʿī school passed by, they incited the blind men to strike them with sticks until they almost killed them.

A rescript of the Caliph al-Rāḍī was issued against the Ḥanbalīs, denouncing their actions and accusing them of believing in anthropomorphism and other doctrines, in which it was said: "You claim that your ugly and disgusting faces are in the image of the Lord of the World and that your vile appearance is in the image of His; you talk of His feet and fingers and legs and gilded shoes and curly hair and going up to heaven and coming down to the world—may God be raised far above what wrongdoers and unbelievers say about Him. Then you revile the best of the Imams and ascribe unbelief and error to the party of the family of Muḥammad, may God bless and save him. Then you summon the Muslims to religion with manifest innovations and erroneous doctrines, not attested by the Qur'ān, and you reject visits to the tombs of the Imams and abuse those who visit them, accusing them of innovation, but at the same time you yourselves assemble to visit the tomb of a man of the common people, without honor or descent or reason in the Prophet of God, may God bless and save him, and you order people to visit his tomb and you claim for him the miracles of the prophets and the favored of God. May God curse the devil who enticed you with these abominations and that which led him astray. Now the Commander of the Faithful swears by God a mighty oath which must be fulfilled, that if you do not turn away from that which is pernicious in your doctrines and crooked ways, he will surely punish you with beating, exile, death, and dispersal and use the sword against your necks and fire against your dwellings."

Ibn al-Athīr, *Kāmil,* viii, pp. 229–231.

6. On Belief (Eleventh Century)

Among the most extreme and extravagant of men are a group of scholastic theologians who dismiss the Muslim common people as unbelievers and claim that whoever does not know scholastic theology in the form they recognize and does not know the prescriptions of the Holy Law according to the proofs which they have adduced is an unbeliever.

These people have constricted the vast mercy of God to His servants and made paradise the preserve [*waqf*] of a small clique of theologians. They have disregarded what is handed down by the *Sunna*, for it is clear that in the time of the Prophet, may God bless and save him, and in the time of the companions of the Prophet, may God be pleased with them, the Islam of whole groups of rude Arabs was recognized, though they were busy worshipping idols. They did not concern themselves with the science of analogical proof and would have understood nothing of it if they had.

Whoever claims that theology, abstract proofs, and systematic classification are the foundation of belief is an innovator.

Rather is belief a light which God bestows on the hearts of His creatures as the gift and bounty from Him, sometimes through an explainable conviction from within, sometimes because of a dream in sleep, sometimes by seeing the state of bliss of a pious man and the transmission of his light through association and conversation with him, sometimes through one's own state of bliss.

Al-Ghazālī, *Fayṣal al-tafriqa,* p. 202.

3
Pilgrimage

The annual pilgrimage to Mecca and Medina was one of the most powerful unifying forces in Islam, bringing together, in the performance of common ceremonies, Muslims from every part of the far-flung Islamic world. Two accounts of pilgrimages follow, one of an African ruler, the other of a Spanish Arab diplomat.

7. The Pilgrimage of Kankan Mūsā (1324–1325)

We shall now relate some of what we have been able to discover about the history of the Malli-koy Kankan Mūsā.

This Malli-koy was an upright, godly, and devout Sultan. His dominion stretched from the limits of Mallī as far as Sibiridugu, and all the peoples in these lands, Songay and others, obeyed him. Among the signs of his virtue are that he used to emancipate a slave every day, that he made the pilgrimage to the sacred house of God, and that in the course of his pilgrimage he built the great mosque of Timbuctoo as well as the mosques of Dukurey, Gundam, Direy, Wanko, and Bako.

His mother Kankan was a native woman, though some say she was of Arab origin. The cause of his pilgrimage was related to me as follows by the scholar Muḥammad Quma, may God have mercy on him, who had memorized the traditions of the ancients. He said that the Malli-koy Kankan Mūsā had killed his mother, Nana Kankan, by mistake. For this he felt deep regret and remorse and feared retribution. In expiation he gave great sums of money in alms and resolved on a life-long fast.

He asked one of the ulema of his time what he could do to expiate this terrible crime, and he replied, "You should seek refuge with the Prophet of God, may God bless and save him.

Flee to him, place yourself under his protection, and ask him to intercede for you with God, and God will accept his intercession. That is my view."

Kankan Mūsā made up his mind that very day and began to collect the money and equipment needed for the journey. He sent proclamations to all parts of his realm asking for supplies and support and went to one of his shaykhs and asked him to choose the day of his departure. "You should wait," said the shaykh, "for the Saturday which falls on the twelfth day of the month. Set forth on that day, and you will not die before you return safe and sound to your residence, please God."

He therefore delayed and waited until these two coincided, and it was not until nine months later that the twelfth of the month fell on a Saturday. He set forth when the head of his caravan had already reached Timbuctoo, while he himself was still in his residence in Malli.

Since that time travelers of that people believe it is lucky to set out on a journey on a Saturday which falls on the twelfth of a month. It has become proverbial that when a traveler returns in a bad state, they say of him, "Here is one who did not set out on the Malli-koy's Saturday of departure!"

Kankan Mūsā set out in force, with much money and a numerous army. A scholar told me that he heard from our shaykh, the very learned qāḍī Abu'l-'Abbās Sīdī Aḥmad ibn Aḥmad ibn Anda-ag-Muḥammad, may God have mercy on him and be pleased with him, that on the day when the pasha 'Alī ibn al-Qādir[1] left for Twāt, announcing that he was going on the pilgrimage to Mecca, he asked how many persons were going with him and was told that the total number of armed men the pasha had with him was about eighty. "God is great! Praise be to God!," said the qāḍī. "Everything in the world grows less. When Kankan Mūsā left here to go on pilgrimage he had with him 8,000 men. The Askia Muḥammad[2] made the pilgrimage later with 800 men, that is, one-tenth of that. Third after them came 'Alī ibn 'Abd al-Qādir, with 80 men, one-tenth of 800." And he added, "Praise be to God, other

[1] Governor of Timbuctoo, 1628–1632.
[2] Ruler of the Songay people, 1493–1538.

than Whom there is no God! ʻAlī ibn ʻAbd al-Qādir did not even achieve his purpose."

Kankan Mūsā went on his journey, about which there are many stories. Most of them are untrue and the mind refuses to accept them. One such story is that in every town where he stopped on Friday between here and Egypt he built a mosque on that very day. It is said that the mosques of Gundam and Dukurey were among those he built. Both at lunch and at dinner, from when he left his residence until he returned, he ate fresh fish and fresh vegetables.

I was told that his wife, called Inari Konte, went with him, accompanied by 500 of her women and serving women. One day they halted in the middle of the desert between Twāt and Tegāza and made camp. This wife of his lay with him in his tent, but she remained awake while he slept. Then he woke up, and finding that she was wakeful and had not yet slept he asked her "Haven't you slept? What is the matter with you?" She did not reply and remained thus until the middle of the night. Then he woke up again and, finding that she was still awake, adjured her in God's name to tell him what troubled her. "Nothing," she replied, "except the dirt and filth that soil my body. I long for the river—to bathe and plunge and dive and swim. Can you get it for me? Is it in your power to achieve such a thing?"

Vexed by these words, Kankan Mūsā sat up and thought for a while. Then he sent for his slave Farba, who was the chief of his slaves and of his henchmen. Thus summoned, Farba appeared and gave him the greeting due to the king. For this greeting their custom required him to take off his shirt, wrap it round himself, then bow deeply while striking his breast, and then crawl on his knees. In all his realm only the qāḍī could shake his hand. The qāḍī was known by the title of Anfaro-Quma, Quma being the name of the clan from which their qāḍīs came. They did not know the word qāḍī, but called them *anfaro*.

When Farba had completed his greeting, Kankan Mūsā said to him, "Farba, since I married this wife of mine she has never asked me for anything which was beyond my capacity nor for anything which was not within my power and which I could not accomplish, until this night, when she has asked me for the river, to bring it out of nothing into these deserts. Between us and the river lies half a month's travel. Only God alone can accomplish this, for it is beyond my powers."

"Perhaps God will arrange it for you," said Farba, who then went out, weeping and beating his chest, and returned to his quarters. There he summoned the slaves who came in the twinkling of an eye. They numbered 8,700 according to Baba, the *Asarmundio* of the town of Dienné, but according to another source there were exactly 9,000. Farba gave each of them a scoop, then, having paced out a thousand paces, he ordered them to dig. They dug down, removed the soil and dug again, to a depth of three times the height of a man. Then Farba ordered them to line the trench all the way with sand and stones. Over this he told them to lay firewood, and over that kernels of shea butter [*bulanga*]. He then set fire to it. The fire blazed, the shea butter melted on to the stones and the sand and fused them, and the trench became as smooth as pottery. Then Farba ordered them to bring their large and small waterskins. They opened the mouths of these waterskins and the water was poured and flowed into the trench until it was full, rippling and undulating like waves on a great river.

Then Farba returned to Kankan Mūsā and found him and his wife seated together, having been awakened by the blaze and the smoke. After the appropriate greeting, Farba said to him, "My lord, God has come to your help and has removed your care. Where is Inari? Let her come, for God has given you the power to bring the river, by the blessing of that one to whom we are going on pilgrimage, the Prophet of God, may God bless and save him."

This was the moment of the high dawn after that night. She went with her women, to the number of 500, and rode on her mule to the river. They arrived there, full of joy and delight, and bathed, and then they departed. Some of them were drowned in the waters of that trench.

Silmān bana Niahate went with him. He was one of his servants who rode ahead of the caravan with a large group. One day when they were very thirsty they came upon a well in the midst of the desert. They lowered a pail into the well, but as soon as the pail reached the water the cord was cut. A second and a third were cut in the same way, and they thought that there was someone down there who was cútting the cords. They were extremely thirsty, and they gathered round the top of the well, not knowing what to do. Then Silmān bana Niahate rolled up his sleeves, took his knife under his arm and went down the well, leaving the others waiting round the mouth of the well in great distress. At the bottom of the well he found a brigand who had got to the well before them and wanted to keep them from the water so that they would all die of thirst, and he would then come out and collect all their property for himself. He did not expect that anyone would dare to come down against him. Silmān bana Niahate killed him, then he shook the cord and they drew it up—and there was the body of the dead man whom he had killed. After pulling him up they threw the corpse back into the well.

Our shaykh, the Mōri Bukar ibn Sāliḥ, the Wangarbe, may God have mercy on him, told me that Kankan Mūsā took forty muleloads of gold with him when he went on his pilgrimage and visited the tomb of the Prophet.

It is said that he asked the shaykh of the noble and holy city of Mecca, may Almighty God protect it, to give him two, three, or four *sharīfs* of the kin of the Prophet of God, may God bless him and save him, to go with him to his country, so that the people of these parts might be blessed by the sight of them and by the blessing of their footsteps in these lands. But the shaykh refused, it being generally agreed that such things should be prevented and refused out of respect and regard for the noble blood of the *sharīfs* and for fear lest one of them fall into the hands of the infidels and be lost or go astray. But he persisted in his request and urged them very strongly, until the shaykh said, "I will not do it, but I will neither command nor forbid it. If anyone wishes, let him follow you. His fate is in his own hands, I am not responsible."

The Malli-koy then sent a crier to the mosques to say, "Whoever wishes to have a thousand *mithqāls* of gold, let him follow me to my country, and the thousand is ready for him." Four men of the tribe of Quraysh came to him, but it is claimed that they were freedmen [*mawlā*] of Quraysh and not real Qurayshīs. He gave them 4,000, 1,000 each, and they followed him, with their families, when he returned to his country.

When the Malli-koy reached Timbuctoo on his way back, he collected ships and small boats on which he transported their families and luggage, together with his own women, as far as his country, for the riding animals were too exhausted to use. When the ships, carrying the *sharīfs* from Mecca, reached the town of Kami, the Dienné-koy and the Kuran attacked the ships and plundered all that they contained. They took the *sharīfs* ashore and revolted against the Malli-koy. But when the people of the ships told them about the *sharīfs* and informed them of their high station, they attended them, and installed them in a nearby place called Shinshin. It is said that the *sharīfs* of the town of Kay are descended from them.

This is the end of the story of the pilgrimage of the Malli-koy Kankan Mūsā.

Now the Dienné-koy was one of the least of the Malli-koy's slaves and one of his humblest servants. Suffice it to say that he was only admitted to the presence of his wife, that is the Malli-koy's wife, that it was to her that he paid the tax of the region of Dienné, and that he never saw the Malli-koy himself. Praise be to God Who raises up and casts down, Who honors and Who humbles.

If it is asked what difference there is between *mallinke* and *wangara,* then know that the *wangara* and the *mallinke* are of the same origin but that *mallinke* means the warriors while *wangara* means the merchants who carry goods from place to place. As for Malli, it is a vast region and an immense country, containing many towns and villages. The authority of the Sultan of Malli extends over all with force and might. We have heard the common people of our time say that there are four sultans in the world, not counting the supreme Sultan,[3] and they are the Sultan of Bagdad, the Sultan of Egypt, the Sultan of Bornu, and the Sultan of Malli.

attributed to
Maḥmūd Kaʿti ibn al-Ḥāj al-Mutawakkil Kaʿti,
Taʾrīkh al-Fattāsh, pp. 32–38.

[3] Presumably the ruler of Constantinople.

8. A Pilgrimage from Spain (1440)

It was the month of Dhu'l-Ḥijja. People were preparing to enter the city, and the amir of Mecca and the *sharīfs* came out to meet the caravans. It is the custom of the pilgrims when they enter Mecca and Medina to drape their howdahs and litters with beautiful covers of gold-braided silk, colored draperies, and the like. They adorn their camels with gold and silver bracelets on their feet, put helmets of silver mail on their brows, and display great pomp and splendor, which gladden souls and fill hearts with joy. Praise be to God for the glory and greatness of Islam.

Our journey from Egypt to Mecca took thirty-seven days. We entered Mecca, may God ennoble it, by the Mi'lā gate in the al-Thaniyya quarter. We were already in a state of sanctity [*iḥrām*],[1] having pronounced the *talbiya*,[2] taken off our ordinary clothes, and carried out the other acts necessary to the pilgrimage. The amir lodged us in the Ḥaram al-Sharīf,[3] in a *ribāṭ* near the Ḥaram mosque called Ribāṭ al-Sidra, where we left our luggage.

Then we made for the Holy Ka'ba, entering by the al-Salām gate of the Ḥaram al-Sharīf. We performed the *ṭawāf*[4] of arrival and the two prostrations before the station of [Ibrāhīm] the Friend of God,[5] upon him blessing and peace! Then we came out by the gate of al-Ṣafā in order to perform the *sa'y*[6] between al-Ṣafā and Marwa, which we did in accordance with the prescriptions of the Holy Law regarding pace and prayer. Then we shaved

[1] A technical term for the state of temporary consecration required of one performing the pilgrimage. The attainment of this state involves a statement of intention, followed by the completion of certain rites and the wearing of the pilgrim's ritual garment. A person in a state of *iḥrām* is called *muḥrim*. See *EI*², "Iḥrām," and, on the pilgrimage in general, "Ḥadjdj."

[2] A formula of religious devotion, beginning with the word *labbayka*, used on various occasions and especially during the pilgrimage. See *EI*¹, s.v.

[3] The Noble Sanctuary, that is, the area including the sacred mosque in Mecca.

[4] The circumambulation of a sacred object. See *EI*¹, s.v.

[5] The patriarch Abraham, regarded by Muslims as the founder or renovator of the monotheistic cult of the Ka'ba.

[6] An ambulation, part walking, part running, performed by pilgrims after visiting the Ka'ba. See *EI*¹, s.v.

our heads and ended our *iḥrām* by resuming our ordinary clothes and cleansing ourselves, and the like.

In the morning and the evening we went to the Ḥaram al-Sharīf, seeking to come as near to God as was possible by means of *ṭawāf*, prayers, invocations, and the contemplation of these holy places, until the eighth day of the month of Dhu'l-Ḥijja, which is the day of *tarwiya*.[7] We performed the major ablution, so as to enter into the state of sanctity for the pilgrimage, took off our ordinary clothes, and carried out the obligations of the *muḥrim*. Then we went back to the holy Ka'ba and there entered into a state of ritual consecration, as required for the pilgrimage.

The same evening we went out to Minā, which we reached at sunset. We stayed in that place for a while to feed our mounts and to have some rest. Then we walked to 'Arafa, which we reached shortly before midnight. We rose next morning and went to visit its holy places, such as the dome of Adam, peace be upon him, the 'Alamān, and the Baṭn 'Urāna, calling upon God and drawing as near to Him as we could, until it was time for the midday prayer. We went to the mosque and were with the Imam during the time between the midday and afternoon prayers. Then he rose and preached to the people and reminded them of their ritual and other duties. Then we returned to our lodgings and stayed there until the time of the afternoon prayer. The sun grew pale, and people gathered, on foot and mounted, on the holy mountain. We stood and prayed to God, with the special prayers for this noble occasion, until the sun set and the shadows spread. We then dispersed, passing between the two towers to Muzdalifa where the pilgrims foregather between the evening and night prayers. From there we went to the Mash'ar al-Ḥarām, where we spent the night and rose for the morning prayer. We made our way to al-Muḥaṣṣib and collected the pebbles which we needed to throw in Minā. Then we went to Minā, where we arrived at sunrise on the day of the Feast of Sacrifice. We found lodgings in Minā and then we made for Jamrat al-'Aqaba, at which we threw pebbles in accordance with commandments and then we made sacrifice and offering.

[7] The day on which the pilgrimage formally begins. See *EI*[1], s.v.

Then we lodged in Mecca, where we made the *ṭawāf al-ifāḍa* as prescribed and performed the *sa'y* between al-Ṣafā and Marwa. Then we returned to Minā and stayed there until the third day after the Day of Sacrifice to throw the rest of the prescribed pebbles. Then we went back to Mecca and made the *ṭawāf* of farewell; then we left the city, our Pilgrimage being completed, may God be greatly praised, as befits His glory.

. . . .

Description of 'Arafa, May God Ennoble It

It is said that the reason why it is called by this name is that Adam and Eve, peace be on both of them, met and recognized one another [*ta'arrafā*] here. It is a large hill. The place of assembly of the pilgrims is in the middle, extending towards Mecca, may God ennoble it. At the end of the plain there is a hill connected with the mountain, and at the top is the noble dome called the dome of Adam [*Qubbat Adam*], peace be upon him. It has three open doors through which people jostle to enter in order to seek the blessing of this place. Sometimes some of them die in the crush. We ourselves saw something of the kind.

On one side of this plain there is a small village which has begun to fall in ruins. In the plain there was a mosque in which people gathered between the midday and afternoon prayers and of which only some traces remain. Here, too, are the 'Alamān,[8] two towers between which people pass when they disperse at nightfall on the day of 'Arafa. In this place there are many wells of sweet water.

It is a great place of assembly where people from all lands foregather, in numbers that God alone knows. When they stand there and their voices rise in prayer and supplication to Almighty God, you would think that the Day of Judgment had come and that all mankind had come together as one. We pray to Almighty God to treat us with His universal kindness at the time of this great gathering.

[8] Literally the two signs, or marks. These mark the limit of the sacred territory.

Muzdalifa is a place between ʿArafa and Minā, where people gather between the sunset and evening prayers. It adjoins the Mashʿar al-Ḥarām, where there is a fine, great mosque and where people pass the night of the Day of Sacrifice, until the time for the morning prayer. But most of these votive practices have been abandoned.

Minā is a village between Mecca and ʿArafa. It contains a great mosque, called the Mosque of al-Khayf, in which pilgrims meet for prayer during the days of their stay in Minā. There is also a large dome in which people come to pray, called the dome of Ismāʿīl. In the center of this village there is a great market where untold quantities of cloth, jewels, and Indian and Syrian merchandise are sold. Dealings take place only during the time that the pilgrims spend in Minā.

In the middle of this market are the three *jamras*[9] against which people throw their pebbles. The first, Jamrat al-ʿAqaba, is at the far end of the market near the road to Mecca, may God ennoble it, very near the dome of Ismāʿīl, peace be upon him. It is cubic in shape, 2 fathoms high, and 4 spans wide on each side. The second *jamra* is in the middle of the market and is similar in construction to the first, and the third is near the end of the market which leads to ʿArafa and is similar in construction to the other two. Every year the pebbles reach nearly half way up the *jamras,* yet by the following year only a few remain. The people say that those that are accepted are raised up [to heaven] and that if this were not so, the pebbles would overtop them. God knows best whether this is the truth.

The people stay in Minā until the midday prayer on the second day after the Day of Sacrifice, when they begin to leave. The military detachments leave on this day; the "First" at noon on the third day; the *Maḥmal*[10] at noon on the fourth day, and the Syrian pilgrimage at noon on the fifth day.

[9] Jamra, a pebble, is the name given to three halts in the vale of Minā, where the ceremony of lapidation takes place. See *EI*², "Djamra."

[10] The *maḥmals* were elaborately ornamented empty litters sent by Muslim rulers to lead the pilgrim caravans from their countries. The sending of a *maḥmal,* and the precedence assigned to it during the ceremonies, were of some political importance. See *EI*¹, s.v.

Description of Mecca, May God Ennoble It

Mecca is a great city enclosed within a valley. It is surrounded by three great mountains. One of them is the mountain of Abū Qubays, which according to tradition was the first mountain that God created. In it the black stone was deposited at the time of the flood. The Quraysh used to call this mountain al-Amīn [the faithful] because it gave the stone to Ibrāhīm, peace be upon him. In this mountain are the tomb of Adam, peace be upon him, and the place where the Prophet, may God bless and save him, stood when the moon was parted in two.[11] It is one of the noteworthy features of Mecca.

Mount al-Muḥaṣṣib is on the western side of Mecca and also adjoins Minā. Mount Thabīr is near Mecca.

Mecca is very hot because it is near the north [sic], and nobody can wear clothes during the summer. During the hot season the wells produce hot water, unlike other countries. Most of the inhabitants have dark skins and lean bodies. They have no foodstuffs or other supplies, apart from what is brought to them by pilgrims and by Indian and Egyptian ships, for as God has said, Mecca is barren and has no tillage.[12] They drink well water. A Syrian merchant called Ibn al-Muzliq brought them water quite recently. He built a very large cistern outside the city to catch this water, which the pilgrims drink and with which they water their camels. This is a good work. It is said that the cistern was ancient and that the merchant rebuilt it.

The Ḥaram mosque is in the center of the city. Its length is 400 . . . [manuscript ends here].

From the Narrative of the Ambassadors of the Sultan of Granada to the Sultan of Egypt, 1440.
Published in the *Bulletin of the Faculty of Arts of the University of Cairo*, vol. xvi/1, 1954, pp. 106–110.

[11] An allusion to Qur'ān, liv, 1.
[12] Cf. Qur'ān, xiv, 40.

4
The Law and Its Upholders

The holy law is one of the greatest and most characteristic achievements of Islam. The following excerpts illustrate some aspects of its content and administration. The first, from the great jurist al-Shāfiʿī, states the principle of consensus, which is central to Islamic law and doctrine. The second deals with some points of criminal law, the third and fourth with the administration of justice. The last two are selected from the vast Islamic biographical literature and deal with two individual qāḍīs, an early medieval Spaniard and a late medieval Turk.

9. The Doctrine of Consensus. (*Ijmāʿ*) According to al-Shāfiʿī (d. 820)

Al-Shāfiʿī said, may God have mercy on him: Someone said to me: I have understood your rule concerning the prescriptions of God and the prescriptions of his Prophet, may God bless and save him, and I have understood that whoever follows the Prophet follows God in that God has enjoined obedience to His Prophet. There is also proof of what you say, that no Muslim who knows a Qur'ānic text or a *Sunna* may maintain the contrary of either of them, and I have understood that this, too, is a prescription of God. But what is your proof for following that on which the people are agreed when there is no text to that effect, either as a revelation from God or as a tradition handed down from the Prophet? Do you believe as some others do, that their consensus [*ijmāʿ*] can only rest on a firm *Sunna*, even when it is not handed down?

I answered him: That on which they are in agreement and say that it is a tradition handed down from the Prophet is as they say, if it please God. As regards that which they do not report on the authority of the Prophet but maintain, perhaps on the basis of a tradition ascribed to the Prophet, is perhaps not so, so that we may not consider it as a tradition from the Prophet, given that one may only transmit further that which one has heard oneself and that if anyone transmits anything on the basis of a guess, the contrary of what he says may also be the case; we maintain what they maintain, following their authority, because we know that even though the *Sunna* of the Prophet may be forgotten by some of them, it cannot be forgotten by all of them, and we know that all of them cannot come to agreement on something contrary to the *Sunna* of the Prophet or on any error, please God.

He asked: Is there anything which proves or supports this?

I answered: Sufyān ibn 'Uyayna informed us, on the authority of 'Abd al-Malik ibn 'Umayr, on the authority of 'Abd al-Raḥmān ibn 'Abdallāh ibn Mas'ūd, on the authority of his father, that the Prophet, may God bless and save him, said: "May God prosper a man who hears what I say, remembers it, keeps it, and hands it on. One may transmit jurisprudence without being a jurist or transmit learning to one who is more learned than oneself. There are three things by which the heart of a Muslim cannot go wrong: sincere behavior toward God, good counsel to the Muslims, and keeping to the community of the Muslims; and their preaching encompasses them entirely."

Al-Shāfi'ī, may God have mercy on him, said: Sufyān informed us, on the authority of 'Ubaydallāh ibn Abī Lubayd, on the authority of Sulaymān ibn Yasār, on the authority of his father, that 'Umar ibn al-Khaṭṭāb, may God be pleased with him, rose in al-Jābiya to make a speech and said: The Prophet rose among us as I rise among you and said, "Honor my Companions, then those who come after them, then those who come after them. Then falsehood will appear, so that a man will swear without being called upon to swear and bear witness without being summoned to bear witness. He who would like to dwell in the midst of Paradise should keep close to the community, for the devil is with the isolated and even keeps away from two together. No man should be alone with a [strange] woman for the devil will be the third with them. He who delights in his good deeds and is grieved by his bad deeds is a believer."

Al-Shāfi'ī said, may God have mercy on him: The man asked, "What is the meaning of the Prophet's command to keep close to the community?"

I replied: It has only one meaning.

He asked: How can it have but one meaning?

I replied: Since the community is scattered through many lands, no one person can keep close to the physical community of scattered peoples, and since the physical community embraces Muslims and unbelievers, pious and sinners, therefore it follows that keeping close to the physical community has no meaning because it is not possible and because the physical community serves no purpose. Therefore, keeping close to the community can have as its only meaning that one should follow the community with regard to what is permitted and what is forbidden and obey in both respects. He who maintains what the community of the Muslims maintains is keeping close to the community, and he who deviates from what the community of the Muslims maintains deviates from that community to which he is commanded to remain close. Error arises in separation. In the community there can be no total error concerning the meaning of the Book of God, of *Sunna*, or of *qiyās*,[1] please God.

Al-Shāfi'ī, *Kitāb al-Umm, Kitāb al-Risāla,* i, p. 65.

10. Discretionary Punishment (ca. 1311–1315)

Offenses for which there is no prescribed specific penalty [*ḥadd*] nor any expiatory compensation, such as he who kisses or caresses a young boy or a strange woman without intercourse; who eats what is forbidden, like blood or carrion; who makes false accusations of offenses other than fornication; who steals unguarded property or property of a value less than the minimum specified for punishment; who betrays a trust, as custodians of the property of the Treasury, of *waqfs*, of orphans and the like or who embezzle; trustees or partners who betray their trust or

[1] Reasoning by analogy.

commit fraud; traders who cheat in food, clothing, or the like, who give short measure; those who give or procure false witness; those who accept bribes in judgment, or who do not judge in conformity with God's command, or who oppress their subjects; those who mourn the dead with heathen practices or who answer the call of heathenism; and other similar transgressions—all are subject to punishment at the discretion of the ruler, taking account of the following:

The prevalence or rarity of the offense among people. If it is common, the punishment is greater; if it is rare, the reverse.

The position of the culprit. If he is a habitual offender, his punishment is greater; if he offends rarely, the reverse.

The greatness or littleness of the offense. He who assaults many women or many boys shall be more severely punished than he who assaults only one woman or one boy.

No limit [*ḥadd*] is set for the lightest penalty. Punishment consists of inflicting pain on a man, whether by words or acts or by abstaining from words or acts. A man may be punished by admonition, rebuke, or censure. He may also, if expedient, be punished by the ban and the withholding of greeting until he repents. Thus the Prophet, may God bless and save him, and his Companions laid a ban on the three men who had held back [at the time of the expedition to Tabuk]. He may be punished by dismissal from office, as was done by the Prophet, may God bless and save him, and his Companions. He may be punished by not being employed in the army [*jund*] of the Muslims, as is the case with deserters from battle, for this is a mortal offense. Cancellation of the grant is also a form of punishment. Likewise, if an amir commits a serious offense, he should be dismissed.

A man may also be punished by imprisonment or by flogging; he may be punished by having his face blackened and being paraded mounted backwards on an ass. It is related that 'Umar ibn al- Khaṭṭāb, may God be pleased with him, used this punishment for a false witness. Because the liar blackened a reputation, his face was blackened; because he turned words backwards, he was mounted backwards.

As regards the maximum discretionary punishment, some jurists hold that discretionary punishment must always be less than the prescribed specific penalty [*ḥadd*]. Among these there are two opinions. One group says that the discretionary punishment must always be less than the minimum prescribed penalty. Thus a free man must always receive less than the minimum prescribed penalty for freemen, which is forty or eighty lashes; a slave, less than the minimum prescribed penalty for slaves, which is twenty or forty lashes. Some even hold that the discretionary punishment to which either of them is liable must always be less than the minimum prescribed penalty to which a slave is liable. Others hold that a discretionary punishment for any offenses must always be less than the prescribed penalty for offense of the same type but may exceed the prescribed penalty for offenses of another type. Thus a man who steals an unguarded object suffers a lesser punishment than having his hand cut off but may be given a flogging greater than that given to a slanderer. The man who commits a moral offense short of fornication suffers a lesser punishment than that prescribed for a fornicator but may be more severely punished than a slanderer. Thus, it is told of 'Umar ibn al-Khaṭṭāb, may God be pleased with him, that when a man had a false seal engraved on his ring and thus cheated the public Treasury, 'Umar gave one hundred lashes on the first day, the same on the second, and the same on the third. It is told of the righteous [patriarchal] Caliphs that when a man and a woman were found under the same blanket, they were given one hundred lashes. It is told of the Prophet, may God bless and save him, that if a man committed fornication with his wife's slave-girl when his wife had given her to him, he gave him one hundred lashes, but if she had not given her to him, he had him stoned.

These last doctrines are accepted in the school of Aḥmad ibn Ḥanbal and other schools. The first two are the doctrines of the school of al-Shāfi'ī and others.

Mālik and some other jurists are quoted as saying that certain crimes incur death. Some Ḥanbalīs agreed, as in the case of a Muslim spy who spied on the Muslims on behalf of the enemy. Aḥmad ibn Ḥanbal hesitates to apply the death penalty to him, but Mālik and some Ḥanbalīs, such as Ibn 'Aqīl, authorize it. Abū Ḥanīfa, Shāfi'i, and some Ḥanbalīs, such as the qāḍī Abū Ya'lā, prohibit it.

A group of Shāfi'is, Ḥanbalīs, and some other jurists consider it lawful to put to death those who spread innovations contrary to the book of God and to the *Sunna*. So do a large number of Mālikīs. They say that Mālik and other jurists held it lawful to put the Qadariyya to death, not for apostasy but for spreading evil [*fasād*] in the land.

The same has been said concerning the execution of the sorcerer. Most jurists are of the opinion that he should be put to death. A tradition is related, on the authority of Jundub, with a full chain of transmitters, that "the prescribed penalty for the sorcerer is that he be put to the sword." This tradition is also found in Tirmidhī. 'Umar, 'Uthmān, Ḥafṣa, 'Abdallāh ibn 'Umar, and other Companions, may God be pleased with them, are also cited for the execution of sorcerers. According to some jurists, this death penalty is for unbelief [*kufr*]; according to others, for spreading evil [*fasād*] in the land; but all agree that this is a prescribed penalty [*ḥadd*].

Abū Ḥanīfa authorizes death as a discretionary punishment for offenses which are repeated if they are of the kind which incurs the death penalty. Thus the death penalty may be imposed for habitual pederasty, robbery with violence, or the like.

The authority for the execution of an evildoer whose evil deeds can only be stopped by his death is in a tradition given by Muslim in his *Ṣaḥīḥ*, as transmitted by 'Arfaja al-Ashja'ī, may God be pleased with him, who said, "I heard the Prophet of God, may God bless and save him, say, 'If, when you are all united under one man, someone comes and tries to sow discord among you and disrupt your unity, kill him!' " Another version reads "There will be much deterioration. If anyone seeks to disrupt this community when it is united, kill him with the sword, whoever he may be." Similarly, the Prophet is quoted as authorizing the execution of a drunkard at the fourth offense. The authority for this is a tradition related by Aḥmad ibn Ḥanbal in his *Musnad*, as transmitted by Daylam al-Ḥimyarī, may God be pleased with him, who said, I asked the Prophet of God, may God bless and save him, " O Prophet of God! Here we are in a country where we have hard work to do. We take a drink made from wheat which fortifies us in our work and also against the cold of our country."

"Does it intoxicate?" asked the Prophet. "Yes," I replied. "Then do not drink it," he said. "But people will not give it up," I said. "If they do not give it up, kill them," said the Prophet. "This is because the promoter of evil is like one who attacks people with violence. If his violence can only be stopped by death, he is put to death."

It follows from all this that there are two kinds of punishment. One kind is for an offense already committed and is a well-earned retribution from God, such as flogging a drunkard or a slanderer or cutting off the hand of a brigand or a thief. The other is a punishment to ensure the discharge of a duty or the cessation of an offense in the future. Thus an apostate is called upon to repent and return to Islam, and if he does not, he is put to death. Similarly, any who fail to pray, to pay the alms tax, or respect the rights of others are punished until they carry out their obligations. Discretionary punishments of the second type are more severe than those of the first. Thus, a man may be flogged again and again until he performs the necessary prayer or carries out his other duties. There is a tradition in the two *Ṣaḥīḥs*,[1] on the authority of the Prophet of God, may God bless and save him, that no man shall be given more than ten lashes except in one of the limits [*ḥadd*] of God. To explain this, some jurists say that the meaning of "*ḥadd* of God" is all that which is forbidden by God's right. Indeed, the term *ḥadd* in the vocabulary of the Qur'ān and in the *Sunna* means the delimitation of the permitted and the forbidden. It also means the end of what is permited and the beginning of what is forbidden. With the first meaning, "These are the bounds drawn by God; do not transgress them!" [Qur'ān, ii, 229]. With the second meaning, "These are the bounds drawn by God; keep well within them" [Qur'ān, ii, 187]. The use of the term *ḥadd* for legal punishment is modern. The meaning of the tradition cited above is, therefore, that if any person flogs another to enforce a right which he has over him, as for example when a husband beats his wife for misbehavior, he should not exceed ten lashes.

Ibn Taymiyya, *Al-Siyāsa al-Shar'iyya*, pp. 112–127.

[1] Two standard collections of *ḥadīths*.

11. On Qāḍīs (Eleventh Century)

Nobody may be appointed to the office of qāḍī who does not comply fully with the conditions required to make his appointment valid and his decisions effective. They are seven in number.

1. The first condition is that he must be a man. This condition consists of two qualities, puberty and masculinity. As for the child below puberty, he cannot be held accountable, nor can his utterances have effect against himself; how much less so against others. As for women, they are unsuited to positions of authority, although judicial verdicts may be based on what they say. Abū Ḥanīfa said that a woman can act as qāḍī in matters on which it would be lawful for her to testify, but she may not act as qāḍī in matters on which it would not be lawful for her to testify. Ibn Jarīr al-Ṭabarī, giving a divergent [*shādhdh*] view, allows a woman to act as qāḍī in all cases, but no account should be taken of an opinion which is refuted by both the consensus of the community and the word of God. "Men have authority over women because of what God has conferred on the one in preference to the other" [Qur'ān, iv, 38], meaning by this, intelligence and discernment. He does not therefore, permit women to hold authority over men.
2. The second condition is intelligence, the importance of which is universally recognized. It is not enough to have the intelligence which qualifies for legal responsibility [*taklīf*], that is to say, the use of the five necessary senses. He must also have discriminating judgment and great perspicacity, be far from forgetfulness and negligence, and have sufficient acumen to clarify difficulties and resolve obscure cases.
3. The third condition is freedom, since the slave, having no authority over himself, cannot have authority over others. Moreover, since his state of slavery makes his testimony unacceptable, all the more does it prevent his holding authority and giving valid judgments. The rule is the same for one whose freedom is incomplete, such as the slave whose liberation will be completed by the death of his master [*mudabbar*] or by contract [*mukātab*], or the partial slave. But the state of slavery does not prevent a man from giving juridical rulings [*fatwā*]

or from relating traditions, since neither of these involves the exercise of authority. When freed, he can act as qāḍī, though bound by the obligations of patronage [*walā'*], because descent [*nasab*] is not taken into account in conferring judicial authority.

4. The fourth condition is Islam, because this is a necessary condition for the right to testify and because of the word of God, "God will not give the unbelievers the advantage over the believers" [Qur'ān, iv, 140]. It is not lawful for an unbeliever to exercise judicial authority over Muslims or over unbelievers. Abū Ḥanīfa said that an unbeliever may be appointed to dispense justice among his coreligionists. Though it is common practice for rulers to appoint unbelievers in this way, it is an appointment as chief or head and not an appointment conferring judicial authority. His decisions bind them because they voluntarily submit to him, not because he has binding authority over them, and the Imam does not assent to his rulings in judgments rendered by him among his coreligionists. If his people do not resort to his jurisdiction, they are not compelled to do so, and they will then be subject to Islamic judicial authority.
5. The fifth condition is rectitude [*'adāla*], which is a requirement for any position of authority. This means that a man speaks truth, is manifestly trustworthy, virtuously refrains from forbidden things and avoids sin, is beyond suspicion, can be trusted in both approval and anger, and conducts himself as befits a man like him in both religious and worldly matters. The fulfillment of all these requirements constitutes rectitude, which qualifies him to testify and to exercise authority. If any of these qualities is lacking, he may neither testify nor exercise authority; his words shall not be heard nor his judgment executed.
6. The sixth condition is soundness of sight and hearing, so that by their means he may determine rights, distinguish between plaintiff and defendant, and differentiate between those who affirm and those who deny in such a way that the difference between truth and falsehood may be clear to him and that he may know the speaker of truth from the liar. If he is blind he is disqualified to exercise authority, but Mālik considers that a blind man may be a qāḍī just as he can bear witness. As to deafness, there are the same differences of opinion as for the Imamate. Soundness of limb is not a requirement, though it is

for the Imamate. A chronic invalid may therefore sit as qāḍī, although freedom from physical defects gives greater dignity to those exercising authority.

7. The seventh condition is that he must be learned in the rules of the Holy Law, his knowledge covering both general principles and specific applications.

   The sources of the rules of the Holy Law are four:

   1. Knowledge of God's book, so that he has a sound understanding of the rules contained in it, both abrogating and abrogated, both precise and equivocal, both general and specific, and both unexplained and clearly interpreted.
   2. Knowledge of the authentic tradition [*Sunna*] of the Prophet of God, may God bless and save him, of his words and his deeds, how they were transmitted, by many or by few, which are genuine and which false and which refer only to a specific occasion and which are of general application.
   3. Knowledge of the interpretations of the first generation of Muslims, whether unanimous or divergent, conforming to the consensus or exercising independent judgment [*ijtihād*] in cases of disagreement.
   4. Knowledge of analogy, the method used to deduce implicit consequences from explicit and agreed principles, so as to attain the knowledge required to settle lawsuits and to distinguish true from false.

If he masters these four sources of the rules of the Holy Law, he becomes a *mujtahid* in religion, and is allowed to act as muftī or qāḍī, and may be asked to act in either capacity. But if he is deficient in them or in any part of them, he cannot be a *mujtahid* and may not act as muftī or qāḍī, and if despite this he is appointed as a judge and gives decisions, whether right or wrong, his appointment is invalid and his decisions, even if they are sound and just, are rejected, and the sin for whatever he adjudges falls both on him and on the one who appointed him as qāḍī.

Al-Māwardī, pp. 61–63.

12. Administrative Justice (Fourteenth–Fifteenth Centuries)

Under the Turkish dynasty the rank of chamberlain was very high, ranking immediately after that of the deputy of the Sultan. The chief chamberlain had the title of Chamberlain of Chamberlains. The duties of this office were that he who held it should dispense justice among the amirs and the military, sometimes acting on his own, sometimes in consultation with the Sultan, sometimes in consultation with the deputy. It was his duty to present petitioners and visitors and to arrange parades of the troops. When there was no deputy, he was the principal functionary at court and replaced the deputies in most of their duties. The judicial authority of the chamberlain, was, however, limited to disputes and litigation among the military about grants [*iqṭāʿ*] and other such matters. No chamberlain in the past presumed to adjudicate in matters falling within the scope of the Holy Law, such as matrimonial disputes or the claims of creditors. Such matters were the exclusive concern of the qāḍīs. We always used to see scribes, tax farmers [*ḍāmin*], and suchlike fleeing from the door of the chamberlain and having to resort to that of a qāḍī in order to seek the protection of the Holy Law, nor would anyone after that dare to take him from the door of the qāḍī. Some even stayed for months or years under the control of the qāḍī protecting them from the hands of the chamberlains. Then things changed. Today many amirs use the title of chamberlain and set themselves up to adjudicate between people for no other purpose than to farm out, in the form of *ḍamāns,* their financial resources for a fixed sum, collected by [imposed on?] their bailiffs daily. There is more than one amir who has no grant with his amirate and whose sole income is from the "inspection of grievances." Today the chamberlain adjudicates among all people, great and small, both in matters of Holy Law and of what they call *siyāsa,* administrative justice. If a qāḍī tries to seize a litigant from the door of the chamberlain, he is unable to do so. The chamberlain's bailiff, on the other hand—whatever the chamberlain's baseness, turpitude, and scandalous public debauchery such as in other days the lowest rabble would not have committed—can seize a litigant from the door of the qāḍī and beat him or extort money from him as he pleases, and none protest.

Al-Maqrīzī, *Khiṭaṭ*, ii, pp. 219–220.

13. The Qāḍī 'Abd al-Raḥmān ibn Ṭarīf al-Yahṣubī (Eighth Century)

Aḥmad ibn Khālid said: It was the custom of the Caliphs, may God have mercy on them, to enquire into reports about people, to seek out men of learning and worth, and to get to know the places where they lived, both in Cordova and elsewhere in the provinces. Then, when they needed a suitable man for some purpose, they sent for him.

The amir 'Abd al-Raḥmān ibn Mu'āwiya, may God have mercy on him, had need to appoint a qāḍī for the district of Cordova. He had heard of a man in Merida, of probity, firmness, and piety. He sent for him and appointed him, and he conducted himself worthily in the office of qāḍī.

Muḥammad ibn 'Abd al-Malīk ibn Ayman said: One of those who served as qāḍī for 'Abd al-Raḥman ibn Mu'āwiya, may God be pleased with both of them, was 'Abd al-Raḥmān ibn Ṭarīf, an inhabitant of the city of Merida and an honorable man of praiseworthy conduct. . . .

Muḥammad said: Khālid ibn Sa'd said: I heard Muḥammad ibn Ibrāhīm ibn al-Jabbāb repeat the following story: Ḥabīb al-Qurashī appeared before the amir 'Abd al-Raḥmān ibn Mu'āwiya, may God have mercy on him, to complain against the qāḍī 'Abd al-Raḥmān ibn Ṭarīf. He said that the qāḍī intended to record a verdict against him in a case about an estate on which al-Qurashī was living and concerning which a claim had been brought against him, alleging that he had misappropriated it by force. The amir sent a messenger to the qāḍī, who spoke with him on the matter. He ordered him to proceed with caution and forbade him to act in haste. Thereupon the qāḍī Ibn Ṭarīf went out immediately, sent for the jurisconsults and legal witnesses, pronounced a verdict against Ḥabīb, recorded it, and had it witnessed. Ḥabīb went to the amir and incited him against the qāḍī, saying that he hated the amir and made light of him. The amir was very angry and sent for the qāḍī Ibn Ṭarīf. He had him brought into his presence and said to him, "Who impelled you to pronounce a verdict after I had ordered you to proceed with caution?"

"I was impelled to do it," replied Ibn Ṭarīf, "by the same one who seated you on this throne, but for whom you would not sit there."

"Your words," said the amir, "are even stranger than your deeds. Who seated me on this throne?"

"The Prophet of the Lord of the Universe," replied the qāḍī. "Were it not for your kinship with him, you would not sit on this throne. He was sent with the Truth to dispense justice to all, far and near. O amir," said the qāḍī, "what induces you to favor one of your subjects at the expense of another? You could find a way of satisfying the one who interests you by using your own money."

"If those," said the amir, "who are the rightful owners of the estate are willing to sell it, I would buy it for Ḥabīb with my own money and satisfy them in the price."

"I shall send for them," said Ibn Ṭarīf, "and put this to them. If they are willing to sell, well and good, but if not, my verdict stands."

The qāḍī went away and sent for the owners. He spoke to them about the estate and they agreed to sell it if the price were good.

Ḥabīb used to say thereafter, "May God reward Ibn Ṭarīf for my sake. I held an estate unlawfully, and Ibn Ṭarīf made it lawful for me."

Muḥammad ibn al-Ḥārith al-Khushanī,
Kitāb al-Quḍāt bi-Qurṭuba, pp. 42–44.

14. The Biography of an Ottoman Jurist (1350–1431)

Among the scholars of the time of Sultan Bāyezīd was the learned, excellent, and worthy Mollā Shams al-Dīn Muḥammad ibn Ḥamza ibn Muḥammad al-Fanāri, may God sanctify his noble spirit.

Al-Suyūṭī said: I heard from our learned shaykh Muḥyi'l-Dīn the rhymester (al-Kāfiyeji) that the designation Fanārī refers to the craft of lantern maker. But I heard from my father, may God have mercy on him, who heard from my grandfather, that the name comes from a village called Fanār. God knows best.

Al-Suyūṭī said: Our learned shaykh Muḥyi'l-Dīn al-Kāfiyeji was constantly in his company and spoke very highly indeed in his praise.

Ibn Ḥajar al-ʿAsqalānī said: Mollā al-Fanārī was skilled in the arts of the Arabic language and learned in the sciences of rhetoric and exposition, as also of the recitation of the Qur'ān. He also participated in many other branches of knowledge.

He was born, may God have mercy on him, in the month of Ṣafar in the year 751 [April–May 1350] and attended the lectures of the learned 'Alā' al-Dīn al-Aswad, who wrote commentaries on the *Mughnī* and on the *Wiqāya*. In his own country he attended the lectures of Mollā al-Jamāl Muḥammad ibn Muḥammad ibn Muḥammad al-Aqsarāyī, studying assiduously. Then he traveled to Egypt to continue his studies there. He attended the lectures of shaykh Akmal al-Dīn and others. Then he returned to the land of Rūm, where he was appointed to the office of qāḍī in Bursa. His status rose greatly in the eyes of the Ottoman ruler, with whom he occupied the highest position and became, in effect, a vizier. His name became famous and his merits widely known. He lived a good life, of great virtue and beneficence. When he came to Cairo on his way to the pilgrimage, the great scholars of that time gathered around him and discussed and debated with him, and testified to his excellence. Then he returned home.

He became very wealthy, to the point when it was said that he had 150,000 gold pieces in cash in his personal possession.

He went on pilgrimage in the year 822 [1419]. On his way back the Sultan al-Mu'ayyad [of Egypt] invited him. He therefore went to Cairo where he met the great scholars of that city. Then he went to Jerusalem, visited the mosque there, and returned home. In the year 833 [1429–1430] he made the pilgrimage by way of Antioch and then returned home, where he died in the month of Rajab. He suffered so badly from eye disease that he became almost blind; some say quite blind. Then God restored his eyesight to him, and he made his last pilgrimage in thanksgiving to God for this.

He compiled a book on the principles of jurisprudence which he called *Fuṣūl al-Badā'i fī Uṣūl al-Sharā'i'*, which he put together from the *Manār*, Pezdevi, the *Maḥṣūl* of the Imam al-Rāzī, the *Mukhtaṣar* of Ibn al-Ḥājib, and other works, a task which took him thirty years. He also wrote a commentary on the first chapter of the Qur'ān [*al-Fātiḥa*] and a treatise in which he considered problems from a hundred sciences, with added complexities. He named this *Anmūdhaj al-'Ulūm.*

Ibn Ḥajar [al-'Asqalānī] said: Al-Fanārī wrote me a license to teach [*ijāza*] in his own hand when he visited Cairo. He died in Rajab of the year 834 [March–April 1431]. That is what Ibn Ḥajar said.

However, I heard from one of his grandchildren that the treatise on problems from one hundred sciences was the work of his son Muḥammad Shāh. I have also seen twenty pieces of verse by Mollā al-Fanārī, each on a problem from a science. He concealed the names of these sciences in the form of enigmas so as to test the scholars of his time, but they could not even identify the sciences, let alone solve the problems. He himself said in the proem to this treatise that "what you see is the hasty product of a day." His son Muḥammad Shāh wrote a commentary on this treatise, in which he identified the various sciences and explained the connection between the enigmas and the solutions of the difficult problems. To each piece of verse he added a sequel in the same rhyme and meter. Of some of these he said, "I spoke to confirm," and of others, "I spoke to answer." His answers are very apt.

Mollā al-Fanārī also wrote an excellent commentary on the treatise of Athīr al-Dīn on logic in the poem, of which he said, "I began this work on the morning of the shortest day, and I finished it with God's help by the call to sunset prayer." He also wrote a commentary on the *Farā'iḍ* of Sirāj al-Dīn, an excellent commentary which is one of the best on this work. When he saw the commentary of al-Sayyid al-Sharīf on the *Mawāqif*, he wrote additional notes containing cogent arguments against al-Sayyid al-Sharīf. He also wrote many treatises and glosses, which however remained as drafts, since his work as muftī, professor, and qāḍī prevented him from putting them into final form.

I heard from reliable authorities that Mollā Ḥamza, the father of Mollā al-Fanārī, was a pupil of shaykh Ṣadr al-Dīn al-Qonawī and had read his book the *Miftāḥ al-Ghayb* under him. He then passed it on to his son Mollā al-Fanārī, who wrote a detailed commentary on this work, containing Ṣūfī knowledge such that ears do not hear and minds fall short of understanding. I heard from my father, may God have mercy on him, on the authority of my grandfather, that Mollā al-Fanārī was a professor in Bursa in the Manastir *medrese*. In addition, he was qāḍī in Bursa and muftī for the whole Ottoman realm. He had great wealth and a high position and was a man of pomp and power. When he went to the mosque on Friday, people thronged around his door so that there were crowds all the way from his house to the mosque. He also had innumerable slaves. It is said that Mollā Khaṭībzāde remarked to Sultan Meḥmed Khan, "One of the best works of Mollā al-Fanārī is the *Fuṣūl al-Badā'i'*, and I can show it up at a mere glance; yet al-Fanārī has twelve slaves in splendid clothes and fine furs as well as innumerable slave-girls in his house, forty of them wearing gold-braided caps."

It is also related that despite all this pomp and glory, he himself dressed modestly, wearing ordinary clothes and a small turban on his head, in the garb of Ṣūfī shaykhs. He used to explain this by saying, "My clothes and my food are from the earnings of my own hands, and I do not earn enough for anything better than this." He worked as a craftsman in raw silk. His house was situated between the mosque and the palace of Sultan Bāyezīd Khan. A *medrese* and a mosque in the city of Bursa bear his name. His grave is in front of the mosque. It is said that he left 10,000 volumes.

It is related that one day the above mentioned Sultan came to testify before him in a law case, but he refused his testimony. The Sultan asked the reason for his refusal, and he replied, "You abandon [that is, do not perform the prayer with] the community." Thereupon the Sultan had a mosque built in front of his palace and appointed himself a place in it, and from that time onward he did not abandon the community. Later, when differences arose between them, Mollā al-Fanārī left all his offices and went to the land of Karāmān, where the lord of Karāmān assigned him 1000 dirhams a day for himself and 500 for his pupils. Mollā Ya'qūb al-Aṣfar and Mollā Ya'qūb al-Aswad studied under him there. Mollā al-Fanārī used to boast about them and say that two learned Ya'qūbs had studied under him. Then Sultan Bāyezīd regretted what he had done regarding Mollā al-Fanārī and sent to the lord of Karāmān, requesting the Mollā's return. He responded to his wish and resumed his former positions. It is related that he also studied under the pious Ṣūfī shaykh Ḥamīd, the teacher of al-Ḥājj Bayrām, and studied Sufism under him.

. . . .

Until the time of Mollā al-Fanārī the students used to have Fridays and Tuesdays free. Then he also gave them Mondays free. The reason for this was that in his time the works of the learned al-Taftazānī enjoyed great fame, and the students were anxious to read them. But these books were not available for sale because too few copies of them were in circulation. The students were therefore obliged to copy them themselves. As they had not enough time to copy them, Mollā al-Fanārī also gave them Mondays free.

Ibn Tāshköprüzāde, *Al-Shaqā'iq al-Nu'māniyya,* pp. 23–31.

2 Heresy and Revolt

From an early date, there were some who believed that Islam had taken a wrong turning, that its leaders were usurpers who had brought tyranny instead of justice and had led the Islamic community into error. God, they believed, would send a true Imam who would end the time of troubles, overthrow the kingdom of evil, and establish the true Imamate and the true Islam on earth. This messianic deliverer came to be known as the Mahdī, *the rightly guided one, and it was generally agreed that he would be of the seed of the Prophet. Many pretenders arose to claim the office. Most of them failed; a few succeeded and established new dynasties, which differed little from those they had overthrown.*

The following excerpts illustrate various aspects of these messianic movements. They begin with some passages from the Qur'ān, often quoted by opponents of the existing order, and a selection of messianic ḥadīths. *Then come some extracts from chronicles, indicating the grievances, aims, and methods of Mahdist rebels in the Umayyad period. A passage from the essayist Jāḥiẓ tries to defend the right of rebellion against evil government in order to justify the violent overthrow of the Umayyads by the 'Abbasids. Two extracts follow, which, though probably not authentic in detail, vividly express the complaints and attitudes of many rebels. The remaining three passages deal with specific movements: the rebellion and defeat of the heretic Bābak, the spread of Carmathian propaganda, and the policies of the Carmathians in power, as seen by a sympathetic Persian traveler.*

15. From the Qur'ān

Pharaoh rose high in the land and divided its people into parties; he abased one group by slaughtering their sons and letting their daughters live. He was one of the workers of evil.

But We wish to bestow favor on those who have been abased in the land, to make them leaders [imam] and to make them heirs.

And We shall set them up in the land, and We shall show Pharaoh and Haman and their armies, on their side, that against which they were on guard.

xxviii, 3/4–5/6.

We have never sent a warner to a city, but the affluent among its inhabitants said, "We do not believe in the message with which you are sent."

And they said, "We have more possessions and more children, and we are not punished."

Say: My Lord bestows sustenance on whom He pleases, and measures it, but most men do not know.

Neither your possessions nor your children are what will bring you near to Us. Only those who believe and do good works have a double recompense for what they have done, and they shall be safe in the mansions [of Paradise].

But those who strive against Our signs, seeking to make Us of no avail, will be brought to punishment.

xxxiv, 33/34–37/38.

What God has assigned as booty to His Prophet from the people of the cities belongs to God and the Prophet and the kinsman, the orphans, the poor, and the wayfarer that it may not become a perquisite circulating among those of you who are rich. What the Prophet has given you, take; from what he forbids you, abstain! Be pious toward God, for God is severe in punishment.

lix, 7.

16. Sayings Ascribed to the Prophet

'Abdallāh said: We were with the Prophet of God, may God bless and save him, when some young men of the Banū Hāshim appeared. When the Prophet saw them, his eyes filled with tears and his color changed. I said to him, "For some time past we have seen something in your face which we do not like."

He answered, "We are members of a family, for whom God has chosen the other world in preference to this world. My family after me will suffer calamity, banishment, and exile until a people comes from the East with black flags. They will ask for good, and it will not be given to them; they will fight and be victorious; they will be given what they ask and not accept it until they deliver the world to a man of my family who will fill it with equity as they had filled it with tyranny. Those of you who live till then will come to them, even crawling through snow."

The Prophet, may God bless and save him, said: There will be a Mahdī in my community; if his time is short, for seven years; otherwise, for nine years. Through him my community will enjoy well-being the like of which they have never enjoyed before. Their food will be brought to them, and the earth will withhold nothing from them, and money in that time will lie in heaps. Then a man will rise and say, "O Mahdī, give me!" and the Mahdī will say, "Take!"

Ibn Māja, *Sunan*, ii, pp. 1366–1367.

The Prophet said: After me there will be Caliphs, and after the Caliphs, amirs, and after the amirs, kings, and after the kings, tyrants, and then a man of my family will arise who will fill the world with justice as it is now filled with tyranny. . . .

Ibn al-Athīr, *Usd al-Ghāba*, v, p. 155.

His justice will fill as much of the world as his authority reaches, and his successors will fill the remainder. . . .

Qāḍī Nuʿmān, *Sharḥ al-Akhbār*, p. 9.

In the last days of my community there will be a Caliph who will scatter money around and will not count it.

Ibn Khaldūn, *Muqaddima*, p. 316.

At the end of time there will be tyrannical amirs, vicious viziers, treacherous judges, and lying jurists. Whoever lives to that time should not serve them, not as inspector, nor as collector, nor as treasurer, nor as policeman.

When the black flags appear, the beginning is sedition, the middle is delusion, and the end is unbelief.

There will be four seditions. In the first they will make free with blood; in the second, with blood and money; in the third, with blood, money, and sex. The fourth will be Antichrist [*al-Dajjāl*].

There will be rulers after me, such that to be with them is calamity; to leave them is unbelief.

Ḥudhayfa said: The Prophet said: A man will come out of the East who will preach in the name of the family of Muḥammad, though he is furthest of all men from them. He will hoist black flags which begin with victory and end with unbelief. He will be followed by the discards of the Arabs, the lowest of the *mawālī*, slaves, runaways, and outcasts in remote places, whose emblem is black and whose religion is polytheism, and most of them are mutilated.

Al-Muttaqī, *Kanz al-'Ummāl*, iii, p. 203; vi, pp. 38, 39, 45, 53.

17. Allegiance to a Rebel (685–686)

Then he [Mukhtār] alighted and entered, and we came to him together with the nobles [*sharīf*] among the people, and he stretched out his hand, and the people hurried to him and swore allegiance to him, and he said, "Swear allegiance to me, on the Book of God and the *Sunna* of His Prophet, to seek vengeance for the blood of the Prophet's kin and to wage Holy War against those who treat that blood as licit,[1] to defend the weak, to fight against those who fight us and be at peace with those who are at peace with us, to be faithful to our pact of allegiance, from which we shall neither give nor seek release."

Al-Ṭabarī (citing Abū Mikhnaf), ii, pp. 623–623.[2]

18. Incitement to Sedition (685–686)

Mukhtār also wrote to Mālik ibn Misma' and Ziyād ibn 'Amr as follows, "Hear me and obey me and be steadfast. I shall give

[1] That is, those who condone the massacre of the Prophet's family at Karbalā' in 680.

[2] An Arabic historian who died in 774.

you whatever you wish of this world and guarantee you paradise if you die." When Mālik read the letter he laughed and said to Ziyād, "He has dealt very generously with us, giving us both this world and the next." Ziyād laughed and said, "We shall not fight on credit. We shall fight for whoever sends us the cash."

Al-Balādhurī, *Ansāb*, v. p. 245.

19. Program of a Rebel (738)

Zayd ibn 'Ali said . . .

"We summon you to the Book of God, to the *Sunna* of His Prophet, may God bless and save him, to wage Holy War against oppressors and defend those who have been abased[1], to give pay to those who are deprived of it and to share the booty equally among those who are entitled to it, to make good the wrongs done by the oppressors, to recall those who have been kept too long on campaigns, and to aid the House of the Prophet against those who obstruct us and disregard our rights. Do you swear allegiance on this?" If they said yes, he placed his hands on theirs, and said, "Do you swear, by the oath and pact and covenant of God and the covenant of His Prophet, to be faithful to my allegiance and fight against my enemy and be loyal to me in secret and in public?" And if they said yes, he stroked their hands, and said, "I call God as witness!"

Al-Ṭabarī, ii, pp. 1687–1688.

20. Complaint of a Rebel (Mid-Eighth Century)

Sudayf, a *mawlā* of the Banū Hāshim, said, "By God, our booty, which was shared, has become a perquisite of the rich[1]; our leadership, which was consultative, has become arbitrary; our succession, which was by the choice of the community, is now by inheritance. Pleasures and musical instruments are bought with the portion of the orphan and the widow. The *dhimmīs* lord it

[1] An allusion to Qur'ān, xxviii, 3–5. See above, p. 50.

[1] An allusion to Qur'ān, lix, 7. See above, p. 51.

over the persons of the Muslims, and evildoers everywhere govern their affairs. O God, the seed of falsehood is ripe; it has reached its limit and assembled its scattered ones. O God, open the hand of the Reaper of the Right to split falsehood asunder and destroy its being, so that right may appear in the fairest form and most perfect light."

Ibn Qutayba, *'Uyūn al-akhbār,* ii, p. 115.

21. On Tyranny and Revolt (ca. 840)

The evildoer is accursed, and whoever forbids the cursing of the evildoer is himself accursed.

But the upstarts of our time and the innovators of our age allege that to abuse bad rulers is sedition [*fitna*] and that to curse tyrants is an innovation [*bid'a*], even if these rulers take the eminent as hostages for the eminent, the friend for the friend, and the kinsman for the kinsman, terrorize the good and reassure the wicked, and rule by favoritism and caprice, the flaunting of power, contempt for the people, repression of the subjects, and accusations without restraint or discretion. If this misconduct reaches the degree of unbelief [*kufr*], if it passes beyond error to irreligion, then it becomes an error greater even than that of whoever refrains from condemning them and dissociating himself from them.

However, he who earns the name of unbeliever by murder is not the same as he who earns it by rejecting the *Sunna* and destroying the Ka'ba. He who earns the name of unbeliever by these offenses is not the same as the polytheist and anthropomorphist. He who earns the name of unbeliever by anthropomorphism is not the same as he who earns it by ascribing evil to God. Now in this respect the upstarts . . . agree that anyone who kills a believer, whether with clear intent or with specious pretexts, is accursed; but if the killer is a tyrannical ruler or a fractious amir, they do not consider it lawful to curse him, depose him, banish him, or denounce him, even if he has terrorized the good, murdered the learned, starved the poor, oppressed the weak, neglected the frontiers and marches, drunk fermented drinks, and flaunted his depravity.

Then the Muslims did not cease to dance attendance on the Umayyads, to fawn on them, to ingratiate themselves with them, and to join with them, except for a remnant whom God preserved from sin until the time of ʿAbd al-Malik ibn Marwān, his son al-Walīd, their governor al-Ḥajjāj ibn Yūsuf, and his freedman Yazīd ibn Abī Muslim, who once again destroyed the holy house, invaded the sanctity of Mecca, demolished the Kaʿba, looted the holy places, changed the *Qibla* of Wāsiṭ, and delayed the Friday prayer until sunset. If a man said to any one of them, "Fear God, for you have delayed the prayer beyond its proper time!" he killed him for these words by public execution, not by stealth, and openly, not in secret. Such an execution is surely worse than the reproof for which it was imposed. How can a man be treated as an unbeliever for one offense and not for a far greater offense?

Some of the righteous sometimes admonished tyrants and warned them of the consequences, showing them that there was still a remnant of mankind to resist wickedness on earth. But when ʿAbd al-Malik ibn Marwān and al-Ḥajjāj ibn Yūsuf appeared, they suppressed this and punished and killed those who practiced it, so that they were not restrained in the evil which they did.

Granted that the change of the *Qibla* was a mistake and the destruction of the Kaʿba due to a misinterpretation [of orders]; granted that the common rumors according to which the Umayyads claimed that the Caliph stands higher than the Prophet are false and invented; granted that branding the hands of the Muslim men and tattooing the hands of Muslim women, driving migrants back to their villages, murdering scholars, reviling the Imams of true guidance, and opposing the family of the Prophet, may God bless and save him, is not unbelief, what do you say to combining three prayers, including the Friday prayer, in one, and of not beginning the first until the hour when the sun is at the height of walls and colors them yellow? If a Muslim said a word, he was struck with swords, beaten with rods, and pierced with lances. If anyone said, "Fear God!" he was accused of a crime, and they were not content until after they had spilt his brains over his chest and crucified him where his family could see him.

What proves that these people were on the path of rebellion against God, making light of religion, despising the Muslims, and spurning the worthy is that their amirs ate and drank in the pulpit on Fridays and days of public assembly. This was done by Ḥubaysh ibn Dulja, Ṭāriq the freedman of 'Uthmān, al-Ḥajjāj ibn Yūsuf, and others.

Al-Jāḥiẓ, *Rasā'il*, 1933, pp. 295–297.

22. Rebellion in North Africa (740–741)

The North Africans were among the most obedient and compliant of the provincials, the most peaceful and submissive of peoples, until the time of Hishām ibn 'Abd al-Malik, when the Iraqis crept in among them. When the Iraqi emissaries [*dā'ī*] infiltrated and incited them to revolt, they broke their ties [with the Caliphate] and have remained separate to this day.

The circumstances of their separation were as follows: At first they rejected the agitators and said, "We shall not deny the Imams for the misdeeds of their agents, nor blame them for them." "But the agents only do what the Imams order them," said the agitators, to which they replied, "We shall not accept this until we have tested them."

Maysara and some ten other men, therefore, set out in order to call on Hishām. They asked for an audience, but finding this difficult, they went to al-Abrash and said, "Inform the Commander of the Faithful that when our amir goes raiding with us and his army and is successful, he distributes the booty to them and leaves us out, saying that they have a better right to it. To this we say "Very well, our holy war is purer if we earn nothing by it. If it is ours, we make it lawful for them to take it; if it is not ours, we do not want it.' "

Then they continued, "When we besiege a town, the amir orders us to advance and holds his army back. Then we cry "Forward!" increasing our merit in the holy war. We shield them with our own persons and save them.

"Then they want our sheep. They slit them open for the unborn lambs, to take their white fleece for the Commander of the Faithful, and they kill a thousand ewes for the skin. And we say, 'It is a small thing for the Commander of the Faithful,' and we put up with it.

"Then they make us give them the most beautiful of our daughters, and we say, 'We have not found this in the Book or in the *Sunna*. We are Muslims and we wish to know: is this with the approval of the Commander of the Faithful or not?'"

"I shall deal with it," replied al-Abrash. But they found the time long, and their money was running out. They therefore wrote their names on petitions, gave them to the viziers, and said, "Here are our names and pedigrees. If the Commander of the Faithful asks about us, inform him." They then returned to North Africa, where they rose against Hishām's governor and killed him and became masters of North Africa. When this was reported to the Caliph, and he asked about the rebels, their names were shown to him, and they were the ones of whom it was reported that they had risen in revolt.

Al-Ṭabarī, i, pp. 2815–2816.

23. A Rebel Sermon (747–748)

Hārūn said: Yaḥyā ibn Zakariyā informed me that Abū Ḥamza preached this sermon when he ascended the pulpit [*minbar*] in Medina. He praised God and thanked Him and then said: Do you know, O men of Medina, that we did not leave our homes and our possessions in exuberance or wantonness or folly or play, nor in quest of new dominion, nor in search of old vengeance. But when we saw the lamps of truth extinguished, the speaker of truth suppressed, and the upholder of justice killed, then the land seemed narrow before us, and when we heard the summoner [*dā'ī*] calling to the obedience of the merciful God and the judgment of the Qur'ān, we answered the summoner of God, "For he who does not answer the summoner of God can not make Him powerless on earth" [Qur'ān, xlvi, 31].

And so we have come from different tribes, several of us on one camel bearing both our food and our persons, taking turns with a single blanket, few and weak in the land. But God sheltered us and strengthened us with His victory, and by God, we all became brothers in His grace.

We met your men at Qudayd and summoned them to the obedience of the Merciful and the judgment of the Qur'ān, and they summoned us to the obedience of the Devil and the judgment of Marwān[1] and the house of Marwān. By God, what a difference between Good and Evil! They came rushing gaily at us, for the Devil had taken a firm hold on them, and his cauldrons were boiling with their blood, and he had convinced them of the truth of his errors. Then God's helpers came in troops and squadrons, all with flashing Indian swords. Then our mill turned, and theirs was turned with blows, which alarmed the men of vanity.

And you, O men of Medina, if you help Marwān and the house of Marwān, then God will destroy you with a punishment from Him or by our hands and "will heal the breasts of those who believe" [Qur'ān, ix, 14]. O men of Medina, the first among you are the best of the first, and the last among you are the worst of the last. O men of Medina, the people are ours and we are theirs. Is he not a polytheist idol-worshipper, a polytheist of the People of the Book, or a tyrannical Imam, O men of Medina, who claims that God imposes on man that which is beyond his strength or asks about what was not given? He is an enemy against whom we must make war. O men of Medina, tell me about the eight shares which God assigned in His book to the strong and, in His love, to the weak. If there comes a ninth, who has no part of them, not a single share, and he takes them all for himself, arrogantly and at war against his Lord—what do you say of him and of those who abet him in his deeds?

O men of Medina, I am told that you belittle my companions, saying that they are callow youths and rough Bedouins. Woe to you, men of Medina! What were the Companions of the Prophet, may God bless and save him, but callow youths? Youths, by God, who in their youthfulness were ripe men, whose eyes were averted from evil, whose steps were too heavy for vanity, who had exchanged their mortal souls for immortal souls. . . .

Abu'l-Faraj al-Iṣfahānī, *Al-Aghānī*, xx, p. 104.
(Cf. al-Ṭabarī, ii, pp. 2009–2011.)

[1] The last Umayyad Caliph.

24. Bābak the Heretic (ca. 815–838)

In [al-Muʿtaṣim's] reign there were conquests the like of which had not occurred under any of the Caliphs before him.

One of these was the defeat, capture, and crucifixion of Bābak. Another was the defeat of Māzyār, lord of the castle of Ṭabaristān. He fortified himself in the castles and mountains, but he was not left alone until he was captured, killed, and crucified at the side of Bābak. Another was Jaʿfar the Kurd, who had devastated the land and taken the people captive. The Caliph sent armies against him and did not desist until he was captured, killed, and crucified at the side of Bābak and Māzyār. . . .

The affair of Bābak began when he started his activities toward the end of the reign of al-Ma'mūn. People differ concerning his pedigree and his religion, but what we have established and confirmed is that he was from the family of Muṭahhar, the son of Fāṭima bint Abī Muslim. It is from her that the Fāṭimiyya group of the Khurramiyya take their name, and not from Fāṭima the daughter of the Prophet of God, may God bless and save him.

Bābak grew up in a time of disorder and continuous strife. He began his career by killing those who were around him in Badhdh and by devastating the surrounding towns and villages, so as to dominate the country, to hinder pursuit, and to obstruct access to him. His power grew, and his cause prospered.

When al-Ma'mūn heard about him, he sent ʿAbdallāh ibn Ṭāhir ibn al-Ḥusayn against him with a great army.

He marched against him and camped on his way by Dīnavar, outside the city, at a place known at the present day as Qaṣr ʿAbdallāh ibn Ṭāhir. It is a famous vineyard and a well-known place.

From there he continued until he came to Badhdh. At that time Bābak had become very powerful, and people feared him. They fought him but could not overcome him. He scattered them and killed their brave men.

Among those killed in that battle was Muḥammad ibn Ḥumayd al-Ṭūsī, for whom Abū Tammām[1] wrote an elegy, in which he said:

[1] A famous Arabic poet (804–845 or 846).

On the day of his death, the tribe of the Banu Nabhān
were like stars in a sky from which the full moon had fallen.

and

He set firm his foot in the quagmire of death
and said to it, "Resurrection is under your sole."

When Abū Isḥāq al-Mu'taṣim billāh[2] succeeded to the Caliphate, he had no other concern but Bābak. He prepared money and men and sent his freedman al-Afshīn Ḥaydar ibn Kāwus. Al-Afshīn marched with his army and reached Barzand, where he stayed until the weather improved and the snow vanished from the passes. Then he sent forward his deputy Yūbāra and Ja'far ibn Dīnār, known as Ja'far al-Khayyāṭ, with a large force of horsemen to the place where there was a camp and ordered them to dig a fortified trench. They went there, made camp, and dug the trench.

When the trench was ready, al-Afshīn appointed al-Marzabān, the freedman of al-Mu'taṣim, as his deputy in Barzand, with a number of commanders, and marched until he reached the trench and halted there. Then he dispatched Yūbāra and Ja'far al-Khayyāṭ, with a strong force, to the source of a large river and ordered them to dig another trench there. They went there and dug it.

When they had finished, al-Afshīn came and joined them. Then he appointed Muḥammad ibn Khālid Bukhārākhudā in his place and set out for Darvad with 5,000 horse and 2,000 foot, as well as 1,000 laborers. He halted at Darvad and dug a great trench with a high wall over it. Meanwhile Bābak and his people were standing on the high mountains, looking down on al-Afshīn's soldiers, and uttering loud cries.

Then on Tuesday, 26 Sha'bān [222/August 3, 837], al-Afshīn advanced with his supplies and mangonels. Bābak ordered Ādhīn to fortify a hill dominating the town [Badhdh]. He had 3,000 men with him and had already dug pits around his positions to prevent horsemen from reaching him.

On a certain day al-Afshīn went back to his trench, and on the following day, Friday, 1 Ramaḍān [222/August 7, 837], he set

[2] Reigned 833–842.

up mangonels and onagers [*'arrāda*] against the town, which the commanders and chiefs surrounded on all sides.

Bābak appeared amid his warriors, whom he arranged in order of battle. The commanders fought bitterly against him until the afternoon, and then they withdrew, having inflicted much damage on his followers.

Al-Afshīn stayed for six days and then joined battle with Bābak on Thursday, 7 Ramaḍān [August 13, 837] Bābak was ready for him and had prepared a huge wagon above Badhdh to roll down on to al-Afshīn's men.

Then Bābak sent a man called Mūsā al-Aqṭa' to al-Afshīn to ask him to come out and talk with him face-to-face. If he could achieve his purpose, well and good; if not, he would fight him. Al-Afshīn agreed, and Bābak went out and came near to al-Afshīn at a place where there was a wadi between them.

When Bābak saw al-Afshīn, he bowed to him, and al-Afshīn spoke to him straightforwardly and told him of the advantages of obedience in this world and the next, but he did not accept this.

He therefore returned to his own place and gave his men the order for battle. They hastened to comply and rolled down the wagon which they had prepared. The wagon broke, and al-Afshīn's men returned and drove them up to the top of the mountain.

Yūbāra and Ja'far al-Khayyāṭ stood facing 'Abdallāh, the brother of Bābak. They attacked, and the commanders also attacked from every side. They killed immense numbers of them. They were driven back into the town, and the attackers followed in pursuit of them, and the battle was fought in the central square of the town.

So fierce a battle had never been seen. They fought in houses and gardens, and 'Abdallāh the brother of Bābak fled.

When Bābak saw that the soldiers had surrounded him, that his escape routes had become narrow, and that his companions had been killed or put to flight, he made for Armenia and traveled until he crossed the river Rass on his way to Byzantium [*Rūm*].

When he crossed the river Rass, Sahl ibn Sunbāṭ, the lord of that part, came to find him. Al-Afshīn had written to the rulers of those parts, to the Kurds in Armenia, and to the *patricii* to intercept him on his way.

Sahl ibn Sunbāṭ came upon him. Bābak had changed his dress and disguised himself, had put rags on his feet, and was riding a mule with a pack-saddle. Sahl ibn Sunbāṭ fell upon him, took him prisoner, and sent him to al-Afshīn who, after making sure of him, wrote to al-Muʿtaṣim to report his victory and to request permission to come to him. The Caliph granted permission, and he came, bringing Bābak and his brother. The story of how al-Muʿtaṣim killed Bābak, cut off his hands and feet, and crucified him is well-known.

Al-Dīnawarī, *Al-Akhbār al-ṭiwāl,* pp. 402–405.

25. Communism in Iraq (Late Ninth Century)

The first thing which he imposed on them, and by which he tested them, was the payment of one dirham. He called this the *fiṭra* and levied it from every man, woman, and child. They hastened to pay it.

He left them a while and then imposed on them the *hijra,* which was one dinar for every person who had reached the age of discretion, and he read them God's words, "Collect an alms tax from their possessions, by which you will cleanse and purify them. Pray for them, for your prayers are a repose for them. God hears and knows all" [Qur'ān, ix, 104]. He told them that this was the interpretation of this verse, and they paid at once, helping one another and succoring the poor.

He left them for a while, and then he imposed on them the *bulgha,* which was seven dinars. He alleged that this was the proof intended in God's words, "Say to them, 'Bring your proofs if you speak truth'" [Qur'ān, xxvii, 65]. He also alleged that this was the tidings [*balāgh*] of those who desire to have faith and to enter among "those who go before, who are those who are brought near" [Qur'ān, lvi, 9–10].

Then he made them a tasty, delicious dish, divided it into pieces the size of hazelnuts, and gave one to everyone who had paid him seven dinars. This, he alleged, was the food of the dwellers in Paradise, which had been sent down to the Imam. He adopted it as seals and transferred a hundred portions [*bulgha*] of it to the missionary [*dā'ī*], from whom he asked 700 dinars.

When he had settled this, he imposed on them a levy of one-fifth of what they owned and of what they earned, and he read them God's words, "Know that of whatever booty you take, one-fifth belongs to God and to the Prophet, the kinsman, the orphans, the poor, and the wayfarer" [Qur'ān, viii, 42]. They therefore assessed all that they owned, in clothing and other effects, and paid one-fifth of it to him. The woman even paid one-fifth of her weaving, and the man one-fifth of what he earned.

When this was completed and established, he imposed on them the duty of union [*ulfa*]. This meant that they assembled their possessions in one place and held them in common, no man enjoying any advantage over his friend because of any property which he owned. He read them God's words, "Remember God's grace to you when you were enemies, when He united [*allafa*] your hearts so that by His grace you became brothers" [Qur'ān, iii, 98]. Then he read them God's words, "Had you spent all the wealth in the world, you would not have united their hearts, but God united them, for He is mighty and wise" [Qur'ān, viii, 64]. He told them that they had no need of possessions because the earth in its entirety would be theirs and no one else's. "This," he told them, "is the test by which you are proved so that we may know how you will act." He called on them to buy weapons and to prepare to use them. This was in the year 276 [889–890].

In every village the missionaries chose and appointed a man whom they trusted to collect all the possessions of the villagers, by way of cattle, sheep and goats, jewelry, effects, and other things; he then clothed the naked and supplied their needs, so that no poor man remained among them, nor any that was needy and deprived. Every man worked diligently at his trade to earn more by his endeavors, and to gain superior rank; the woman brought him what she earned by weaving, and the child brought his wages for scaring away birds. No one owned anything but his sword and his arms.

When all this was established and they acted in conformity

with it, he ordered the missionaries to assemble all the women on a certain night to mix with the men. This, he said, was true love and union between them. Often a husband offered his friend his own wife if he desired.

When he was master of their affairs and was sure of their obedience, and had taken the measure of their minds, he began to lead them astray in successive stages. He brought them arguments from the teachings of the dualists. They followed him in this until he made them cast off the Holy Law. Then he abrogated his own previous injunctions to them to practice humility and piety. He removed all restraints from them concerning property and sexuality and freed them from fasting, prayer, and the commandments. He taught them that they were relieved of all this, that the possessions and the blood of their opponents were lawful to them, that the knowledge of the Master of Truth, for whom he preached, dispensed them from everything, and that with him they need have no fear of sin or punishment.

Al-Nuwayrī, *Nihāyat al-arab,* Ms. Paris, fol. 48b–49b.

26. Revolutionaries in Power (Eleventh Century)

In Laḥsā, the town, the outskirts, and the neighboring villages are all enclosed by fortifications. They are surrounded by four strong concentric walls built of hardened clay, at a distance of about a parasang from each wall to the next. In this town there are great springs of water, each of them able to turn five waterwheels, and they use all this water in the area so that none of it flows outside the walls. A fine town stands at the center of the fortified enclosure, equipped with everything that is found in great cities and with more than 20,000 male inhabitants able to bear arms.

They said that the Sultan of that place was a *sharīf* and this man had turned the people away from Islam. He told them that he had freed them from prayer and fasting, and he preached to that people that they should have no recourse to any but him. His name was Abū Saʿīd. If the people of this town are asked what religious doctrine they follow, they reply that they are Abū Sa'īdīs. They do not perform the prayer or observe the fast, but they profess belief in Muḥammad the Chosen One, may God bless and save him, and in his apostolate. Abū Sa'īd told them that he would return to them after his death. His grave is in the town of Laḥsā, and they have built a fine tomb over it. In his final instructions to his sons, he said, "Let six of my descendants always hold and conduct this government, and govern the people with justice and equity and without opposing one another until I return."

Today the descendants of Abū Sa'īd have a great palace, which is their seat of government, and a throne on which six kings sit in one place, give orders in mutual agreement, and govern. They have six viziers. The six kings sit on one throne, and the six viziers sit behind them on another, and whatever business arises they deal with in consultation.

At that time they had 30,000 Zanjī or Ethiopian slaves, bought for money, engaged in agriculture and gardening. They take no tithes or other taxes from the people. If anyone becomes destitute or falls into debt, they look after him until his affairs go better. If anyone lends money to another, he asks for nothing beyond the principle. If a stranger, knowing a trade, arrives in that town, they give him enough capital to set him up, so that he can buy the materials and tools of trade and, when he is ready, return the exact sum which had been lent to him. If any property belonging to one of the owners of property and appurtenances is ruined and he lacks the means to restore it, they send some of their own slaves to make good the ruined property and appurtenances and ask for nothing from the owner.

There are mills in Laḥsā which are the property of the government and in which they turn wheat into flour for the people without taking any fee. They pay for the upkeep of these mills and the wages of the millers from the money of the government.

The Sultans are addressed as Sayyid, and the viziers, as Shā'ira [counselor].

There was no mosque in Laḥsā for the Friday prayer, no sermon, and no public prayers. However, a certain Persian built a mosque there. The name of that man was 'Alī ibn Aḥmad. He was a Muslim, a pilgrim, and a rich man, and he took care of pilgrims who arrived in this town.

They buy and sell in this town with lead, which is kept in baskets, each weighing 6,000 dirhams. When they make a transaction, they count baskets and take them away. They do not take the lead out of the basket.

They weave fine aprons there, which they take to Basra and elsewhere.

If anyone performs the prayer, they do not prevent him, but they themselves do not. If, when one of the Sultans mounts his horse and goes out, anyone speaks to him, he gives a pleasant answer and behaves with modesty. They never drink wine. They keep a horse, with girths, collar, and saddle, always on duty, day and night, by the gate of Abū Sa'īd's tomb, for him to mount when he rises again. They say that Abū Sa'īd said to his children, "If, when I come back, you do not recognize me, let this be the sign. Strike my neck with my sword. If it is I, I shall come back to life at once." He made this rule so that no one might pretend to be Abū Sa'īd.

In the time of the Caliphs of Baghdad, one of the Sultans [of Laḥsā] led an army against Mecca. He seized Mecca, and killed a number of the pilgrims who were going round [*ṭawāf*] the Ka'ba. He ripped the Black Stone from its corner and carried it off to Laḥsā. They said that this stone was a magnet which drew men to itself from all parts of the world. They did not know that it was the honor and glory of Muḥammad the Chosen, may God bless and save him, that drew them there. In fact, the Black Stone remained in Laḥsā for many years, but no one went there. Finally, it was bought back from them and restored to its place.

In Laḥsā they sell the meat of all kinds of animals, such as cats, dogs, donkeys, oxen, sheep, etc. But whatever meat they sell, they put the head and skin of the animal next to it so that the buyer may know what he is buying. They fatten dogs, as they fatten sheep, until they become so fat that they can no longer walk. Then they kill them and eat them.

Seven parasangs east of Laḥsā one comes to the sea. If one crosses the sea, one comes to Baḥrayn, which is an island fifteen parasangs long. There is a large town with many groves of date palms. They fish for pearls in that sea. Half of what the divers collect belongs to the Sultans of Laḥsā.

Nāṣir-i Khusraw, *Safar-nāma,* pp. 123–126.

3 The Lands of Islam and Beyond

5

Capital and Provinces

Medieval Islam produced a geographical literature of great interest and diversity, including practical manuals for the post and other government services, personal narratives of travel, and vast works of geographical scholarship. The examples given include descriptions of the capital and the Islamic provinces, travelers' tales, and accounts of the strange peoples who lived beyond the frontiers of the Islamic world in Africa, Asia, and Europe.

27. Baghdad (Late Ninth Century)

I begin with Iraq only because it is the center of this world, the navel of the earth, and I mention Baghdad first because it is the center of Iraq, the greatest city, which has no peer in the east or the west of the world in extent, size, prosperity, abundance of water, or health of climate, and because it is inhabited by all kinds of people, town-dwellers and country-dwellers. To it they come from all countries, far and near, and people from every side have preferred Baghdad to their own homelands. There is no country, the peoples of which have not their own quarter and their own trading and financial arrangements. In it there is gathered that which does not exist in any other city in the world. On its flanks flow two great rivers, the Tigris and the Euphrates, and thus goods and foodstuffs come to it by land and by water with the greatest ease, so that every kind of merchandise is completely available, from east and west, from Muslim and non-Muslim lands. Goods are brought from India, Sind, China, Tibet, the lands of the Turks, the Daylam, the Khazars, the Ethiopians, and others to such an extent that the products of the countries are more plentiful in Baghdad than in the countries from which they come. They can be procured so readily and so certainly that it is as if all the good things of the world are sent there, all the treasures of the earth assembled there, and all the blessings of creation perfected there.

Furthermore, Baghdad is the city of the Hashimites, the home of their reign, the seat of their sovereignty, where no one appeared before them and no kings but they have dwelt. Also, my own forbears have lived there, and one of them was governor of the city.

Its name is famous, and its fame widespread. Iraq is indeed the center of the world, for in accordance with the consensus of the astronomers recorded in the writings of ancient scholars, it is in the fourth climate, which is the middle climate where the temperature is regular at all times and seasons. It is very hot in the summer, very cold in the winter, and temperate in autumn and in spring. The passage from autumn to winter and from spring to summer is gradual and imperceptible, and the succession of the seasons is regular. So, the weather is temperate, the soil is rich, the water is sweet, the trees are thriving, the fruit luscious, the seeds are fertile, good things are abundant, and springs are easily found. Because of the temperate weather and rich soil and sweet water, the character of the inhabitants is good, their faces bright, and their minds untrammeled. The people excel in knowledge, understanding, letters, manners, insight, discernment, skill in commerce and crafts, cleverness in every argument, proficiency in every calling, and mastery of every craft. There is none more learned than their scholars, better informed than their traditionists, more cogent than their theologians, more perspicuous than their grammarians, more accurate than their readers, more skillful than their physicians, more melodious than their singers, more delicate than their craftsmen, more literate than their scribes, more lucid than their logicians, more devoted than their worshippers, more pious than their ascetics, more juridical than their judges, more eloquent than their preachers, more poetic than their poets, and more reckless than their rakes.

In ancient days, that is to say in the time of the Chosroes and the Persians, Baghdad was not a city, but only a village in the district of Bādūrayā. The city in Iraq which the Chosroes had chosen for their capital was al-Madā'in, seven parasangs from Baghdad. The audience chamber of Chosroes Anushirvan is still there. At that time there was nothing in Baghdad but a convent situated at a place called Qarn al-Ṣarāt, at the confluence of the Ṣarāt and the Tigris. This convent is called al-Dayr al-'Atīq [the ancient convent] and is still standing at the present time. It is the residence of the Catholicos, the head of the Nestorian Christians.

Nor does Baghdad figure in the wars of the Arabs at the time of the advent of Islam, since the Arabs founded Basra and Kūfa. Kūfa was founded in the year 17 [638] by Sa'd ibn Abī Waqqās al-Zuhrī, one of 'Umar ibn al-Khaṭṭāb's governors. Basra, too, was founded in the year 17 by 'Utba ibn Ghazwān al-Māzinī of the tribe of Māzin of Qays, also a governor of 'Umar ibn al-Khaṭṭāb at that time. The Arabs settled down in these two places, but the important people, the notables, and the rich merchants moved to Baghdad.

The Umayyads lived in Syria and did not stay in Iraq. Mu'āwiya ibn Abī Sufyān, who had been governor of Syria in the name of 'Umar ibn al-Khaṭṭāb and then of 'Uthmān ibn 'Affān for twenty years, lived in Damascus with his family. When he seized power and sovereignty passed to him, he kept his residence and capital in Damascus, where he had his authority, his supporters, and his faction. The Umayyad kings after Mu'āwiya stayed in Damascus, since they were born there and knew no other place, and its people were their sole supporters.

Then the Caliphate came to the descendants of the paternal uncle of the Apostle of God, may God bless and save him and also his family, the line of ʿAbbās ibn ʿAbd al-Muṭṭalib. Thanks to clear discernment, sound intelligence, and perfect judgment, they saw the merits of Iraq, its magnificence, spaciousness, and central situation. They saw that it was not like Syria, with its pestilential air, narrow houses, rugged soil, constant diseases, and uncouth people; nor was it like Egypt, with changeable weather and many plagues, situated between a damp and fetid river, full of unhealthy mists that engender disease and spoil food, and the dry, bare mountains, so dry and salty and bad that no plant can grow nor any spring appear; nor like Ifrīqiya, far from the peninsula of Islam and from the holy house of God, with uncouth people and many foes; nor like Armenia, remote, cold and icy, barren, and surrounded by enemies; nor like the districts of the Jabal, harsh, rough, and snow-covered, the abode of the hard-hearted Kurds; nor like the land of Khurāsān, stretching to the east, surrounded on every side by rabid and war-like enemies; nor like the Ḥijāz where life is hard and means are few and the people's food comes from elsewhere, as Almighty God warned us in His book, through His friend Ibrāhīm, who said, "O Lord, I have given to my descendants as dwelling a valley without tillage" [Qur'ān, xiv, 40]; nor like Tibet, where, because of the foul air and food, the people are discolored, with stunted bodies and tufty hair.

When they understood that Iraq was the best of countries, the ʿAbbasids decided to settle there. In the first instance the Commander of the Faithful, Abu'l-ʿAbbās, that is ʿAbdallāh ibn Muḥammad ibn ʿAlī ibn ʿAbdallāh ibn ʿAbbās ibn ʿAbd al-Muṭṭalib, stayed in Kūfa. Then he moved to Anbār and built a city on the banks of the Euphrates which he called Hāshimiyya. Abu'l-ʿAbbās, may God be pleased with him, died before the building of this city was completed.

Then, when Abū Jaʿfar al-Manṣūr. succeeded to the Caliphate, he founded a new city between Kūfa and Ḥīra, which he also called Hāshimiyya. He stayed there for a while, until the time when he decided to send his son, Muḥammad al-Mahdī, to fight the Slavs in the year 140 [757–758]. He then came to Baghdad and stopped there, and asked, "What is the name of this place?" They answered, "Baghdad." "By God," said the

Caliph, "this is indeed the city which my father Muḥammad ibn 'Alī told me I must build, in which I must live, and in which my descendants after me will live. Kings were unaware of it before and since Islam, until God's plans for me and orders to me are accomplished. Thus, the traditions will be verified and the signs and proofs be manifest. Indeed, this island between the Tigris in the east and the Euphrates in the west is a marketplace for the world. All the ships that come up the Tigris from Wāsiṭ, Basra, Ubulla, Ahwāz, Fārs, 'Umān, Yamāma, Baḥrayn, and beyond will anchor here; wares brought on ships down the Tigris from Mosul, Diyār-Rabī'a, Ādharbayjān, and Armenia, and along the Euphrates from Diyār-Muḍar, Raqqa, Syria, the border marches, Egypt, and North Africa, will be brought and unloaded here. It will be the highway for the people of the Jabal, Iṣfahān, and the districts of Khurāsān. Praise be to God who preserved it for me and caused all those who came before me to neglect it. By God, I shall build it. Then I shall dwell in it as long as I live, and my descendants shall dwell in it after me. It will surely be the most flourishing city in the world. Then I shall found four other cities, none of which shall ever be ruined."

The Caliph did indeed found them. They were Rāfiqa (which he did not name), Malaṭya, Miṣṣīṣa, and Manṣūra in Sind.

The Caliph gave orders to summon engineers, men expert in building and specialists in measuring lengths and areas and in dividing up lands, to lay out the plan of his city, which was called the city of Abū Ja'far. He summoned masons, laborers and craftsmen who were carpenters, smiths, and diggers. When they were all assembled and complete, he assigned them rations and pay. He had written to all parts, asking them to send him people who knew something about building, and 100,000 different workmen and artisans came to him. Indeed, certain authorities relate that Abū Ja'far al-Manṣūr did not begin the work of building until he had completed his 100,000 workers and artisans.

He laid out the plan in the month of Rabī' I of the year 141 [July–August 758]. He made of it a round city, the only round city known in the whole world. He laid the foundations at the moment chosen by the astronomer Nawbakht and by Māshāllāh ibn Sariya. Before the laying of the foundations, they had made sun-dried mud bricks of a very large size. The whole brick was square, one cubit by one cubit, and weighed 200 *raṭls*. The half-brick, one cubit long by one-half cubit wide, weighed 100 *raṭls*. Wells were dug and a canal made, drawing on the Karkhāyā Canal, which itself draws on the Euphrates. This canal was carefully built and brought water inside the city for drinking, for brick making, and for moistening the clay.

He provided the city with four gates, which he named the Gate of Kūfa, the Gate of Basra, the Gate of Khurāsān, and the Gate of Syria. The distance between each gate and the next was 5,000 black cubits,[1] measured from outside the ditch. Each of the city gates was provided with a double iron door, high and thick, of such weight that to close or open one door several men were needed. Each gate was high enough for a horseman bearing a standard or a lancer with a long lance in his hand to pass through without dipping the standard or couching the lance. He made the main surrounding wall of the large bricks, the size of which we have already described and the like of which had never before been seen, and of clay. The thickness of the walls at the foundation was 90 black cubits. They then become thinner, and at the top they were only 25 cubits thick. The height was 60 cubits, including the battlements. Around the main wall was an outer wall, thick and high, with a distance of 100 black cubits between the two. This outer wall had strong towers, and on it there were circular battlements. Outside the outer wall, all the way round, was a high dike, solidly and carefully made and lined with kiln-burnt bricks set in quicklime. Beyond the dike was a ditch into which water was brought from a canal drawing on the Karkhāyā Canal. After the ditch were wide avenues. For each of the four gates of the city he made a great vaulted hall, 80 cubits long and vaulted with kiln-burnt bricks and plaster. Entering the hall at the outer wall, one crossed a stone-paved courtyard and then came to a hall at the main wall, with thick, high,

[1] The black cubit is estimated at about half a yard.

double iron doors, each door requiring several men to open and close it. The four gates of the city were all like this. Entering the hall at the main wall, one crossed a court to vaulted arcades, made with burnt bricks and plaster and fitted with small Greek windows, through which the sun and light could enter but not the rain. This was where the pages were lodged.

Each of the four gates had arcades, and over each of the gates of the city at the main wall there was a great vaulted gilded dome, around which were places to sit and lean, where one could sit and look down on all that was happening below. Access to these domes was by a ramp over the vaulting, built partly of kiln-burnt bricks and plaster, partly of very large sun-dried bricks. There were rooms with arches of increasing height, in which were the horse guards and foot guards. The ramp leading to the dome above the gate was built over these arches. The ramp, on which one could ride, was fitted with doors which could be closed.

Coming out of the arcades, one came to a courtyard and thence to an immense hall, vaulted with kiln-burnt bricks and plaster with a double iron door through which one reached the great square. The four arcades were all the same.

In the center of the great square stood the palace, the entrance of which was called the Golden Gate, and next to it was the cathedral mosque. Around the palace there was no building, private house, or dwelling except for a building on the side of the Syria Gate for the horse guards and a great, long gallery supported on columns of kiln-burnt bricks and plaster. The chief of police sat in the one, the commander of the guard in the other. This last building is now used for public worship.

All around the central square were the dwellings of the young sons of al-Manṣūr, the black slaves attached to his personal service, the treasury, the arsenal, the chancery, the office of the land tax, the office of the seal, the office of the army, the office of supplies, the office of the palace staff, the public kitchens, and the office of expenditure.

From one arcade to the next there were alleys and streets known by the names of officers or *mawālī* of the Caliph or of the people who lived in the street.

From the Basra Gate to the Khurāsān Gate: the Street of Police, the Street of Haytham, the Street of the Dungeon (al-Maṭbaq), in which was the large prison called al-Maṭbaq, a strong building with thick walls; the Street of the Women, the Street of Sarjis, the Street of al-Ḥusayn, the Street of 'Aṭiyya, the Street of Mujāshi', the Street of al-'Abbās, the Street of Ghazwān, the Street of Abū Ḥanīfa, and the Narrow Street.

From the Basra Gate to the Khurāsān Gate: the Street of the Guards, the Street of Nu'aymiyya, the Street of Sulaymān, the Street of al-Rabī', the Street of Muhalhil, the Street of Shaykh ibn 'Umayra, the Street of the Marwarrūdhīs, the Street of Wāḍiḥ, the Street of the Water Carriers, the Street of Ibn Burayha ibn 'Īṣā ibn Manṣūr, the Street of Abū Aḥmad, and the Narrow Way.

From the Kūfa Gate to the Syria Gate: the Street of al-'Akkī, the Street of Abū Qurra, the Street of 'Abdūya, the Street of al-Sumayda', the Street of al-'Alā', the Street of Nāfi', the Street of Aslam, and the Street of Manāra.

From the Syria Gate to the Khurāsān Gate: the Street of the Muezzins, the Street of Dārim, the Street of Israel, a street which is now called al-Qawārīrī, of which I forget the original name, the Street of al-Ḥakam ibn Yūsuf, the Street of Samā'a, the Street of Sā'id, the mawlā of Abū Ja'far, a street which is now called al-Ziyādī, of which I forget the original name, and the Street of Ghazwān.

These streets led from one portico to the next, inside the city and inside the wall.

In each of these streets lived the chief officers, who could be trusted to live near to the Caliph; also his chief *mawālī* and other persons who were required for important business. Each street was closed at both ends by secure gates. Furthermore, no street was connected with the wall around the central square in which stood the palace of the Caliph, since all the streets ran parallel round the wall of the square.

The measurements were made by the engineers 'Abdallāh ibn Muḥriz, al-Ḥajjāj ibn Arṭāt, 'Imrān ibn al-Waḍḍāḥ, and Shihāb ibn Kathīr in the presence of the astronomers and the mathematicians Nawbakht and Ibrāhīm ibn Muḥammad al-Fazārī and al-Ṭabarī. He divided the suburbs into four quarters and appointed an engineer to take charge of each of them, and he gave them, in each quarter, a statement of the area assigned to each person who had been given a grant, as well as the assigned area to make markets in each quarter.

He assigned the four quarters as follows:

The quarter from the Kūfa Gate to the Basra Gate, including the Muhawwal Gate and Karkh and the adjoining districts; to Musayyib ibn Zuhayr, to his (the Caliph's) freedman Rabī', and to the engineer 'Imrān ibn al-Waḍḍāḥ.

The quarter from the Kūfa Gate to the Syria Gate and from the main road to Anbār up to the district of Ḥarb ibn 'Abdullāh; to Sulaymān ibn Mujālid, to his (the Caliph's) *mawlā* Wāḍiḥ, and to the engineer 'Abdallāh ibn Muḥriz.

The quarter from the Syria Gate to the district of Ḥarb and its environs, to the avenue of the Syria Gate and its environs, as far as the bridge at the furtherst part of the Tigris; to Ḥarb ibn 'Abdallāh, his *mawlā* Ghazwān, and the engineer al-Ḥajjāj ibn Arṭāt.

The quarter from the Khurāsān Gate to the Tigris bridge and extending by an avenue along the Tigris as far as Baghayyīn and the Qaṭrabbul Gate; to Hishām ibn 'Amr al-Taghlibī, 'Umāra ibn Ḥamza and to the engineer Shihāb ibn Kathīr.

He informed those in charge of each quarter of the area of land assigned to each grantee and his followers and of the area allotted for shops and markets in each quarter, so that in each district there should be a general market for the sale of all kinds of commodities. In each district they were to set aside for streets and for open and blind alleys an area equal to that of the buildings and to call each street by the name of the commander or eminent personage who lived there or that of the country of origin of the people living there. They were ordered to lay out the avenues with a width of 50 black cubits and the streets with a width of 16 cubits and to build, in all the district, markets and streets, enough mosques and baths for the inhabitants of every district and neighborhood. He ordered them to take a certain area from the grants of the officers and troops and set it aside for traders to build and live there, for small shopkeepers and for people from the provinces.

Al-Ya'qūbī, *Buldān*, pp. 233–242.

28. On the Characteristics of Different Countries (Late Tenth Century)

The most elegant country is Iraq. It is the one which most lightens the heart and sharpens the mind and in which the soul is most at ease and thought is most refined, if means suffice.

The most distinguished, the richest in fruits, and the most plentiful in knowledge and glory and coolness is the East.

The most plentiful in wool, in silk, and in income for its size is Daylam.

The most excellent in milk and honey, with the tastiest bread and the most potent saffron, is Jibāl.

The most abundant in produce, the cheapest in price, also for meat, but with the dullest people is Riḥāb.

The country with the worst and basest people, root and branch, is Khūzistān.

The country with the sweetest dates and the most submissive people is Kirmān.

The most plentiful in candy, rice, musk, and camphor is Sind.

The country where the people and the merchants are smartest and where there is most vice is Fārs.

The fiercest in heat and drought and with the most palm trees is Arabia.

The richest in blessings, righteous people, holy men, and holy places is Syria.

The richest in worshippers, Qur'ān-readers, wealth, trade, special features, and corn is Egypt.

The country with the most dangerous roads, the best horses, and the most ordinary people is Aqūr.

The country with the most uncouth, doltish, and dishonest people, the most numerous cities, and the vastest territories is the Maghrib.

'Abd al-Raḥmān the nephew of al-Aṣma'ī said: I called on al-Jāḥiẓ and I asked him, "Tell me about the qualities of different countries." He said, "Yes. There are ten cities; manhood in Baghdad, eloquence in Kūfa, craftsmanship in Basra, trade in Egypt, treachery in Rayy, crudity in Nīshāpūr, meanness in Marw, bragging in Balkh, and work in Samarqand." By my life, he spoke truth, but there are skillful workmen in Nīshāpūr too, trade in Basra, eloquence in Mecca, and skill in Marw. Ṣan'ā' has a good climate, Jerusalem has fine buildings, and Ṣughar and Jurjān are plague spots, Damascus has many rivers, Ṣoghd has vast forests, Ramla has delicious produce, Ṭabaristān has constant rain, Farghāna has low prices, Marw and Juḥfa are dens of iniquity, Raqqa is a place of danger, Hamadhān and Tinnīs are the center of freemen, Syria is the land of the worthy, Samarqand is the destination of merchants, Nīshāpūr is the city of grandees, and Fusṭāṭ is the most populous of the garrison cities. Happy are the people of Gharj in the justice of their king and of Iṣfahān for their climate, their cloth, and their pottery. The habits of Shīrāz are a scandal to Islam. Aden is the anteroom of China with deserts around it. Ṣaghāniyān has pasturage of fruit and birds. Bukhārā would be splendid but for its water and its fires. Balkh is the treasure house of jurisprudence, spacious and affluent. Aelia suits religious and worldly folk; the people of Baghdad show little prosperity, while Ṣan'ā' and Nīshāpūr are the reverse. There are none more numerous or vile than the preachers of Nīshāpūr, none greedier than in Mecca, poorer than in Yathrib, more chaste than in Jerusalem, more cultivated than in Herāt and Biyār, cleverer than in Rayy, keener than in Sijistān, more fraudulent than in 'Umān, more ignorant than in 'Ammān. Nor are there any with more accurate weights than in Kūfa and 'Askar Mukram [Samarra], nor handsomer than in Ḥimṣ or Bukhārā, nor uglier than in Khwārazm, nor with finer beards than in Daylam, nor greater tipplers than in Ba'albakk or in Egypt, nor more depraved than in Shīrāz, nor more fractious than in Sijistān and Damascus, nor more turbulent than in Samarqand or Shāsh, nor more submissive than in Egypt, nor more stupid than in Baḥrayn, nor more foolish than in Ḥimṣ, nor more suave than in Fasā, Nābulus, Baghdad, and Rayy, nor better-spoken than in Baghdad, nor worse-spoken than in Ṣayā or Herāt, nor purer in language than in Khurāsān, nor with better Persian than in Balkh or Shāsh, nor more flatulent than in the Marshes, nor with sounder leaders than in Haytal, nor with better people than Gharj al-Shār.

If anyone asks which country is best, the answer would depend. If he is one of those who seek both worlds, then it is Jerusalem; if he is devout and free from ambition, Mecca. If he seeks comfort, affluence, low prices, and fruits, he may be told: "Any country would serve you," or else, "You have five capitals, Damascus, Basra, Rayy, Bukhārā, and Balkh; or five towns, Caesarea, Bā'aynāthā, Khujanda, Dīnawar, and Nuqan; or five districts, Ṣughd, Ṣaghāniyān, Nihāwand, Jazīrat ibn 'Umar, and Sābūr. Choose whichever you please, for these places are the delights of Islam. It is said that Andalusia is a paradise, but the earthly paradises are four in number, the Ghūṭa of Damascus, the river of Ubulla, the Garden of Ṣughd, and Sha'b Bawwān. Whoever desires commerce, should take Aden, 'Umān, or Egypt."

Whenever we speak of the defects of the inhabitants of the provinces, scholars and men of letters are excluded, especially the jurists, whose merits I see. Know that every country the name of which includes the letter *Ṣād* is peopled with fools, except for Basra. If the name include two *Ṣāds,* such as Miṣṣīṣa or Ṣarṣar, then God save us. With every country where the adjectival form of the name ends in *zī*, its bearer is clever, such as the Rāzī (from Rayy), the Marwazī (from Marw), and the Sijzī (from Sijistān). Every country the name of which ends in *ān* has some good or special feature, such as Jurjān, Mūqān, and Arrajān. Every country where it is very cold has the fattest and most corpulent inhabitants with the finest and longest beards, such as Farghāna, Khwārazm, and Armenia. Every place by the sea or a river is full of fornication and sodomy, such as Sīrāf, Bukhārā, and 'Aden. Every country surrounded by rivers has trouble makers and rebels among its people, such as Damascus, Samarqand, and al-Ṣalīq. Every country which is spacious and comfortable is short of accommodation, with the exception of Balkh.

Know that Baghdad was great in the past but is now falling in ruins. It is full of troubles, and its glory is gone. I neither approve nor admire it, and if I praise it, it is mere convention. Fusṭāṭ of Egypt is today what Baghdad was in the past, and I do not know any greater city in all Islam.

Al-Muqaddasī, pp. 32–36.

6
Travelers' Tales

29. An African Adventure (Tenth Century)

Ismāʿīlūya and several sailors told me that he had sailed from ʿUmān on board his ship bound for Qanbaluh in the year 310 [922–923], but the ship was carried off course by a violent wind and taken to Sufāla in the land of the Zanj. "When I had examined the place," said the ship's captain, "I realized that we had come to the land of the man-eating Zanj and that to land in this place was certain death. We therefore made our ablution, repented of our sins to Almighty God, and recited the prayer for the dead for one another. Canoes surrounded us and led us to an anchorage, where we entered, cast anchor, and went ashore with these people. They took us to their king. We found a young man, handsome for a Zanjī and well-built. He asked us about ourselves, and we told him that our destination was his country. 'You lie,' he said, 'you were bound for Qanbaluh and not here. The storm caught you and carried you to our country.' 'It is so,' we said, 'but we spoke as we did only in order to please you.' 'Unload your goods,' he said, 'and carry on your trade. You have nothing to fear.' We therefore opened our bales and did very good business. He imposed no tax on us, in kind or in cash, and when we gave him some presents, he gave us presents of equal or greater value.

"We stayed in his country for several months, and when it was time to go, we asked his permission, which he gave us. We therefore loaded our goods and wound up our business, and when we decided to leave, we informed him. Rising from his throne, he walked with us as far as the shore with a group of his companions and his slaves, embarked on a canoe, and came aboard our ship with us. He came on board with seven of his chief slaves. When they were on board ship I said to myself, 'This king would be worth 30 dinars at auction at 'Umān and his seven slaves 160 dinars. They are wearing clothes worth 20 dinars, which would bring us at least 3,000 dirhams—and this would do us no harm at all." So I shouted to the sailors, and they hoisted the sail and raised the anchors while he was still expressing his friendship and goodwill and inviting us to return and promising to treat us well when we did so.

"When the sails were hoisted and he saw that we were on our way, his face changed. 'You are leaving,' he said. 'I bid you farewell,' and he rose to go back to his canoe. But we cut the cable joining us to the canoe, and we said to him, 'You will stay with us and we will take you to our country and reward you for your kindness to us and repay you for what you have done for us.' 'Good people,' he cried. 'When you came to me I could, as my people desired, have let them eat you and take your goods, as they did to others. But I treated you well; I took nothing from you and even came to bid you farewell on your ship as a mark of esteem from me to you. Therefore give me my due and take me home.' We paid no attention to what he said and took no notice of him. The wind was strong, and before very long his country disappeared from sight, and by nightfall we were in the open sea. The king and his companions were put with the other slaves, about 200 head, and we treated him in the same way as the other slaves. He kept aloof and neither answered nor spoke to us. He ignored us as if he did not know us, nor we him. When we got to 'Umān, we sold him and his companions along with the other slaves.

"In the year 31, we again left 'Umān bound for Qanbaluh, and the wind carried us away to Sufāla in the land of the Zanj, and without telling any lies, we arrived at the very same place. As soon as the people saw us, they came out and their canoes surrounded us. This time we really were convinced that we were lost, and we none of us said a word to one another, so great was our fear. We made our ablution, recited the prayer for the dead, and bade each other farewell.

"They came, seized us, brought us to the dwelling of their

king and led us in—and there was the very same king, seated on his throne as if we had left him but a moment before. When we saw him, we fell prostrate and our strength left us, so that we could not move ourselves to stand up. 'You are my friends,' he said, 'no doubt about it." None of us could speak, and all our limbs trembled. 'Look up,' he said. 'I give you my pledge of safety for your persons and your property.' Some of us looked up; others could not, through weakness and shame. But he spoke to us in a friendly way until we all raised our heads. We did not look at him, in our shame and fear.

"When, thanks to his promise of safety, we had recovered our composure, he said to us, 'Betrayers! I treated you as I did, and you repaid me by treating me as you did!' 'Despise us, O King,' we cried, 'and forgive us.' 'I have already forgiven you,' he replied. 'Carry on your trade as you did that time; there is nothing to stop you.'

"Our joy was such that we could not believe what we heard, and we thought that this was a trick to get our goods ashore. We brought them ashore, and we offered him a present of great value, but he refused it, and said, 'I have not enough regard for you to accept a present from you, nor do I wish to render my own possessions unlawful by taking anything from you, for all that you possess is tainted.'

"We therefore carried on our trade, and when it was time to go, we asked his permission to load the ship, which he gave us. When we had decided to set sail I said, 'O King, we have decided to sail.' And he replied, 'Go under the protection of God.' 'O King,' I said. 'You have treated us better than we could ever repay, and we betrayed and wronged you. But how did you manage to escape and return home?'

" 'When you had sold me in 'Umān,' he said, 'the man who bought me took me to a town called Basra' (which he described). 'There I learned prayer, fasting, and also a little of the Qur'ān. Then my master sold me to another who took me to the city of the king of the Arabs which is called Baghdad' (then he described Baghdad), 'where I learned to speak correct Arabic, learned the Qur'ān, and prayed with everybody in the mosques.

I saw the Caliph who is called al-Muqtadir.[1] I stayed in Baghdad for a whole year and part of the next year. Then some people came from Khurāsān, mounted on camels. Seeing their great number, I asked who they were and why they had come, and they said they were on their way to Mecca. I then asked, "What is this Mecca?" And they said, "In it is the holy house of God, to which people go on pilgrimage," and they told me about this house. I said to myself, "I must follow these people to this house" and I told my master what I had heard, but I saw that he wished neither to go himself nor to let me go. I therefore pretended to think no more of it until the people had left, and when they did so I followed them and accompanied a group of travelers whom I served all the way. I ate with them, and they gave me two garments which I wore as the ritual dress of a pilgrim. They instructed me in the rites of the pilgrimage, and Almighty God helped me to complete my pilgrimage.

" 'Fearing to return to Baghdad, where my master would catch me and put me to death, I left with another caravan bound for Egypt. On the way I served some people, who took me with them and gave me a share in their provisions as far as Egypt.

" 'When I reached Egypt and saw this sea of sweet water which they call the Nile, I asked whence it came and they told me that its source lay in the land of the Zanj. "And in what part?" I asked. "In a part of Egypt," they said, "which is called Aswān, on the border of the land of the black people." So I followed the bank of the Nile, going from place to place, begging from people, and they fed me. Such was my way.

" 'Then I came among some black people who turned against me. They put me in chains and burdened me, along with other slaves, with more than I had the strength to bear. So I fled and fell into the hands of others who seized me and sold me. I fled again, and so I went on, from the time I left Egypt until I reached a certain place in the land of the Zanj.

" 'There I disguised and hid myself, for from the time when I left Egypt, in spite of all my terrifying experiences, I was never

[1] Reigned 908–932.

so much afraid as when I found myself now near to my own country. In my own country, I thought, another king would have gained the kingship and would be sitting in my place. The soldiers would obey him, and it would be hard to wrest the kingship from him. If I showed myself or if anyone got to know of me, I would be taken to him and he would put me to death, or else some loyal supporter would make bold to cut off my head and use it to show his loyalty.

" 'I was frightened beyond endurance. I began to hide by day and hurry by night in the direction of my country, until I reached the seashore. There I took passage in disguise on a ship to such and such a place. Then I embarked again for another place, and the ship landed me at night on the shore of my own country. I made enquiries of an old woman, "Is your present reigning king just?" I asked. "By God, my son," she answered, "we have no king other than Almighty God." And she told me everything that had happened to their king. I expressed my astonishment as if I knew nothing about it and as if I were not myself that king. Then she said, "The people of the kingdom agreed among themselves that they would not have any king after him until they knew what had happened to him and until they despaired of his life, for their diviners had informed them that he was alive and well in the land of the Arabs."

" 'The next morning I came to this my town and entered this my palace and found my family just as I had left them, except they were full of sadness, as were also my subjects. I told them my story, and they marveled and rejoiced and joined with me in entering the religion of Islam. I became their king again one month before your arrival and am now full of joy and happiness that God has blessed me and my subjects with Islam and true faith and with the knowledge of prayer, fasting, and pilgrimage, of what is permitted and what is forbidden, I have thus attained what was never before attained by anyone in the land of the Zanj. Therefore, I forgive you, since you were the cause of my coming to the true religion. There is only one other matter which weighs on me, and I ask God to release me from the sin." I asked him what it was, and he said, "My master. I left Baghdad for the pilgrimage without his permission or his consent, and I did not return to him. If I could find a reliable man I would send him the price which he paid for me and ask him to accord me my liberty. If you had been honest and trustworthy men, I would have paid you my purchase price and asked you to remit it to him, and I would have given him ten times more as a gift in return for the patience which he showed me. But you are men of treachery and cunning."

"We bade him farewell, and he said, 'Go. And if you come again, I will treat you in the same way and even more generously. Tell the Muslims to come to us, for now we are their brothers, Muslims as they are. As for accompanying you on board, I prefer not.' We bade him farewell and left."

Buzurg ibn Shahriyār, *Kitāb 'Ajā'ib al-Hind,* pp. 50–60.

30. Sicily (973)

Among the countries in the hands of the Muslims, Sicily, by virtue of its fine situation, may be put in the same class as Spain. It is an island in the form of an isosceles triangle, with its apex to the west. Its length is seven days' journey; its width, four. It lies in the open sea to the east of Spain and facing that part of the North African coastline which extends from Ifrīqiya, Bāja, and Tabarqa to Marsā al-Kharaz. Westward across the sea lies the island of Corsica, southward, the island of Qawsara [Pantellaria]; and eastward, the seashore of the great continent in which stands Constantinople. Here lies the town of Reggio and the districts of Calabria. Sicily consists mainly of mountains, castles, and fortresses. Most of its soil is inhabited and cultivated. The only famous city is Palermo, the capital of Sicily, which is on the seashore. It consists of five quarters, adjoining and not separated by any distance but with their boundaries clearly marked.

The great city called Palermo is surrounded by a huge stone wall, high and strong. It is inhabited by merchants. There is a great cathedral mosque, which was built as a Christian church shortly before the Conquest. In it there is a great sanctuary, and a certain logician claims that the Greek sage, that is to say, Aristotle, is in a wooden casket hung in this sanctuary, which the Muslims have adopted as a mosque; he says that the Christians used to revere his grave and come to seek healing from it because of the respect and veneration which they had seen the Greeks accord him. The reason why it is suspended between heaven and earth is that people used to come to it to pray for rain, or healing, or help in other grave matters such as cause men to seek refuge with God and to draw near to Him in times of stress, fear of death, or mutual violence. I myself saw a wooden casket which could well be this grave.

Facing Palermo there is a town called Khāliṣa, with a stone wall inferior to that of Palermo. Here live the Sultan and his entourage. There are two public baths but neither markets nor inns. There is a small cathedral mosque, the Sultan's garrison, a naval arsenal, and the administrative offices. It has four gates in the north, south, and west, but in the east there is the sea and a wall without a gate.

The quarter known as the Quarter of the Slavs is bigger and more populous than the two cities I have mentioned. In it is the seaport. There are springs which flow between this place and [the capital of] Sicily, and the water serves as a boundary between them.

There is a quarter known by the name of the mosque of Ibn Saqlāb. It is also big but has no streams, and its inhabitants drink from wells. By its edge flows the river called Wādī ʿAbbās, a broad and swift stream on which they have many mills, but their gardens and orchards do not make use of it.

The New Quarter is large and adjoins the quarter of the mosque. There is no division or demarcation between them, and both are unwalled, as is also the Quarter of the Slavs. Most of the markets are between the mosque of Ibn Saqlāb and the New Quarter. They are as follows: the olive oil sellers in their entirety; the millers, the money changers, the apothecaries, the smiths, the sword cutlers [polishers?], the flour markets, the brocade makers, the fishmongers, the spice merchants, a group of butchers, the greengrocers, the fruiterers, the sellers of aromatic plants, the jar merchants, the bakers, the rope makers, a group of perfumers, the butchers, the shoemakers, the tanners, the carpenters, and the potters. The wood merchants are outside the city. In Palermo proper there are groups of butchers, jar merchants, and shoemakers. The butchers have nearly 200 shops for the sale of meat, and there are a few of them inside the city at the beginning of the main road. Near them are the cotton merchants, the ginners, and the cobblers. There also is another useful market in the city. The extent and numbers of the people of Palermo can be seen in their cathedral mosque, where I estimated the congregation, when it was full, at over 7,000 persons. Not more than 36 rows stand in prayer, with not more than 200 men in each row.

In Palermo and Khāliṣa, together with the quarters outside the walls, there are more than 300 mosques, most of them in good condition, with their roofs, walls, and doors intact. Well-informed people among them agree on the identity and number of these mosques. There are also mosques outside the city in the adjoining and surrounding area, amid the gardens and towers and in the quarters that follow one another without interruption along the banks of the stream called Wādī 'Abbās, near a place called Mu'askar, within the urban area, scattered across the plain of 'Abbās, one after another, until the way station called Bāyḍā', a village overlooking the city and about half a parasang away. This village is in ruins, and its owners dead as the result of disorders which befell them. They all know these mosques, and do not disagree about their number, which exceeds 200. I have never seen so many mosques in any place or great city, even in cities double the size, nor have I heard anyone claim such a number, except for the claim of the Cordovans that their city has 500 mosques. I was not able to verify this in Cordova and mentioned it in its place with some expression of doubt, but I can confirm it for Sicily because I personally saw the greater part. One day I was standing near the house of Abū Muḥammad 'Abd al-Waḥīd ibn Muḥammad, known as al-Qafsī, a jurist and notary. From his mosque I could see, at the distance of a bowshot, about ten mosques, all within view, some of them facing one another and separated only by the breadth of the street. I inquired about this and was informed that these people are so puffed up with pride that each one of them wants to have his own mosque, reserved to him and shared by no one apart from his own family and retinue. It even happened that two brothers, whose houses were adjoining with party walls, each built a mosque for himself in which to sit alone. Among the ten mosques which I have mentioned was one in which Abū Muḥammad ibn al-Qafsī performed his prayers. Between this mosque and the house of one of his sons, who was also a jurist, there were less than forty paces, yet his son had built himself a new mosque on the side of his house. The door of this mosque was always closed. When the time of the prayer came, he sat in the hall of his house, adjoining and attached to his mosque, but did not go into it to pray. It seemed that his purpose in building it was that it should be known as the Mosque of the Jurist, the son of the Jurist. He was a young man of immense self-regard and prodigious self-importance. So great was his vainglory that one might have thought that he was his father's father, not his son, or that he had no father at all, because of his boasting, his bragging, his mode of riding, and his dress. Within the forty paces which I mentioned as separating his mosque from his father's mosque, there was yet another mosque with an Imam and a school.

On the seashore there are many convents [*ribāṭ*], full of cant and hypocrisy, fractious idlers and evildoers, old men and youngsters, shabby and seedy ruffians who have made themselves prayer carpets and who rise up only to collect alms and to defame respectable women. They are a disastrous visitation, a general misfortune, and a standing calamity. Most of them are also pimps. Many people do not realize this because of their great hypocrisy and reputation, but most of them are deliberate frauds who make profession of the faith but are so ignorant that they do not know the difference between what is law and what is tradition in the matter of ablution. Their clients are those who lack a place for idleness and for debauchery. To these they give shelter and a trifle of food, in conditions which it would be unseemly to describe, for this is not the kind of book to contain such descriptions. I think that they were not founded in piety, as were the mosques described above. Therefore, they have crumbled and their people have perished because of the upheavals and the insurrections and rebellions of which they have been guilty. But God knows best.

I have described Khāliṣa and its gates and contents, but I have not described Palermo, which is the old city. The best-known gate is the Sea Gate, so called because it is near the sea. Then comes the gate erected by Abu'l-Ḥusayn Aḥmad ibn al-Ḥasan ibn Abi'l-Ḥusayn because the people in this quarter complained that the only place by which they could leave the city was far away. He built it on high ground overlooking a stream and a spring called 'Ayn Shifā', by which name the gate is known at the present time. Those who live near this gate have the advantage of the spring. Then there is the gate of St. Agatha, which is an ancient gate, and by it is the Rūṭa Gate, named after a large stream to which one goes down through this gate and which has its source under the gate. The water is healthy, and on its bank there is a long row of mills. Then there is the Riyāḍ Gate, also a recent one, built by Abu'l-Ḥusayn Aḥmad ibn al-Ḥasan. Nearby there was also a gate called Ibn Qurhab, situated in a poor defensive position. In bygone days there was much fighting over the city, and attackers entered through this opening, causing great dishonor and injury to the inhabitants. Therefore, Abu'l-Ḥusayn closed it and removed the gate. Nearby there is the Gate of Tidings [*Anbā'*], the most ancient in the city. Then there is the Gate of the Blacks, [*al-Sūdan*], facing the smiths market; then the Iron Gate leading to the Jewish quarter; then another gate, also built by Abu'l-Ḥusayn, which has no name, leading to the Abū Jamīn quarter. That makes nine gates in all.

This city is elongated in shape. It has a market which goes from east to west and is known as the main street, paved with stone and in use from beginning to end for various kinds of commerce. It is surrounded by numerous springs which flow from west to east and are fast enough to turn a mill. By these waters there is more than one mill at more than one point. Along these streams, from their source to their outlet into the sea, lie marshes and thickets with many Persian sugar canes, vegetable gardens, and excellent cucumber fields. Among the fields there are groves full of papyrus, from which scrolls are made. I know of no papyrus in the whole world which can be compared with the papyrus of Egypt, except the papyrus of Sicily. Most of it is plaited into ropes for ships' anchors, and a small part is used to make scrolls for the government, but no more is made than is actually required.

The drinking water of the townspeople, those who live near the walls from the neighborhood of the Riyāḍ Gate to the 'Ayn Shifā' Gate, comes from these springs. The rest of the people and the people of Khāliṣa and all the different quarters drink water from wells in their houses. The water is sometimes light and sometimes heavy, but they relish this above the plenitude of sweet running waters which they have because they eat a lot of onions. The drinking water of the people of Mu'askar comes from the spring called al-Ghirbāl, which is good. In Mu'askar there is another spring called 'Ayn al-Tisa', smaller than al-Ghirbal, and another spring called 'Ayn Abī Sa'īd, still smaller, and a spring called 'Ayn Abī 'Alī, named after one of their rulers. The drinking water of the district called Gharbiyya comes from the spring known as the Iron Spring because there is an iron mine belonging to the sovereign. Its products are used for the needs of his ships and his carriages. This mine used to belong to the Aghlabids[1] and was very profitable to them. It is near a village called Balhara from which springs and streams flow into the Wādī 'Abbās and swell it. There are many orchards and vineyards in these parts. Around the urban area there are other less known springs with waters that are used to good advantage, such as Qādūs in the southern quarter, which contains the small fountain and the large fountain on the spur of the mountain which overlooks the town. It is the most plentiful of all their springs. All these waters are used for their gardens. The village of al-Bayḍā' has an excellent spring called al-Bayḍā', adjoining al-Ghirbāl and al-Gharbiyya. The drinking water of the neighborhood called Burj al-Baṭṭāl comes from the spring called 'Ayn Abī Mālik. Most of the waters in the land to the west of the town are used for their gardens by means of waterwheels. They have well-stocked gardens and also fertile orchards watered by the rain, not irrigated as in Syria. Most of the water of the city and its quarters comes from wells and is heavy and unwholesome. That they prefer to drink this water rather than sweet flowing water is because they lack refinement and eat a lot of onion, spoiling their taste by consuming much of it raw. There is nobody among them, of whatever class, who does not eat onion every day and no house in which it is not eaten morning and eve-

[1] A dynasty which ruled in North Africa and, for a while, in Sicily during the ninth century.

ning. This is what has corrupted their imagination, harmed their brains, confused their senses, altered their intelligence, diminished their understanding, stultified their perceptions, spoiled their complexions, and so disturbed their constitutions that they see things, or at any rate most things, as the opposite of what they really are.

What I say on this matter is confirmed and proved by the testimony of Yūsuf ibn Ibrāhīm the scribe in his *History of Physicians,* where he speaks of his call in Damascus on ʿĪsā ibn al-Ḥakam, the Christian physician. "I discussed the onion with him," he says, "and he did not cease to condemn it and describe its defects. Now ʿĪsā and Salūya ibn Bayān lived like monks and did not desire any aphrodisiacs, which they said ruined the body and speeded the soul on its way. I did not therefore think it fitting to adduce the aphrodisiac effects of the onion, and I said to them, "In my travels I have observed that the onion has a certain use." He asked me what it was, and I replied, "It has happened that I tasted the water of a pool or spring and found it bad and then ate onion and drank again and found it less bad." Now ʿĪsā was a man who laughed little, but my words made him roar with laughter. Then, shocked, he recovered his composure, and said, "I find it strange that a man like you should make such a mistake. You have noticed the nastiest feature of the onion, and you have made it a virtue! But my dear fellow, when the brain suffers corruption, are not the senses corrupted so that the senses of smell, taste, hearing, and sight all become deficient?" "Yes indeed," I replied. And he continued, "The property of the onion is to induce corruption in the brain. That you were less able to perceive the saltiness and brackishness of the water was due to the corrupting effect of the onion on your brain."

This is a rational conclusion. The result of eating onions is that in this city there is none who is intelligent, worthy, really competent in any branch of learning, manly, or religious. The riffraff predominate, and most of the people are of low condition, without intelligence or real religion. Most of them are Barqajāna[2] and freedmen claiming a connection with those who conquered the country and then died out.

[2] A Berber tribe.

More than one of them told me about ʿUthmān ibn al-Kharrāz, who was their qāḍī and a pious man. He relied on some witnesses and rejected others. He was petitioned by a woman who was troubled by an unfounded claim on a house which belonged to her. He asked her for proofs and she pleaded possession, adducing witnesses and written evidence which she produced to the judge. He, however, asked for additional witnesses. Now he trusted the testimony of the schoolmaster Abū Ibrāhīm Isḥāq ibn al-Mājalī. He knew about the affair of this woman, and she asked him to act as witness on her behalf. This he refused to do until she promised a bribe of a number of *rubāʿīs*,[3] whereupon he testified in her favor. It happened that ʿUthmān was about to sign the order of judgment which he had given on Isḥāq's testimony and to have it registered, when Isḥāq demanded the money which the woman had promised him. But she dismissed him and refused to pay what she had promised him, believing in her right and trusting that the testimony was established and that she had no further need of Isḥāq or of anyone else. But the judge summoned Isḥāq to confirm his testimony in person, so as to execute judgment in favor of the woman on the basis of his testimony. Isḥāq then said "May God strengthen the judge! I now withdraw my testimony because of certain problems which have arisen concerning it." Now the judge had held Isḥāq's testimony in such esteem that a withdrawal did not seem to him allowable. He began to doubt his story and made a very thorough investigation, by which the truth of the matter appeared. Thereafter he accepted neither his testimony nor anyone else's. He deleted all the witnesses from the official list and nullified their testimony. Thereafter, most of his judgments rested on agreed compromises. He mistrusted the witnesses, and neither desire nor fear could bring him to them until he died. When his end drew near he said, "There is no one in this whole city to whom my work can be entrusted." He therefore gave his office to an immigrant from Qayrawān called al-Ghaḍāʾirī, whom he had trusted. This story became known among the townspeople, and it was one of the means used by Ibn al-Mājalī to win them over to choose him and

[3] A coin, usually equivalent to a quarter of a dinar.

make him their judge and preacher, with the expectation, on the part of some of them, that he would practice the knavery that they desired. Isḥāq, according to what they told me, was a man of little weight and great ignorance, full of admiration for his own deficiencies, with neither presence nor dignity, nor the manner of a qāḍī—he was just a Barqajānī schoolmaster made into a qāḍī.

One of the townspeople, called Abu'l-Ḥārith Fiḥl ibn Falāḥ al-Lahīṣī, also al-Kutāmī, whom I heard tell many stories about the town, told me that he, with another man whom he named, had appeared one day at a hearing of Isḥāq al-Mājalī after he became judge. He sat by the prayer niche of the cathedral mosque and had in his hand a decision in their favor on the subject of a dowry, which he proceeded to read. At each paragraph he paused and dilated in praise of the beautiful expressions which he had used, the elegant phraseology, and the perfections of his style, while they were both silent. He did this at each new paragraph. Then he rose from the prayer niche, where he had installed himself as if in judgment, and went and sat in front of them and continued to read aloud and repeat his own praises. Then he said "I see that you are not listening to this judgment, the like of which, by God, has never been uttered on the face of the earth." Then he continued to read and then returned to his place by the prayer niche.

The same person told me that sometimes he raised his hand against litigants to strike them. Several of them told me about a man who had brought a dispute to him and had been summoned to plead it. There was a large pair of scissors. He took them in his hand and gestured with them toward the man as if to strike him in the face. The man bent down toward Isḥāq's sandals, which were in front of him, and took hold of them. "Why have you grabbed my sandals? To hit me with them?" asked the qāḍī. "No," replied the man, "to defend myself against you, for fear lest you reach my face with these scissors." There are many stories about him about various kinds of folly and madness. He was one of the band of crazy and foolish schoolmasters, and indeed one of the greatest and most famous among them.

The country is full of schoolmasters, and there are schools in every place. They are of different kinds and various grades of madness and foolishness, but surpassing the madness of schoolmasters in all countries and of fools in every region. They even presume to discuss the behavior and predilections of the sovereign, use insulting language about his faults, and treat his good points as bad ones.

There are some 300 schoolmasters in the city, or in any case, not far short of that. Such numbers are not found in any other place or in any other country. The reason why they are so many, though they are of so little use, is their aversion for frontier fighting and their disinclination to the Holy War. Their city is a frontier march against the Romans, a country facing the enemy. The Holy War is permanent there, and the call to arms has not ceased since Sicily was conquered. Their rulers do not slacken, and when they call to arms, they allow none to stay at home save those who pay a commutation or who are excused to stay behind and serve with the ruler's guard. It has long been the custom among them to exempt schoolmasters from these burdens and to pay the indemnity for them. Thus the most stupid among them take refuge in teaching, which their ignorance makes seem attractive, despite its lack of benefit or advantage. Most of them barely earn ten dinars a year from all their pupils, who are, nevertheless, many. What posture is more degraded, what figure more vile and contemptible than that of a man who barters the duty imposed on him by Almighty God, the Holy War, with its honors and its glorious warfare against the infidels, in exchange for the lowest of positions, the meanest of trades, and the vilest of crafts? Among people of note in all countries, teachers, although they instruct the children of the great and rich, are regarded as a shiftless crew from whom only remissness can be expected. In their unanimous opinion and that of every man, the schoolmaster is a fool, condemned to inadequacy, ignorance, triviality, and lack of intelligence. The greatest misfortune, severest trial, and final calamity is that all the people of Sicily, because of their lack of discernment, deficient knowledge, and slowness of understanding, believe that this crew are their notables, their élite, their jurists, their scholars, their jurisconsults, their legal witnesses, and that it is they who can determine what is permitted and what is forbidden, pronounce judgments and legalize testimony, and that they are the men of letters and the orators.

I saw a son of this Isḥāq ibn al-Mājalī, the schoolmaster and qāḍī mentioned above, who gave sermons there for about two years. From the beginning to the end of his sermon, he apocopated every noun and put every verb in the jussive. I spoke to a man of letters of the town who tried and claimed to have knowledge of everything, just after this preacher had used an active verb in a passive sentence, or a nominative noun as the direct object, and I said, "Did you not hear this orator and what he uttered?" and I explained it to him, I no longer remember in what words. "By God," he replied, "it may indeed be as you say, but we don't worry about such things."

Among the most outstanding and preeminent of these schoolmasters in conduct and rectitude [*'adāla*], that is, the opposite, foolishness and ignorance, are Abū 'Abdallāh Muḥammad ibn 'Īsā ibn Maṭar, a schoolmaster of the Zuhrī Mosque in the main street, who traveled to the east and wrote down *ḥadīths,* and Abu'l-Ḥasan 'Alī ibn Bāna, known as Ibn Alf Sawt [the son of a thousand lashes], who is his peer in rectitude and whom some of them consider his superior in knowledge, jurisprudence, and decorum. Both are stupid, purblind, inadequate, and deficient, both in appearance and in reality.

Abū 'Abdallāh Muḥammad ibn 'Īsā, known as al-Nāshī al-Qarawī, the theologian, told me this story when we met in Sicily. "Once," he said, "I was standing in the main street near the school of Ibn Maṭar, in conversation with some of my friends, when Ibn Maṭar came and joined them. They greeted him, he greeted me, and I returned his greeting. Then he started to describe me and my beliefs in the coarsest language and with the most offensive words and gestures. In the course of his remarks he said, "It pains me that you are so far from the truth." I replied, "May God curse whichever of us is farthest from the truth and has least knowledge of it." Then his color changed, and he became pale, but those present said to him, "He has dealt fairly with you, since he has only cursed the one who is farthest from the truth and only attacked the one who has the least knowledge of God." Then he asked, "Are you not of the school of Iraq?" I replied, "No, for the people of Iraq are called Murji'a[4] and were so called because they did not believe in the eternal damnation of those who commit a mortal sin." I then began to explain the problem at issue between us. He said, "I see that your doctrine is very close to ours." "But my man," I said, "I was explaining to you the doctrine of the Iraqis, which in my view is damnable and I am against them." He asked how, and I said, "We maintain that those who commit a mortal sin are doomed to eternal hellfire." He said, "I thought it was only the Iraqis who held this doctrine." Thus, in his ignorance, from morning to night, at every meeting and in every gathering, he accused them of unbelief. He condemned the Muʿtazilīs as unbelievers without even knowing their doctrine of the intermediate position, though this is one of the best known of doctrinal schools, and he cursed both the Waʿīdī and the Murjiʿ without distinguishing between them." This is the very summit of stupidity, and may God have mercy on the narrator to whom the transmitters of narratives wrongly ascribe a monopoly of ignorance.

On Friday, 10 Rajab of the year 362 [April 16, 973] I was sitting in Sicily by the shop of one Ibn al-Anṭākī in the main street of Palermo. It was a rainy day, at the sixth hour, and I was about to go with Ibn al-Anṭākī to the cathedral mosque which was a bowshot away. Suddenly Ibn Alf Sawṭ came toward us from the direction of the mosque, for his house was nearby. We asked where he was going, and he replied, "The people have already prayed, and I am going to watch the funeral of the preacher." Indeed, the preacher Ibn al-Mājalī, whose shortcomings I have already described, had died that Thursday night. He continued in the direction of the Sea Gate. After some time he returned, when he had already made us give up hope of the prayer. We asked him where he was going, and he answered, "I hear that they have not yet prayed, so I came back. Perhaps I can catch up with the prayer," and off he went. We were appalled by his behavior and were discussing his ignorance and the fate of people when one such as he was a legal witness when

[4] An early theological school in Islam. See *EI*[1], "Murdjiʿa."

he came back again. We said, "What now?" He replied, "They have already prayed, so I am now going to pray at the open-air oratory [*muṣallā*]." And this man is the most esteemed among them for his rectitude and holds the most respected position! That is how he is.

In a book arranged in ten chapters I have dealt at length with this person, with Ibn Maṭar, and the rest of their crew, describing their slight intelligence, dull understanding, extreme ignorance, quick frivolity, dead awareness, and proficient villainy, as well as their persistent heedlessness, offensive practices, numerous vices, and the nasty food which reinforces their ignorance and constipation. I began by describing the qualities in which the peoples of different towns, tribes, and countries take pride, the merits connected with them, how they are connected with districts and cities, as also the vices which diminish the pride and excellence and beauty of some of them. I called it the *Book of Sicily*. I left out none of their virtues or vices, but included all their characteristics, qualities, and deficiencies, what was given to them and what withheld, their coarse natures and bad morals, the stinking food and filthy, dirty objects which are peculiar to them, their great surliness and endless wrangling. I gave the names of all their schoolmasters with the stories which I heard about them, their ranks in impertinence, and their intermittent fractiousness against the authority of the sovereign. I described their sect, which is unlike any other sect in Islam or any creed in any [Muslim] land or any heresy, nor indeed does it resemble the beliefs of any other religion at all. They are tricksters [?]. The majority of the inhabitants of the cities, countryside, and the villages practice marriage with Christian women, the male children being tricksters [?] like their fathers, while the females are Christians like their mothers. They do not perform the prayer; they do not observe ritual purity; they do not give legal alms; they do not go on pilgrimages. Some of them observe the fast of Ramaḍān and then commit uncleanliness and wash themselves after it during the fast. It is a peculiarity which no one else shares with them and a unique quality by which they have gained preeminence in ignorance. I included a description of these people in my book. The minds of the noble and the hearts of the worthy desire full knowledge of all things, and the account of them in general works does not correspond to their true position.

One of the shabbiest and seediest things that I saw was a group of five schoolmasters in one school, teaching the children in partnership and squabbling among themselves. The school was near the 'Ayn Shifā' Gate. Their head was a *shaykh* called Milṭāṭ, a red-headed, blue-skinned profligate villain, always ready to bear false witness. There were his two sons, a man called Ibn al-Wadānī, and another called Akhū Rajā, with different places in their partnership. When I left Sicily, Ibn al-Wadānī had just died and if the most melancholy, the most demure, and the most staid of men had seen them when he died, their grief for him, their longing for him, their extravagant weeping at the funeral, he would either have roared with laughter or have been struck dumb with embarrassment at their ignorance.

As regards their livelihood, although they have light burdens, small expenses, and rich crops, there is not a man among them who owns a fortune in money or who has ever seen one, except with the ruler, if he is one of those who have access to the ruler and whose position is such that he is admitted to his presence. Now it is by wealth, tax revenue, and affluence that one may judge the condition of the people of towns, districts, and provinces, as also their merit, honor, and other qualities. The wealth of the island of Sicily at this time, which is for this place the most thriving and the most copious, amounts in all, from all kinds of taxes and dues, including the fifth, the *mustaghallāt*, the poll tax on non-Muslims, maritime dues, the annual tribute from the people of Calabria, the tax farm on fisheries, and other imposts, to a total of [figure missing in manuscript]. In its crops and fertility, its range of food and drink, Sicily is comparable with the countries mentioned earlier in my book as having been fertile and prosperous in the past. When I entered Sicily, its condition had passed from fertility to dearth. Its country gentry are like the barbarian islanders, stuttering, deaf, and mute; its country people, those of them who have not been refined by travel, in addition to a bestiality which overwhelms their human attributes, a manifest neglect of rights and duties in their dealings, utterances remote from the truth, and a fierce and mighty hatred of the stranger and visitor, neither practice nor endure any form of social life, but imitate their townspeople, who also hate merchants and strangers traveling in business to a degree not found among any savage tribe in the world or among brutish, uncouth mountain peoples—and this despite their dependence on importers and their need of traders. For the island lacks the resources of other countries and has only wheat, wool, pelts, wine, a small quantity of cane sugar, and some linens, which, to do them justice, are without equal in quality and cheapness. A manufactured piece, double size, is sold at between 50 and 60 *rubāʿīs*, and it is much better than similar cloths sold in Egypt at between 50 and 60 dinars. All other requirements and necessities are imported into the island from outside. To the corruption of their minds and religious beliefs, I would add the corruption of the soil, of wheat and of grain, for hardly a year passes without these being spoiled. Sometimes the grain even rots on the threshing floors before it has been put in the mattamores and granaries. The dirt in their houses is beyond the filth of the Jews, and the darkness and blackness of their dwellings, beyond that of kilns and ovens. Even among the highest class, chickens wander over the seats, and birds foul their prayer rugs and cushions.

Ibn Ḥawqal, *Ṣūrat al-Arḍ*, pp. 118–131.

31. The Sultan of Birgi (1333)

He is the Sultan Muḥammad ibn Aydin, one of the best, most generous, and most worthy of rulers. When the professor sent to inform him about me, he sent me his deputy to ask me to go and visit him. The professor advised me to wait until he sent for me a second time. The professor had a boil on his foot at that time, so that he could not ride and even stopped going to the *madrasa*. Then the Sultan sent for me a second time. This distressed the professor, who said, "I cannot ride, but I want to go with you so as to ensure that the Sultan gives you your due." So he braced himself, wrapped his foot in rags, and mounted without putting his foot in the stirrup. My companions and I also mounted, and we rode up the mountainside on a path which had been hewn out of the rock and leveled.

We reached the Sultan's camp just after midday and dismounted by a stream in the shade of some walnut trees. We found the Sultan worried and preoccupied because of the flight of his younger son, Sulaymān, who had fled to his father-in-law the Sultan Orkhān Bey. When he heard of our arrival, he sent us his two sons Khiḍr Bey and 'Umar Bey. These two princes greeted the jurist, who ordered them to greet me. They did so, questioned me about myself and my coming, and went away. The Sultan sent me a tent of the kind which they call *kharqa,* consisting of wooden slats put together in the form of a dome and covered with felt. The top can be left open to let in light and air, like a ventilator, or closed when necessary. They brought a rug and spread it on the ground. The jurist sat down, and I with him, together with his companions and mine, outside the tent in the shade of the walnut trees. This place is very cold, and one of my horses died that night of the extreme cold.

The next day the professor rode to see the Sultan and spoke about me as his own generous nature indicated. Then he came back to me and informed me of this. After a certain time the Sultan sent for both of us. We went to his place of residence, where we found him standing, and greeted him. The jurist then sat down on his right, and I next to the jurist. He asked me about myself and about my coming and questioned me about the Ḥijāz, Egypt, Syria, Yemen, the two 'Iraqs,[1] and the lands of the Persians. Then food was served, we ate and took our leave. The Sultan sent us rice, flour, and cooking fat in sheeps' stomachs. Such is the custom of the Turks.

We stayed in this way for several days, the Sultan sending for us every day to join him at his meals. One day he came to visit us in the afternoon. The jurist sat in the place of honor, with me sitting on his left and the Sultan on his right. This is because of the high regard in which the doctors of the law are held among the Turks. He asked me to write down some traditions of the

[1] Iraq proper and the western province of Iran, then known as 'Irāq 'Ajamī —Persian Iraq.

Prophet of God, may God bless and save him, for him. I wrote some down for him, the jurist presented them to him at the same time, and the Sultan commanded him to write him an explanation of them in the Turkish language. Then he rose and left. As he was going, he saw our servants cooking our food in the shade of the walnut trees, without spices or vegetables. Because of this he gave orders to punish his storekeeper and sent us spices and cooking fat.

Our stay on this mountain lasted a long time, and I became bored and wanted to leave. The jurist, too, was bored with this place and sent a message to the Sultan to inform him that I wished to continue on my way. Next day the Sultan sent his deputy who spoke to the professor in Turkish, which I did not then understand. The professor replied, and the deputy went away. "Do you know what he said?" the professor asked me. "I do not know," I replied. "The Sultan," he said, "sent to ask what he should give you. I told his messenger, 'The Sultan has gold, silver, horses, and slaves. Let him give whatever he pleases of these.' " The deputy went back to the Sultan and then returned to us and said, "The Sultan commands that you both stay here today and that you go with him tomorrow to his residence in the city."

The next day he sent a fine horse from his stable and went down into the city, and we with him. The townspeople came out to welcome him, among them the qāḍī whom we have already mentioned and others. The Sultan thus made his entry, and we with him. When he dismounted at the gate of his residence, I set off with the professor in the direction of the *madrasa*, but he called us back and ordered us to go into the residence with him. When we reached the vestibule, we found about twenty of his servants of strikingly beautiful appearance and dressed in silk garments. Their hair was parted and hanging down, and their color was a radiant white tinged with red. "Who," I asked the jurist, "are these beautiful forms?" "These," he replied, "are Greek pages."

Together with the Sultan we went up many steps until we reached a fine audience hall in the middle of which there was an artificial pool of water, with a copper lion in each corner spouting water from its mouth. All the way round the hall there were benches covered with rugs, on one of which was the Sultan's cushion. When we reached this bench the Sultan put aside his cushion with his own hands and sat with us on the rugs. The doctor sat down on his right, the qāḍī sat next to the doctor, and I sat next to the qāḍī. The Qur'ān-readers sat below the bench, for they never leave the Sultan wherever he may hold audience. They brought gold and silver bowls filled with diluted sherbet into which lemon juice had been squeezed and with small pieces of biscuit added. In these bowls there were gold and silver spoons. At the same time they brought porcelain bowls containing the same drink with wooden spoons. Those who had religious scruples used the porcelain bowls and wooden spoons.[2] I addressed some words of thanks to the Sultan and praised the jurist. I went to great lengths in this, so that it delighted the Sultan and gave him pleasure.

While we were seated with the Sultan, an old man arrived, wearing a turban with a tassel. He greeted the Sultan, and the qāḍī and the doctor rose in his honor. He sat in front of the Sultan on the bench and the Qur'ān-readers were below him. "Who is this shaykh?" I asked the jurist. He smiled and was silent. But I repeated my question and he answered, "This is a Jew physician. We all have need of him, and that is why we stood up for him as you saw." At this my old indignation overcame me again, and I said to the Jew, "You accursed son of an accursed father, how dare you sit above the readers of the Qur'ān, you who are a Jew?" and I berated him in a loud voice. The Sultan was astonished and asked what I was saying. The professor told him, while the Jew became angry and left the audience in ignominy. When we went away the doctor said to me, "Well done! God bless you! Nobody else would have dared to speak to him that way. You have let him know just what he is!"

During this audience the Sultan asked me whether I had ever seen a stone that had fallen from the sky. I replied that I had neither seen one nor heard of one. "This stone," he said, "fell from the sky near our city." Then he sent for some men and ordered them to bring the stone. They brought in a massive black stone,

[2] The pious tradition disapproves of the use of gold and silver.

very hard and with a glitter. I estimated its weight at about a quintal. The Sultan sent for stone hewers. Four of them came, and he ordered them to strike the stone. All four struck together as one man, four times, with iron hammers, and left no mark on the stone. I was astonished at this. The Sultan ordered them to take it back where it had been.

On the third day after our entry into the city with the Sultan, he gave a great feast to which he invited the jurists, the shaykhs, the chiefs of the army, and the leading townspeople. They ate, the Qur'ān-readers gave beautiful recitations from the Qur'ān, and we returned to our quarters in the *madrasa*. Every night the Sultan sent us food, fruits, sweetmeats, and candles. Then he sent me a 100 *mithqāls*[3] of gold, a thousand dirhams, a complete suit of clothes, a horse, and a Greek slave called Michael. To each of my companions he gave a suit of clothes and some dirhams. We owed all this to the good offices of the professor Muḥyi'l-Dīn, may God reward him. He bade us farewell and we left. The length of our stay on the mountain and in the city was fourteen days.

Ibn Baṭṭūṭa, *Riḥla*, ii, pp. 298–307.

[3] The *mithqāl* of gold was about 65.5 grains (4.25 grams).

7
Neighbors

32. Nubia and the Black Lands (Late Ninth Century)

The Gold Mines

He who wishes to go to the gold mines proceeds from Aswān to a place called al-Ḍayyiqa, between two mountains, then al-Buwayb, then Bayḍiyya, then Bayt Ibn Ziyād, then Udhayfir, then Jabal al-Aḥmar, then Jabal al-Bayāḍ, then Qabr Abī Mas'ūd, then 'Afār [?], and finally to Wādī al-'Allāqī. All these places are gold mines, and treasure-hunters make for them.

Wādī al-'Allāqī is like a large town. There are many people there, a mixture of Arabs and non-Arabs, all seekers after treasure, and there are markets and trade. Their drinking water comes from wells dug in the Wādī al-'Allāqī. Most of the inhabitants of al-'Allāqī are of the tribe of Rabī'a, a group of Banū Ḥanīfa from Yamāma who moved here with their wives and children.

The Wādī al-'Allāqī and its neighborhood consist of gold mines, and people work in all those that are near. Each group, traders and others, have negro slaves who do the digging. They bring out the ore, looking like yellow arsenic, and it is then made into ingots.

From al-'Allāqī to a place called Wādī al-Ḥil [?] is one day's journey. Then to a place called 'Anab [?], then to a place called Kiyār [?], where people gather to seek gold. In this place there are tribesmen of Rabī'a from Yamāma.

From al-'Allāqī to the mine called Baṭn Wāḥ, one day's journey. From al-'Allāqī to a place called A'mād, two days' journey. To a mine called Mā al-Sakhra, one day's journey; to a mine called al-

Akhshāb, two days; to the mine called Mizāb, where live tribesmen of Bali and Juhayna, four days; and to a mine called 'Arba Baṭhā' [?], two days.

From al-'Allāqī to 'Aydhāb is four days' journey. 'Aydhāb is on the seashore, and from there men take ships for Mecca, the Ḥijāz, and the Yemen. Merchants come there and carry away gold, ivory, and other goods on ships.

From al-'Allāqī to Barkān [?], the farthest gold mine to which the Muslims reach, is four days' journey. From al-'Allāqī to a place called Daḥ [?], where tribesmen of the Banū Sulaym and other tribal groups of Mudar live, ten days; from al-'Allāqī to a mine called al-Sanṭa where tribesmen of Muḍar and others live, ten days; from al-'Allāqī to a mine called al-Rifq, ten days; from al-'Allāqī to a mine called Sakhtīt, ten days.

These are the mines to which the Muslims go and where they seek for gold.

Nubia

The traveler from al-'Allāqī to the land of the Nubians who are called 'Alwa must travel thirty days, through Kūbān [?], then to a place called al-Abwāb [the gates], and so to the chief town of the 'Alwa, which is called Sūba, where lives the king of the 'Alwa. The Muslims come and go there, and from there comes the first news of the Nile's flood. It is said that the island of 'Alwa is connected with the island [peninsula] of Sind and that the Nile flows behind 'Alwa to the land of Sind into a river called Miḥrān [Indus] in the same way as it flows into the Nile of Egypt. It floods at the same time as the flood in Egypt. In the island of the 'Alwa, as in the islands of Sind there are elephants and rhinoceros and such, and in the Indus there are crocodiles as in the Nile of Egypt.

From Aswān one proceeds to the beginning of the land of the Nubians who are called Muqurra, at a place called Māwa. This is the place where Zakariyyā' ibn Qirqī lived as representative of his father Qirqī, the king of Nubia. From Māwa to the chief town and royal residence of the Nubians, called Sayāl [?], to Dongola, thirty days' journey.

The Land of the Bujja

From al-ʻAllāqī to the land of the Bujja, who are called the Ḥadāriba and the Kadabīs [?], twenty-five days' journey. The capital of the king of the Ḥadāriba Bujja is called Hajar, and Muslims come there for trade.

The Bujja live in skin tents and pluck their beards. They remove the nipples of young men so that they should not resemble the breasts of women. They eat millet and suchlike and ride camels on which they fight as one fights on horseback. They throw spears and do not miss.

From al-ʻAllāqī to the land of the Bujja, who are called Zanāfija, twenty five stages. The residence of the king of the Zanāfija is called Baqlin. Muslims sometimes go there to trade. Their religious beliefs are like those of the Ḥadāriba. They have no holy law, but they worship an idol which they call Ḥaḥākhū.

. . . .

Zawīla

Further to the south [from Libya] is the land of Zawīla. They are Muslim people, all of them Ibāḍīs[1] who make the pilgrimage to the Holy City. Most of them belong to the tribe of Rawāya [?].

They export black slaves originating from Mīra, Zaghāwa, Maruwa, and other black races near them, whom they capture. I was told that the kings of the blacks sell blacks without any pretext or war.

From Zawīla come the skins called zawīla.

It is a land of palm groves, planted with millet and suchlike. The people are mixed, coming from Khurāsān, Basra, and Kūfa.

Fifteen days' journey beyond Zawīla is the town of Kuwwār, with a Muslim population of mixed origins, mostly Berbers, who sell blacks.

Al-Yaʻqūbī, *Buldān*, pp. 334–337, 345

[1] A branch of the Kharijites. See *EI*², "Ibāḍiyya."

33. The Blacks (Tenth Century)

The blacks and Ethiopians live in the country opposite that part of the heavenly mansions which is between Aries and Cancer. The sun in its rising and setting, when it comes to these mansions, is in mid-sky at its zenith over their heads. It thus boils their air and burns them and causes great heat and dryness among them. That is why their color is black, their hair woolly, their bodies dry and thin, and their natures hot. So, too, are their animals and their trees. Among the characteristics of the people of this region are roughness and cleverness.

Ibn Rusteh, p. 102.

The land of the blacks is a vast land but is desolate and very poor. In their mountains they have the usual kinds of fruit found in the lands of Islam, but they do not eat them. They have other foodstuffs which they eat—fruit and other plants unknown in the lands of Islam.

The black eunuchs who are sold in the lands of Islam are from these people. They are not Nubians, nor Zanj, nor Ethiopians, nor Bujja, but are of a separate race, of a darker and purer black than any of them.

Al-Iṣṭakhrī, p. 40.

[The land of the blacks] is a great and vast land, stretching from the Western sea to the sea of Qulzum [Red Sea], and it is immense and tremendous. Between the realm of Ghāna and the country of the Nubians there is a land of many deserts and sands. The land of the Nubians is very hot and has little rain and few rivers or plants or trees. Its people go naked because of the great heat, and the women cover their private parts and nothing else. They bring up their children in holes which they make in the sand. It is a country with many lions and wild animals and huge beasts of burden. Their country is rich in gold, but they prefer brass to gold and use it to make adornments for their women, which they wear round their waists. . . . They take mule skins and wear them for years; these are so strong that they do not wear out. The chief city of Ethiopia is the town of Jarmī, the seat of government of Ethiopia, belonging to the Negus. There pure gold is sold for copper, and its people do not understand.

Isḥāq ibn al-Ḥusayn, p. 410.

On their [the Berbers'] borders are various kinds of blacks called Zaghal and Zaghāwa, and from there those black eunuchs are brought.

The Ethiopians are black people, and their country has scorched plains and coasts. Their religion is Christianity; their food, honey and millet. To the east of them is the Ḥijāz; to the west, the Nile. In their country giraffes are hunted.

The Bishriyya are black people. Their country is hot, their water is from the Nile, their religion is Christianity, and they live in tents. The Bujja are of this group. Above them [that is, upstream] is a place called 'Abarāt al-Salāḥif [tortoise crossings]. It is said that there is no marriage among them, that the child does not know his father, and that they eat people. God knows best.

The Zanj are people of black color, with flat noses, kinky hair, and little understanding or intelligence. To the east of them is Western India; and to the west, the river. Their country is broken and ruined; it bears no plant and grows no tree. Food and clothing are imported to them; from them come gold, slaves, and coconuts.

Al-Maqdisī, iv, pp. 69–70.

34. Details on Africa (Twelfth Century)

The first climate begins to the west of the Western Ocean, which is called the Sea of Darkness. What lies beyond this sea is unknown. There are two islands in this sea called al-Khālidāt, [the fortunate islands], from which Ptolemy began to reckon longitude and latitude. In each of these islands, it is said, there is a stone idol, 100 cubits high. On each there is a copper figure pointing backward with its hand. There are said to be six of these idols. One of them is the idol of Cadiz in the west of Andalus. No inhabited land is known beyond this.

The towns in this section are Awlil, Sillā, Takrūr, Barīsā, Daw, and Mūra. These places are part of the country of the Maqzāra blacks. The island of Awlil is in the sea near the shore. In this island are the famous saltworks, no other saltworks being known in the land of the blacks. From here salt is taken to all the lands of the blacks by means of ships which come to the island and take a cargo of salt. From here they sail to the mouth of the Nile,[1] a distance of one day's journey, and then they sail up the Nile to Sillā, Takrūr, Barīsā, Ghāna, and the other towns of Wanqāra, Kūgha, and all the lands of the blacks. Most of these countries are unsettled except along the banks of the Nile and of its tributaries; the rest of the country adjoining the Nile is empty desert and uncultivated.

In these deserts there are waterless tracts where one may travel two, four, five, six or twelve days before finding water. One such is the area of Tīsar, on the road from Sijilmāsa to Ghāna, in which there is no water for fourteen days' journey, so that caravans crossing these tracts carry a supply of water in leather bottles on the backs of camels. There are many such tracts in the land of the blacks. Most of the country is sand, blown and carried by the winds from place to place. There is no water at all, and the heat in those countries is intense so that the inhabitants of the first climate, the second, and part of the third, because the heat is great and the sun burns them, are of black color and have woolly hair, contrary to the color of the people of the sixth and seventh climates.

From the island of Awlil to the town of Sillā is sixteen days' journey. The town of Sillā is on the north bank of the Nile. It is a populous town, a meeting place for the blacks, and a thriving center of trade. The inhabitants are brave and courageous. It is subject to the ruler of Takrūr, a powerful sultan with slaves and troops. He is firm, steadfast, and famous for his justice. His country is safe and peaceful. His residence is the town of

[1] Arab geographers use the name Nile for various rivers. Idrīsī applies it to both the Senegal and Niger.

Takrūr, south of the Nile, at two days' journey from Silla by land and water.

Takrūr is larger and has more trade than Sillā. The Moroccans come there; they bring wool, copper, and beads and take away gold and eunuchs. The food of the people of Sillā and Takrūr is millet, fish, and milk stuffs. Their flocks are mostly camels and goats. The common people wear woollen *qadāwīr*[2] and woollen *karāzī*[3] on their heads; the upper class wear cotton garments and bonnets.[4]

From Sillā and Takrūr to Sijilmāsa is forty days' journey by caravan. The nearest to these of the lands of the Lamtuna of the desert is Azuqqa, which is twenty-five days' journey away. In making this journey, water supplies are taken on every two, four, five, or six days. Similarly, from the island of Awlil to the town of Sijilmāsa is about forty days' journey by caravan.

From Takrūr to Barīsā, going eastward along the Nile, is twelve days' journey. Barīsā is a small, unwalled town resembling a populous village. Its people are traveling merchants who obey the ruler of Takrūr.

To the south of Barīsā is the land of Lamlam, about ten days distant. The people of Barīsā, Sillā, Takrūr, and Ghāna raid the Lamlam country, capture its people, take them to their own country, and sell them to the merchants who come there and who take them to other parts. In all the country of Lamlam there are only two small towns, like villages. One of them is called Mallal, the other, Daw, and they are four days' journey apart. According to what the people of this region say, the inhabitants are Jews, but unbelief and ignorance prevail among them. Among all the people of Lamlam, when one reaches the age of puberty, he brands his face and temples with fire. This is a sign for them. Their country and all their habitations are in a valley which leads into the Nile. Beyond Lamlam, toward

2 Singular *qādūr or qandūr*; a word of Berber origin denoting a long, broad, sleeveless shirt.

3 Singular *kurziyya* or *karziyya;* a word widely used during the Middle Ages, denoting a light woolen material. Its origin is unknown but may be connected with the English village of Kersey, in Suffolk.

4 *Mi'zar.* This word also, at various times and places, denotes cloaks and drawers.

the south, no inhabited country is known. The land of Lamlam adjoins Maqzāra in the west, Wanqāra in the east, Ghāna in the north, and empty deserts in the south. The language of the inhabitants of Lamlam does not resemble either that of Maqzāra or that of Ghāna.

From Barīsā to Ghāna, going eastward, is twelve days' journey. Barīsā is half way between Ghāna and the towns of Sillā and Takrūr. Likewise, from Barīsā to Awdaghosht to the north is twelve days' journey.

In the country of the blacks there is no fresh fruit apart from the dates brought from Sijilmāsa and from the Zāb country by the people of Warqalān of the desert. In this country the Nile flows from east to west. On its banks, prickly [?] reeds, ebony, boxwood, willows, and varieties of tamarisk grow in unbroken forests. Their flocks come here to rest at midday and seek shade when the heat is great. In the forests there are lions, giraffes, gazelles, hyenas, elephants, hares, and porcupines. In the Nile there are various kinds of fish, both large and small, on which the black people live. They catch, salt, and store them. These fish are very fat and thick.

The weapons of the people of this country are the bow and arrow, on which they rely. They also use clubs which they make from ebony, and in this they have skill and perfect craftsmanship. The bows and arrows and bowstrings are all made from the prickly [?] reed. They build their houses of clay, since broad and long pieces of wood are scarce. Their adornments are copper, beads, glass necklaces, the stones known as *bādhuq* [or *bādharūn*] and *lu'āb al-shaykh* [old man's spit], and various kinds of cut glass colored like onyx.

What we have said about their food, drink, clothing, and adornments applies to most of the blacks in all their country, for it is a very dry and hot country. The townspeople plant onions, gourds, and watermelons, which grow very big there. They have no wheat nor any grain other than millet, from which they make a strong drink. Their main flesh foods are fish and jerked camel meat, as has already been described. This is the end of the first section of the first climate. Praise be to God for this. . . .

The Second Section of the First Climate

The towns in this section are Mallal, Ghāna, Tīraqqā, Madāsa, Saghmāra, Ghiyāra, Gharbīl, and Samaqanda. The town of Mallal in the land of Lamlam, which we have mentioned above, is a small town, unwalled like a large village. It stands on a hill of red earth, in a strong defensive position. The people of Mallal are secure there from attacks by other blacks. Their drinking water is from a rippling spring which comes from the mountain to the south. But its water is brackish, not really sweet.

To the west of this town, by the stream from which they drink, along its course to the point where it flows into the Nile, there are many black peoples who are naked, do not cover themselves with anything, and mate without marriage contract and without law. They are the most prolific of mankind in children. They have camels and goats on whose milk they live. They also eat the fish they catch and jerked camels' meat. The people of neighboring countries constantly take them captive by various tricks and carry them off to their own countries to sell them to the merchants in gangs. Large numbers of them go to Morocco every year. All the people of Lamlam have branded faces. It is their sign, as already stated.

From the town of Mallal to the great town of Ghāna is about twelve days' journey through soft, waterless sands. Ghāna consists of two towns on the two banks of the river, and it is the biggest town in the country of the blacks in area, population, and trade. Rich merchants come there from all the surrounding countries and from Morocco. The people are Muslims and the king, according to what is stated, is descended from Ṣāliḥ ibn 'Abdallāh ibn al-Ḥasan ibn al-Ḥasan ibn 'Alī ibn Abī Ṭālib. The *khuṭba* is recited in his name only, but he recognizes the suzerainty of the Abbasid Commander of the Faithful. He has a palace on the bank of the Nile; strongly built and skillfully constructed; its rooms are adorned with various sculptures, paintings, and glass windows. This palace was built in the year 510 of the Hijra [1116]. The territory of this king adjoins the country of the Wanqāra, which is the famous gold country, known for the quantity and excellence of its gold. What the people of Morocco know, certainly and indisputably, is that this king has in his palace an ingot of gold weighing thirty *raṭls* in a single piece, made as it is by Almighty God and neither cast in fire nor worked with a tool. A hole was made in it to which the king's horse is tethered. It is a wonderful thing, which he alone has and may use, and he boasts of it to the other kings of the blacks. He is the most just of men, according to what is told about him. One of his customs, which shows his accessibility and justice, is that he has a number of officers who ride to his palace every morning, each carrying a drum and beating it. When they arrive at the palace gate, they stop this noise, and when all the officers have joined the king, he rides, with the rest of them following, through the streets and around the town. If anyone has a grievance or some misfortune has befallen him, the king stays there until he has dealt with his grievance. Then he returns to his palace and his officers disperse. In the afternoon, when the heat of the sun abates, he rides out again, with his troops around him, but this time no one can approach or reach him. His riding twice a day is a well-known custom, and this is famous about his justice.

He wears a silken garment [*izār*] around his waist or else wraps himself in a cloak, with drawers over his middle and leather [?] shoes on his feet. He rides a horse; he has beautiful adornments and splendid attire which he has carried in front of him on festival days. He has many flags but only one banner. Before him walk elephants, giraffes, and other wild animals of the kinds found in the country of the blacks. They have solidly built ships on the Nile, which they use for fishing and for travel between the two towns. The garments of the people of Ghāna are the *izār,* the *fūṭa,* and the *kisā,* each as he chooses.

To the west, the land of Ghāna adjoins the land of Maqzāra; to the east, the land of Wanqāra; to the north, the Sahara, which lies between the land of the blacks and the land of the Berbers; to the south, the country of the unbelievers of Lamlam and others.

From the town of Ghāna to the beginning of the land of Wanqāra is eight days' journey. Wanqāra is the land of gold, famous for its excellence and quantity. It is an island 300 miles long by 150 miles wide, surrounded by the Nile on all sides and throughout the year. In the month of August, when the heat is great and the Nile floods, the island, or most of it, is flooded and remains so for the usual period. Then the river begins to fall, and when this happens they foregather from all the lands of the blacks and come to this island in search of gold. They search throughout the period of the low Nile, and each finds that quantity of gold, be it much or little, that God grants him, and none are disappointed. When the Nile returns to its bed, they sell whatever gold they have acquired, trading among themselves. The greater part is bought by the people of Warqalān and by those of Morocco, who take it to the mints in their country, have it struck in dinars, and use it for trade and merchandise. It is like this every year. This is the most important product of the land of the blacks, on which they live, great and small alike. In the country of Wanqāra there are thriving towns and famous fortresses. The people are rich, with gold in plenty, and good things are brought to them from the remotest parts of the world. Their garments are the *izār, kisā, and qadāwīr*. They are very black.

One of the towns of Wanqāra is Tīraqqā, a large town with many people but without walls or palisades. It is subject to the ruler of Ghāna, in whose name the *khuṭba* is pronounced and to whom they have recourse for legal judgments. From Ghāna to Tīraqqā is six days' journey following the Nile. From Tīraqqā to Madāsa is also six days' journey.

Madāsa is a medium-sized town, populous and with thriving provinces. Its people are intelligent. It is on the north bank of the Nile, whose water they drink. They have rice and millet, large grained and good to eat. Most of their livelihood comes from fishing and dealing in gold.

From Madāsa to Saghmāra is six days' journey. Between Madāsa and Saghmāra, toward the north and by the desert, is a tribe called Baghāma. These are nomadic Berbers of no fixed place who pasture their camels on the banks of a stream coming from the east and flowing into the Nile. They have plenty of milkstuffs on which they live.

From Saghmāra to Samaqanda is eight days' journey. Samaqanda is a pleasant little town on the river bank. From there to Gharbīl is nine days' journey. From Saghmāra to Gharbīl is six days' journey, traveling southward.

The town of Gharbīl is on the bank of the river. It is a pleasant little town on the slope of a mountain which overlooks it from the south. Its people drink Nile water, wear wool, and live on millet, fish, and camel's milk. The people of this country trade in various commodities current among them.

From Gharbīl proceeding westward to Ghiyāra is eleven days' journey. Ghiyāra is on the bank of the Nile, with a ditch all round it. It has many inhabitants, who have courage and intelligence. They raid the country of Lamlam, take the people captive, bring them back, and sell them to the merchants of Ghāna. From Ghiyāra to the land of Lamlam is thirteen days' journey. They ride excellent camels, stock themselves with water, march by night and rest by day until they get their booty and return to their own country with as many Lamlam captives as God allots to them. From Ghiyāra to the town of Ghāna is eleven days' journey, with very little water. All these countries which we have mentioned are subject to the ruler of Ghāna. It is to him that they pay taxes, and it is he who protects them. This is the end of the second section of the first climate. Praise be to God.

. . . .

The Seventh Section of the First Climate

This section comprises part of the Indian Ocean and a number of scattered islands in which are various peoples. In the south of this section there is also the remainder of the country of the black infidels and adjoining coastal areas of the land of the Zanj. We intend with God's help to describe all this clearly and subject it to thorough examination.

We say that this sea is the Indian sea, and on its shore is the town of Barawa [Brava], the last of the lands of the infidels who have no religious creed but take standing stones, anoint them with fish-oil, and bow down before them. Their worship and their depraved beliefs consist of this and similar absurdities, but they are steadfast in them.

Part of this country is subject to the king of Berbera and part to the Ethiopians. From Barawa following the coast to Badhūna is three days' journey by sea. It is a ruined, thinly populated town, with wretched houses and full of dirt. Its inhabitants live on fish, shellfish, frogs, snakes, mice, lizards, the creature called Umm Ḥubayn,[5] and other creatures which are not eaten.

Although they live in poverty and want and privation, Almighty God makes countries dear to their inhabitants, and they are therefore satisfied with this and contented. They are subject to the Zanj.

From this town to Malindi, in the land of the Zanj, along the coast, is three days, by sea three days and nights. The town of Malindi is on the sea shore at the mouth of a sweet water stream. It is a large town, and its people's occupations are hunting and fishing. They hunt leopards and wolves and fish in the sea for various kinds of fish, which they salt and sell. They have an iron mine where they dig and work and which provides most of their livelihood and trade. The people claim that they bewitch dangerous beasts so that they only harm those on whom they wish to inflict harm and vengeance, and they claim that lions and leopards do not attack them because of their spells. The name of these enchanters in their language is *Mqanqa*.[6]

From this town to the town of Manbasa [Mombasa] along the coast is two days' journey. It is a small town of the Zanj, and the occupations of its people are iron mining and leopard hunting. They have red dogs who overcome all wolves and even lions. This town is by the sea, on the shore of a great bay which ships enter to a distance of two days' sailing and along which there is no settlement, but only wild beasts living in the forests on both shores. They hunt these beasts there, as we have already stated. In this town is the residence of the king of the Zanj. His soldiers go on foot, for they have no riding animals; they do not live in this country.

[5] According to the Arabic lexicographers, a small, evil-smelling lizard.

[6] The word *mganga* still occurs in Bantu languages, with the same meaning.

From Manbasa to the village of al-Bānas is six days' journey by land and one and half sailings [150 miles] by sea. Al-Bānas is a large and populous village. Its people worship al-Raḥīm. This means for them a big drum, like a barrel, covered with skin on one side. They tie a strap to the skin and pull it tight. This drum makes a fearsome noise which can be heard for a distance of three miles or thereabouts.

Al-Bānas is the last of the lands of the Zanj. It adjoins the land of Sufāla, the gold country. From there along the coast to a town called Butahna is eight days' journey by land and one and a half sailings by sea. The reason is that between these two towns there is a great bay which stretches southward and compels the traveler to make a detour. Between the two towns in the sea there is a high and broad mountain called 'Ajrad. The water has eroded it on every side, and the waves make a fearsome noise. This mountain attracts ships to itself, and travelers avoid it and flee from it.

The town of Butahna is also in the land of Sufāla. Many villages adjoin the land of the Zanj, each of them on an inlet.

The products of all the lands of the Zanj are iron and Zanjī leopard skins, which are reddish in color and very soft. They have no riding or pack animals, but dispose only of their own persons. They carry their goods on their heads and backs to the towns of Manbasa and Malindi, where they buy and sell. The Zanj have no ships on which to travel, but ships from 'Umān and elsewhere come to the islands of the Zānij,[7] where they sell their goods and buy Zanjī goods. The people of the islands of the Zānij sail to the Zanj in small boats and carry goods in them because they understand each other's languages.

The Zanj are in great fear and awe of the Arabs, so much so that when they see an Arab trader or traveler, they bow down before him, treat him with great respect, and say in their language, "Greeting, O people from the land of the dates!" Those who travel to this country steal the children of the Zanj with dates, lure them with dates, and lead them from place to place until they seize them, take them out of the country, and transport them to their own countries. The Zanj people have great numbers

[7] This may refer to the island of Zanzibar, or possibly to Madagascar.

but little gear. The ruler of the island of Kish in the sea of 'Umān raids the Zanj country with his ships and takes many captives.

Al-Idrīsī, pp. 17–26, 58–61.

35. Neighbors in the East (Early Ninth Century?)

The Chinese and the Indians kill the animals they want to eat. They do not slaughter them but hit them on the head until they die. The Indians and the Chinese do not wash themselves after sexual intercourse,[1] and the Chinese, after stool, only wipe themselves with paper. The Indians wash every day before breakfast and then eat. The Indians do not come to their wives during their periods, but expel them from their houses in aversion. The Chinese come to their wives during their periods and do not expel them. The Indians use toothpicks, and no one among them eats without using a toothpick and washing himself. The Chinese do not do this.

India is twice as big as China and has more kings, but China is more populous. Neither the Chinese nor the Indians have date palms, but they have other trees and fruits which we have not. In India they have no grapes, and in China they have few; other fruits are numerous among them, and there are very many pomegranates in India.

The Chinese have no science[2] [*'ilm*], but the basis of their cult comes from India; they believe that the Indians gave them their Buddhas and that they are the people of religion. In both countries they believe in reincarnation and differ only in the details of their religion.

There is medicine and philosophy in India, and the Chinese also have medicine. Their medicine consists chiefly of cauterization.[3] They have knowledge of astronomy, but the Indians have

[1] According to Muslim law, major ablution is required after sexual intercourse.

[2] Science (*'ilm*) is used here in the sense of religious knowledge—scripture, theology and holy law.

[3] A possible reference to acupuncture.

more. I know of no one on either side who is a Muslim or who speaks Arabic.[4]

The Indians have few horses; the Chinese have more. The Chinese have no elephants and do not allow them in their country, regarding them as ill omens.

The armies of the kings of India are numerous and do not receive regular pay. The king only summons them to make war, and then they campaign at their own expense and the king is not liable for any of it. As for the Chinese, their army pay is like that of the Arabs.

The land of China is more agreeable and more beautiful. In most of India there are no cities, while the Chinese have great walled cities everywhere. China is healthier and has fewer diseases and has better air. One hardly ever sees a blind man or a one-eyed man or anyone disabled by disease. There are many such in India.

The rivers of both countries are huge. There are rivers greater than our rivers, and the rains in both countries are plentiful.

In India there are many deserts, while China is all cultivated.

The Chinese are better-looking than the Indians and more closely resemble the Arabs in dress and in the animals which they ride. In their appearance and in their ceremonies they resemble the Arabs. They wear coats [*qabā*] and belts, while the Indians wear two pieces of cloth, and both men and women adorn themselves with gold bangles and precious stones.

Beyond China, on the land side, are the Toquz Oguz,[5] who are Turks, and the Khāqān of Tibet, the latter adjoining the land of the Turks. Beyond China, on the sea side, are the islands of Sila.[6] These are white men who send gifts to the ruler of China, believing that if they did not send gifts to him, the rain would not fall on them from the skies. None of our people has reached them to tell us about them. They have white falcons.

Akhbār al-Ṣīn wa'l-Hind, pp. 25–27.

4 An indication of the early date of this text, before the introduction of Islam into India or China.

5 The Toquz Oguz or Nine Oguz are a group of Turkish tribes.

6 Probably a reference to Korea, where the Silla dynasty reigned from 670 to 935. The same Arabic word serves for both island and peninsula. There may be some confusion with Japan, the northern part of which was inhabited by the Ainu, a people usually described as white.

36. Neighbors in the North (Tenth Century)

As regards the people of the northern quadrant, they are the ones for whom the sun is distant from the zenith, those who penetrate to the North, such as the Slavs, the Franks, and those nations that are their neighbors. The power of the sun is weak among them because of their distance from it; cold and damp prevail in their regions, and snow and ice follow one another in endless succession. The warm humor is lacking among them; their bodies are large, their natures gross, their manners harsh, their understanding dull, and their tongues heavy. Their color is so excessively white that it passes from white to blue; their skin is thin and their flesh thick. Their eyes are also blue, matching the character of their coloring; their hair is lank and reddish because of the prevalence of damp mists. Their religious beliefs lack solidity, and this is because of the nature of cold and the lack of warmth.

Those of them who are farthest to the north are the most subject to stupidity, grossness, and brutishness. The farther north, the more this is so. Such are those Turks who penetrate to the north. Because of their distance from the circuit of the sun when it rises and sets, there is much snow among them, and cold and damp have conquered their habitations; their bodies are slack and thick, and their backbones and neckbones so supple that they can shoot their arrows as they turn and flee. Their joints form hollows because they have so much flesh; their faces are round and their eyes small because the warmth concentrates in their faces while the cold takes possession of their bodies. The cold humor produces much blood; then their coloring grows red, since it is a quality of coldness to gather warmth and make it appear outside.

Those who dwell sixty miles beyond this latitude are Gog and Magog. They are in the sixth climate and are reckoned among the beasts.

Al-Masʿūdī, *Kitāb al-Tanbīh waʾl-ishrāf*, p. 22.

37. Neighbors in the West (Thirteenth Century)

Frank-land, a mighty land and a broad kingdom in the realms of the Christians. Its cold is very great, and its air is thick because of the extreme cold. It is full of good things and fruits and crops, rich in rivers, plentiful of produce, possessing tillage and cattle, trees and honey. There is a wide variety of game there and also silver mines. They forge very sharp swords there, and the swords of Frank-land are keener than the swords of India.

Its people are Christians, and they have a king possessing courage, great numbers, and power to rule. He has two or three cities on the shore of the sea on this side, in the midst of the lands of Islam, and he protects them from his side. Whenever the Muslims send forces to them to capture them, he sends forces from his side to defend them. His soldiers are of mighty courage and in the hour of combat do not even think of flight, rather preferring death. But you shall see none more filthy than they. They are a people of perfidy and mean character. They do not cleanse or bathe themselves more than once or twice a year, and then in cold water, and they do not wash their garments from the time they put them on until they fall to pieces. They shave their beards, and after shaving they sprout only a revolting stubble. One of them was asked as to the shaving of the beard, and he said, "Hair is a superfluity. You remove it from your private parts, so why should we leave it on our faces?"

Al-Qazwīnī, *Āthār al-bilād,* p. 498.

4 The Economy

Medieval Islam has left a considerable body of written evidence of economic activity and thought. A large proportion of the surviving documents are concerned with taxation and other aspects of government finances, and an extensive literature deals with economic matters. Jurists, bureaucrats, experts of various kinds, and even practical men wrote books or essays on taxation, fiscal administration, coinage, agriculture, crafts, trade, markets, and occasionally on economic principles.

The following passages fall into four groups. The first group, from the Qur'ān and ḥadīth, *contains examples of religious guidance on economic matters and shows the kind of question to which the relaters of* ḥadīth *found answers. The second, drawn from documents and books, is concerned with government revenue and expenditure. It ends with part of an inventory listing the contents of Hārūn al-Rashīd's palace. The third group, consisting of papyri, inscriptions, and excerpts from books, illustrates various forms of economic activity, mostly private. The final section is concerned with the theory and practice of commerce and concludes with an account from a Persian chronicle of an unsuccessful attempt to introduce paper money.*

38. From the Qur'ān

Those who feed on usury will not rise again [on the Day of Judgment], but will be as those whom the Devil has overthrown by his touch. This is because they claim that trade and usury are the same. But God has permitted trade and forbidden usury. He to whom there comes an admonition from his Lord, and who desists, may keep his past gains, and his case is with God, but those who revert will be dwellers in hellfire for evermore.

God will nullify usury and fructify alms, for God does not love any sinful unbelievers. . . .

O you who believe! Be pious toward God, and forego what is outstanding from usury, if you are believers.

If you do not do this, then expect war from God and His Prophet, but if you renounce [usury], your capital will remain with you, and you will neither inflict nor suffer injury.

ii, 275–279.

O you who believe! Do not consume your property among you in vanity, but let there be trading by mutual consent among you. . . .

iv, 33/29.

It is He who brought forth gardens, both trellised and untrellised, palms, crops giving various foods, olives and pomegranates, like and unlike. Eat their fruit when they fructify, and give what is due from it at harvest time, but do not squander it, for God does not love squanderers.

From your cattle [He has provided] animals for transport and slaughter. Eat what God has provided for you, and do not follow in the footsteps of the Devil, for he is your manifest enemy.

vi, 142–143.

Do not interfere with the property of the orphan, save for the best, until he is of age. Give good measure and fair weight equitably. Do not burden anyone beyond his capacity. When you speak, be just, even with a near kinsman. Keep God's covenant. This is what He commands you. Perhaps you will remember.

vi, 153/152.

39. Sayings Ascribed to the Prophet

The best of works is lawful gain.

The best of gain is from honorable trade and from a man's work with his own hands.

The greatest scarcities in my community at the end of time will be a lawful dirham and a trustworthy brother.

To seek lawful gain is the duty of every Muslim.

To seek lawful gain is Holy War.

Well-being is ten parts: nine in seeking a livelihood and one in everything else.

He who ends the day weary from the work of his hands ends the day forgiven for his sins.

The honest, truthful Muslim merchant will stand with the martyrs on the Day of Judgment.

If a man works for his aged parents, that is in the path of God; if he works for his young children, that is in the path of God; if he works for himself, to be free of want, that, too, is in the path of God.

There is no prophet who has not tended sheep.

I commend the merchants to you, for they are the couriers of the horizons and God's trusted servants on earth.

If a man buys a garment for ten dirhams, of which one dirham was unlawfully obtained, God will not accept his prayer as long as he wears any part of it.

The price of the *ḥarīsa*[1] is unlawful and to eat it is unlawful.

The dupe is neither praised nor paid.

The cowardly merchant is deprived; the brave merchant is rewarded.

[1] A dish made with meat, cracked wheat, and sour milk, regarded as a great delicacy.

God says, "I am the third with two partners as long as neither of them betrays the other. If he does so, I depart from them."

The devils come to the markets early in the morning with their flags; they arrive with the first to arrive, and they leave with the last to leave.

The worst things in cities are their markets.

After you have performed the dawn prayer, do not let sleep keep you any longer from earning your living.

Seek a livelihood in the hidden places of the earth.

Do not be the first to enter the market or the last to leave it, for that is where the devil is hatched and fledged.

O merchants! You have adopted something by which bygone nations perished—weights and measures.

The most worthy of earnings are those of the merchants who if they are spoken to, do not lie, if they are trusted, do not betray, if they promise, do not fail, if they buy, do not condemn, if they sell, do not extol, if they owe, do not delay, and if they are owed, do not press.

Nine-tenths of livelihood is trade; the tenth is livestock.

The work of pious men is sewing, of pious women, spinning.

If God permitted the inhabitants of paradise to trade, they would deal in cloth and perfume.

Keep sheep, for they are a blessing.

People who have twenty black and dun goats need fear no burden.

When God created livelihoods, He put His blessing in tilling and sheep.

You must have straw—its capital is small and its profit is great, and you must have cloth, for in it are nine-tenths of blessing.

O men of Quraysh! Let not the *mawālī* prevail over you in trade. There are twenty kinds of livelihood, nineteen for the merchant and one for the craftsman. . . .

If there were trade in Heaven, they would sell cloth, and if there were trade in Hell, they would sell food. Whoever sells for forty days, mercy is plucked out of his heart.

If you have the price of a slave, buy a slave with it, for good fortune is in the forelocks of men.

Three things are illicit—the earnings of a cupper, the dower of a whore, and the price of a dog, except a hunting dog.

He whose business is food goes to bed with rancor in his heart against the Muslims.

The worst of men are those who buy and sell men.

The biggest liars are the dyers.

If on the Day of Judgment, the Herald cries out, 'Where are the betrayers of God on earth?"—the coppersmiths, money changers, and weavers will come to him.

The owner of a commodity is best entitled to offer it for sale.

Selling is attended by clamor and swearing; therefore, mix it with a little charity.

If you buy a slave, do not sell him until you have him in your possession.

Do not sell food until you have bought it and completed the purchase.

The supplier is rewarded, and the hoarder is accursed.

He who brings supplies to our market is like a warrior in the Holy War for God. He who hoards and corners supplies in our market is like a heretic deviating from the Book of God.

If anyone deprives the Muslims of their food by cornering it, God will strike him with leprosy and bankruptcy.

If anyone hoards a commodity in order to charge the Muslims high prices, he is a wrongdoer, and the covenant [*dhimma*] of God and His Prophet is withdrawn from him.

The dearness and cheapness of your prices are in the hand of God.

It is God who fixes prices. It is my desire to leave you with no man holding a grievance against me for any wrong I have done him, whether to his person or his property.

It is God who raises or lowers prices, but I desire to meet God with none holding a grievance against me.

Dearness and cheapness are two of God's soldiers. One is called greed, and the other is called fear. If God desires dearness, He puts greed in the hearts of the merchants, who become greedy and hoard their wares. If God desires cheapness, He puts fear in the hearts of the merchants, and they release what is in their hands.

When God is angry with a people [*umma*], He makes their prices high, their markets sluggish, their misdeeds many, and their rulers very oppressive, whereupon their rich do not thrive, their sultan does not remit, their poor do not pray.

Al-Muttaqī, *Kanz al-'Ummāl,* ii, pp. 193–203, 212–213.

40. Papyri (710–915)

Tax Demand

In the name of God, the Merciful and the Compassionate.

From Qurra ibn Sharīk to Basil, headman of Ashqūh. I praise God, other than Whom there is no God.

As follows: You know how much time has passed, and you still delay the *jizya*, and now the time has come for the pay of the troops and the families and for the departure of the armies on campaign, please God. When this my letter reaches you, take whatever *jizya* is due from your lands, and send whatever you collect, batch by batch. Let me not learn that you have delayed what you have gathered, and let it not be held back, for the people of your land have already completed their sowing. God is their helper in what is due from them to the Commander of the Faithful. Therefore, let there be no deficiency in your affair and no delay or holding back of what you have. Had the money been in my possession, I would have given the troops their pay, please God. Write and inform me what has accumulated with you, of what you have collected of the *jizya*, and how you have done this. Peace be upon those who follow the right guidance.[1]

Written by Jarīr in the month of Rabīʿ I of the year 91 [January–February 710].

Papyri Schott-Reinhardt, i, no. I, pp. 58–60.

Letter from an Official

From Qurrā ibn Sharīk to Basil, the headman of Ashqūh. I praise God, other than Whom there is no God. As follows: Marcus the son of George informed me that he has a claim of 10½ dinars from a native [?] in your district, and I understand that he has forcibly deprived him of his due. Therefore, when my letter comes to you, if he brings proof of what he says, give him his due, and do not wrong your slave. If his case should be otherwise, write to me about it.

[1] A form of greeting used when addressing non-Muslims.

Greeting to those who follow the right path. Written by Muslim ibn . . . and copied by Al-Ṣalt ibn Mas'ūd in Ṣafar of the year 91 [December 709–January 710].

Becker, *ZA*, pp. 72–73.

Arrears of Taxes

As follows: You know what I have written to you about collecting the money, and [you know] that the time has come for the payment to the troops and their families and the men for the campaign. When my letter comes to you, set to work to collect the money, for the country people have [? been restless] for months. Then send me speedily whatever money you have collected, batch by batch. I do not wish to learn that you have held back from us what is due from you, for the country people have finished their tilling and know what is due from them, and their surplus is available [?] for the sale of whatever part of it they wish to sell. Therefore, send me in haste whatever money you have collected. Indeed, had the money come to me, I would have ordered that the troops be given their pay, please God. And you should not be the last of the officials to send what is due from him, so that I need not blame you.

Greeting to those who follow the right guidance. Written by Yazīd on Friday.

Becker, *Isl*, pp. 251–252.

List of Tax Payers

'Abd al-Qāhir Subsistence . . .
From him: land tax (*kharāj*); two dinars
Collected a quarter of a dinar and a quarter . . .
Two dinars remain . . .
less one *qīrāṭ*

Wahb ibn Yūsuf
Land tax one dinar Palms Subsistence two thirds . . .
a dinar and a third

Sālim ibn Isma'īl
Land tax, one dinar Palms
half of a quarter Subsistence

Ṭāhir	one dinar and a third	
ibn Shihāb	. . .	
Land tax one dinar	Subsistence, a third	. . .
. . . .		

[verso]

. . . three dinars
. . . and a third and a quarter and an [?] eighth
subsistence two-thirds of a dinar
. . . one dinar
. . . and a third and an eighth
. . . Subsistence one third
. . . one dinar
. . . and a third and an eighth
. . . dinar
. . . two dinars
. . . . . .
. . . Subsistence an eighth of a dinar . . .
. . .

Grohmann, *AO*, xii, pp. 13–14.

Land Tax Receipt

3 DINAR
FOLIO 2 ½ + ⅓ + 1/48

In the name of God, the Merciful and the Compassionate. Yohannes al-Samtī [?] has paid the land tax due from him for Basīs, the lease [*qabāla*] of Abū Muḥammad Ḥakīm ibn . . . Freedman of the Commander of the Faithful, two dinars and a half and a sixteenth a dinar *mithqāl* to Stephen [?] son of Buqṭur the treasurer in the presence of Yūnus ibn al-Muwaffaq, the agent of Abū Muḥammad, may God strengthen him, for the land tax of the year two hundred and sixty one, 261 [874–875].

Grohmann, *AO*, xi, p. 252.

Poll Tax Receipt

ON FOLIO 2: SATURDAY ½ + ⅓ + 1/24 (DINAR) + ⅓ (*qīrāṭ*)

In the name of God, the Merciful and the Compassionate. Buqṭur has paid, for Sarmāda the butcher, a half and a quarter and an eighth of a dinar and a third of a *qīrāṭ* in current coin of what is due from him in poll tax [*jāliya*] in Tutun, now administered by the hand of Abū Ja'far, may God strengthen him, for the land tax of the year three hundred and two

Dinar	For the land tax of the year
$\frac{1}{2} + \frac{1}{3} + \frac{1}{24} + \frac{1}{3}$ (*qīrāt*)	302 [914–15]

Grohmann, *AO*, xi, p. 254.

41. On Collecting Taxes (739)

Naṣr [ibn Sayyār][1] raided from Balkh into Transoxania, in the direction of Bāb al-Ḥadīd. Then he returned to Marw, and addressed the people as follows:

Indeed, Bahrāmsīs use to favor the Magians; he favored them and protected them and loaded their burdens [of taxation] onto the Muslims. Ashbdād son of Gregory used to favor the Christians, and Aqīva the Jew used to favor the Jews and do the same thing. But I favor the Muslims; I shall favor them and protect them and load their burdens on to the polytheists. I shall accept nothing less than the full amount of the *kharāj* as recorded and collected. I have appointed Manṣūr ibn 'Umar ibn Abī'l-Kharqā' to govern you, and I have ordered him to deal justly with you. If any man among you, of the Muslims, has been made to pay the *jizya*, or has paid too much *kharāj* while the polytheists have paid too little, let him bring this before Manṣūr ibn 'Umar, who will transfer the burden from the Muslim to the polytheist.

By the following Friday, 30,000 Muslims came to him who were paying a *jizya* poll tax, while 80,000 polytheists had been relieved of their *jizya*. He imposed it on them and removed it from the Muslims. Then he organized the *kharāj* and imposed it where it belonged and levied it in accordance with the terms of the armistice. In the days of the Umayyads, 100,000 was collected from Marw, in addition to the *kharāj*.

al-Ṭabarī, ii, pp. 1688–1689.

[1] The last Umayyad governor of Khurāsān.

42. On Taxation and Its Effects (Ninth–Twelfth Centuries)

Ja'far ibn Yaḥyā said, "The land tax [*kharāj*] is the tent pole of the realm. How great it becomes by justice, how mean by oppression?"

The quickest way to the ruin of the country, the disuse of the cultivated land, the destruction of the subjects, and the cessation of the land tax is by tyranny and extortion. A ruler who burdens his taxpayers until they cannot cultivate the land is like one who cuts off his own flesh and eats it when he is hungry. He grows stronger in one part and weaker in another, and the pain and weakness he brings on himself are greater than the ache of hunger which he remedies. He who taxes his subjects beyond their capacity is like one who coats his roof with earth from the foundations of his house. He who makes a habit of cutting the tent pole will weaken it and bring down the tent. If the cultivators become weak, they cannot cultivate the land, and they leave it. Then the land is ruined, cultivation is weakened, and the tax diminishes. This leads to the weakening of the army, and when the army is weakened, enemies covet the realm.

O King, be more glad at what remains in your subjects' hands than at what you take from them. In prosperity nothing will diminish; in ruin nothing will remain. Protecting what is slight produces might. The bungler has no money; the successful does not suffer poverty.

It is related that al-Ma'mūn lay sleepless one night and summoned a courtier to tell him a story. He said, "O Commander of the Faithful! There was an owl in Basra and an owl in Mosul, and the Mosul owl asked the Basra owl to give her daughter in marriage to her son. The Basra owl replied, 'I will not give my daughter to your son unless you settle on her a marriage portion of a hundred ruined farms.' To this the Mosul owl replied, 'I can't do it now, but if our governor, may God keep him safe, stays another year, I shall do this for you.'" Al-Ma'mūn was roused, and sat to hear grievances [*maẓālim*], dealt equitably with the people, and investigated the actions of the governors.

I heard some of the old men of Spain, from the army [*jund*] and others, who said that the Muslims were victorious over their enemies and their enemies were weak and inferior as long as the land was distributed and assigned to the army in the form of *'iqṭā'*. They exploited it and dealt kindly with the peasants and cared for them as a merchant cares for his merchandise. The land flourished, there was plenty of money, and the armies were well-supplied with equipment and provender and weapons beyond what they needed. So it was, until in his last days Ibn Abī 'Āmir reintroduced a fixed monthly pay for the army, took the money by force, and sent tax collectors to the land to collect it. They devoured the subjects and misappropriated their money and exhausted them, so that the subjects fled and could not cultivate the land. The revenues brought to the Sultan diminished, the armies became weak, and the enemy grew strong against the lands of the Muslims and seized many of them. The Muslims remained inferior and the enemy victorious until the Veiled Ones[1] came to Spain and restored the grants [*iqṭā'*] as they had been in ancient times.

Al-Turṭūshī, *Sirāj al-Mulūk*, pp. 208–209.

43. *Jawālī* (Fifteenth Century)

Jawālī is the poll tax collected from the *dhimmīs* every year. It is of two kinds: that collected in the capital of Egypt, that is in Fusṭāṭ and Cairo, and that collected elsewhere. In the capital of Egypt there is a supervisor [*nāẓir*] appointed by the Sultan by decree and assisted by other officials who are called *shādd, 'āmil,* and *shāhid.* He has at his disposal a collector for the Jews and

[1] The text has al-Ma'mūn, which makes no sense. The reading *al-Mulaththamūn,* the Veiled Ones, is accepted from the Cairo edition of 1306/1888, p. 100. This is a common designation of the Berber Almoravid dynasty, which conquered Spain at the end of the eleventh century.

a collector for the Christians who know the persons whose names are listed in the *dīwān* and those who are added to them, that is to say, the boys who reached the age of puberty every year, known as *nashw,* and the immigrants to the capital from the country, known as *ṭārī'* [strangers in transit], as also those persons listed in the *dīwān* who have become Muslim or who have died. They dictate the changes which have taken place in these respects to the secretaries of the *dīwān.*

The author of the book *Qawānīn al-Dawāwīn*[1] says that in his time the poll tax was levied at three rates, the highest rate at four and a sixth dinars per head per year, the middle rate at two dinars and two *qīrāṭs,*[2] the lowest rate at one dinar, a third of a dinar, a quarter of a dinar, and two *ḥabbas*[3] of a dinar, and that to the poll tax imposed on every person were added two and a quarter dirhams as the pay of the officials in charge of collection. He also said that it was the custom to collect the tax at the beginning of the month of Muḥarram every year, but later it was collected during the month of Dhul'-Ḥijja.

I say: In our day the rate of the tax has fallen so that the highest rate is twenty-five dirhams and the lowest is ten dirhams, but it is collected in advance in the month of Ramaḍān. A fixed amount from the proceeds reaches the treasury every year, and the rest goes to the judges and men of religion, to whom sums are distributed according to what is collected.

As regards other places outside the Egyptian capital, the poll tax on the *dhimmīs* in every place pertains to whoever has been assigned that place as fief [*iqṭā'*], be it the amir or any other, and the tax is considered a part of the income of the fief. If the place is under one of the Sultan's *dīwāns,* then the poll tax collected from the local *dhimmīs* goes to that *dīwān.*

Al-Qalqashandī, *Ṣubḥ,* iii, pp. 462–463.

[1] A book by Ibn Mammātī, an Ayyubid official who died in 1209. The text was published in Cairo by Prof. A. Z. Atiya in 1943.

[2] A *qīrāṭ* is a twenty-fourth part.

[3] A *habba,* literally grain, is variously valued. Here it is probably a quarter of a *qīrāṭ,* that is, one-ninty-sixth of a dinar.

44. Register of Holdings in Ottoman Albania (1431–1449)

A copy of the register of the Sanjak of Arvanid, which was written by order of the Pādishāh, mighty as fate, lofty as Saturn, vast as the heavens, the defender of God's lands, the helper of God's servants, the Sultan of Islam and the Muslims, Sultan Murād Khan,[1] son of Sultan Meḥmed Khan, may God make his Sultanate eternal and make his proofs manifest in the world, by the initiative of Umur Bey, son of Saruja Pasha, and by the pen of the weakest of the weak, the poor Yūsuf, in the year 835 [1431–1432].

I. Appanages of the Sanjak-Bey, in the possession of Ali Bey (32 men-at-arms, 2 sets of horse armor, 2 tents, 1 awning, 1 kitchen).

(a) Vilayet of Aryurikasri, also called vilayet of Zenebish. [In the margin] Transferred to Zaganos Bey, treasurer of the Court, in the first decade[2] of Dhu'l-Qa'da, 843 [April 4–13, 1440] in Edirne.

Aryurikasri proper: market dues with fines, etc. [*niyābet*], 4000 aspers; fines, etc., of the vilayet 6000

Households, 121; bachelors, 15; widows, 27. Revenue, including fines and market dues: 26,938

Village of Kolorçi	Households, 56; widows, 10; bachelors, 8	Revenue: 4157
Village of Manastir, also called Ayo Nikola	Households, 53; widows, 2; bachelors, 6	Revenue: 5217a
Village of Mashkulari	Households, 36; widows, 1; bachelors, 4	Revenue: 2882
Village of Lower Koranji	Households, 35; widows, 2; bachelors . . .	Revenue: 2420
Village of Khristozali	Households 12; bachelors, 4	Revenue: 695a

[1] Sultan Murād II.

[2] In Ottoman chancery usage documents were dated in periods of 10 days, the first, middle, or last decade of the month.

Village of Yuvanishte	Households, 30; widows, 2; bachelors, 4	Revenue: 1922
Village of Vmelos [?]	Domain vineyard, 1; Households, 11; bachelors, 1	Revenue: 953
Village of Guveri	Households, 3	Revenue: 145
Village of Burni Kuk	Households, 11; bachelors, 1	Revenue: 515
Village of Isharat	Households, 12; widows, 1; bachelors, 2	Revenue: 811
Village of [?]	Households, [?]; bachelors, 2	Revenue: 995
Village of Ulyani [?]	Households, 26; bachelors, 3	Revenue: 1544
Village of Užaniko	Households, 11; bachelors, 1; widows, 1	Revenue: 598
Village of Livinye	Households, 32; bachelors, 4	Revenue: 2260a
Village of Nodye	Households, 17; bachelors, 2	Revenue: 1005a
Village of Ayos-Mertini	Households, 19; widows, 2; bachelors, 2	Revenue: 1139a
Village of Bodrishte	Households, 31; bachelors, 5	Revenue: 1823a
Village of Humelije	Domain vineyard, 1; Households, 24; widows, 1; bachelors, 3	Revenue: 1955
Village of Peskopiye	Households, 20; widows, 3; bachelors, 2	Revenue: 1473

[In the margin] Five houses and three houses from this village, with additional population from other places, have been given with the bishopric of Aryurikasri, to the unbeliever called Gönemoryan; in the first decade of Ramaḍān 853 [October 18–27, 1449] in Edirne.

Village of Klazezni	Households 9; widows, 1; bachelors, [?]	Revenue: 741
Village of Haskove	Households, 14; bachelors, 2	Revenue: 840

Village of Istoyani	Households, 18; widows, 1; bachelors, 2	Revenue: 1376
Village of Libahove	Households, 25; bachelors, 3; rice seeds, 12 maunds	Revenue with rice: 9277
Village of Great Labove	Households, 104; widows, 5; bachelors, 10	Revenue : 7820
Village of Zavrikos	Domain windmill, 1; in the village of Könöshay; households, 16; bachelors, 1	Revenue: 1109a
Village of Pizavishte	Households, 7; bachelors, 1	Revenue 450a
Village of [?]	Households [?], bachelors [?]	Revenue: 425 [?]
Village of Zuvyani	Households, 16; widows, 2	Revenue: 1267a
Village of Gorije	Households, 30; bachelors, 2	Revenue: 1485
Village of Frashtani	Households, 35; bachelors, 2	Revenue: 1695
Village of Agline	Households, 25; widows, 1; bachelors, 2	Revenue: 1457a
Village of Upper Goranji	Households, 13; bachelors, 2	Revenue: 836
Village of Vezyo [?]	Not in the original register. Added when Aydin Bey was Sanjak Bey: households, 5	Revenue: 269
Village of Pepeli	Households, 20	Revenue: 1200a
Village of Eflahlar [Vlachs ?]	Households, 12; widows, 1	Revenue: 666a
Village of Bolshani	Households, 17; widows, 1	Revenue: 981
Village of Krushavič	In the original register, 15, now empty	
Village of Valtije	In the original register, 18, now empty	
Village of Mavropol	In the original register, 12, now empty	

Altogether in Aryurikasri proper; villages, 36; untenanted lands, 3; households, 951; widows, 59; bachelors, 103. Revenue: 91,333.

The holding of Yako, given in accordance with a letter from Hamza Bey, has been recorded in the register. It was given to him because it was previously his tenancy. He is in possession and is free from obligation.

Suret-i Defter-i Sancak-i Arvanid, pp. 1–2.

45. The Treasures of Hārūn al-Rashīd (809)

Al-Faḍl ibn al-Rabīʿ said, "When Muḥammad al-Amīn succeeded his father Hārūn al-Rashīd as Caliph in the year 193 [809], he ordered me to count the clothing, furnishings, vessels, and equipment in the stores. I summoned the secretaries and storekeepers and continued counting for four months, during which I inspected treasures which I did not dream the caliphal stores contained. Then I ordered them to set down a total for each kind. The list of contents was as follows:

4,000 embroidered robes,
4,000 silk cloak lined with sable, mink, and other furs
10,000 shirts and shifts
10,000 caftans
2,000 drawers of various kinds
4,000 turbans
1,000 hoods
1,000 capes of various kinds
5,000 kerchieves of different kinds
500 [pieces of] velvet
100,000 *mithqāls* of musk
100,000 *mithqāls* of ambergris
1,000 baskets of Indian aloes
1,000 precious china vessels
Many kinds of perfume
Jewels valued by the jewelers at 4 million dinars
500,000 dinars
1,000 jeweled rings
1,000 Armenian carpets
4,000 curtains

5,000 cushions
5,000 pillows (*mikhadda*)
1,500 silk carpets
100 silk rugs
1,000 silk cushions and pillows
300 Maysānī carpets
1,000 Darabjirdī carpets
1,000 cushions with silk brocade
1,000 inscribed silk cushions
1,000 silk curtains
300 silk brocade curtains
500 Ṭabarī carpets
1,000 Ṭabarī cushions
1,000 pillows (*mirfada*)
1,000 pillows (*mikhadda*)
1,000 washbasins
1,000 ewers
300 stoves
1,000 candlesticks
2,000 brass objects of various kinds
1,000 belts
10,000 decorated swords
50,000 swords for the guards and pages [*ghulām*]
150,000 lances
100,000 bows
1,000 special suits of armor
50,000 common suits of armor
10,000 helmets
20,000 breast plates
150,000 shields
4,000 special saddles
30,000 common saddles
4,000 pairs of half-boots, most of them lined with sable, mink, and other kinds of fur, with a knife and a kerchief in each half-boot
4,000 pairs of socks
4,000 small tents with their appurtenances
150 marquees

Ibn al-Zubayr, *Kitāb al-Dhakhā'ir wa'l-Tuḥaf*, pp. 214–218.

46. Papyri (Eighth–Tenth Centuries)

Reminder (*Eighth–Ninth Centuries*)

From Abū Ḥāzim to. . . .

In the name of God, the Merciful and the Compassionate. May God keep us and you in good health . . . and hold it firm apart from this, please God. I sent to you about this money to buy us what we need with it, and I see you, O . . . that you have detained my messenger. So buy what he needs and send him to us quickly at once. . . . Please God, and send us . . . and gourds and cucumbers and other things, please God.

May God keep us and you in good health.

Grohmann, *AO*, xiv, p. 167.

Expense Account (*Ninth Century*)

For . . .	
for Ḥārith	22¼ . . .
for watering the young	two dirhams
for repairing a coat	two dirhams and a half
for laundering clothes	one dirham
for salves	⅛ [dinar]
for papyrus	half a dirham
for a shoe belonging to ʿIsā	three *dāniqs*
for galbanum oil	one dirham
for Kāmil and others	one dirham and one *dāniq*
for the servant of Abū Ḥātim	19 1/48 [dinar]
for tolls and dues	21⅙ [dinar]
for barley [?]	½ + ⅓ + 1/24 [dinar]
for . . .	½ + ...

Grohmann, *AO*, xiv p. 214.

Lease (*860–861*)

In the name of God, the Merciful and the Compassionate. This writing is from ʿAbd al-ʿAzīz ibn ʿAbd al-Ghaffār al-Kuraydī and

Muḥammad ibn Abī Ya'qūb the cloth merchant to Hāshim ibn Sulaymān the clothes merchant, a resident of the city.

You have asked us and requested of us that we lease you two feddans of the land known as the land of Tara [?] ibn Siya, of [?] Sulqus, the property of 'Abd al-'Azīz ibn 'Abd al-Ghaffār al-Kuraydī and the heirs of al-Muṭalla and the heirs of Muḥammad ibn Abī Ya'qūb, for two dinars and a half and a sixth, at the rate of one dinar and a third per feddan in cash of the treasury as weighed for the land tax of the year 246 [860–861], on condition that you plant it with whatever crops you please except indigo and sugarcane and that you pay your land tax with the installments due to the governor. We grant you this, and we lease you these two feddans for these two dinars and one-half and a sixth. What you do in addition will be accounted in accordance with your registration. For what you leave fallow, you are still liable for the land tax. Therefore plant, with God's blessing and help, in due observance of the terms we have registered for you.

May God bear witness to this, and God is sufficient witness. Two feddans for two dinars and a half and a sixth, at the rate of one feddan for one dinar and a third.

Grohmann, *AO*, x, p. 154.

Expense Account (Ninth–Tenth Century)

In the name of God, the Merciful and the Compassionate,
For an eighth of a dinar, rush-mats; for a quarter of a dinar, . . .
for one dirham, tamarind; for one dirham, sugar;
for one dirham, bananas; for one dirham, apples;
for two dirhams, pomegranates; for one dirham, sour pomegranates;
for half a dirham, candy sugar.

Grohmann, *AO*, xiv, p. 212.

Acknowledgement of a Debt (901)

In the name of God, the Merciful and the Compassionate, Ghalbūn ibn Mufarrij, with the *kunya* . . . acknowledges a debt, *ardabbs* of wheat, round, brown, fat, good, clean from . . . and mud and turf and free of all the harvest which was mine in the month of Payni of the year 298.[1] . . . Khaṭṭāb ibn . . . ʿAbs ibn al-Ḥasan ibn . . . ʿAbdallāh ibn Aḥmad ibn . . . . What is in this writing . . . is attested by Aḥmad ibn . . . .

Grohmann, *AO*, x, pp. 158–159.

List of Effects (Tenth Century)

In the name of God, the Merciful and the Compassionate. List of the effects of Iqbāl, viz: a black, sewn garment . . . a stuffed couch . . . a shirt . . . a worn woollen tunic . . . a linen shirt . . . a carpet . . . an apron . . . a patterned cushion and a white pillow. List of the effects of . . . a black, sewn garment . . . a plaited cloak . . . buckets [?] . . . old . . . a linen shirt . . . a white lining . . . a plaited apron . . . a face kerchief . . . a Dābiqī kerchief . . . smocks . . . a patterned mattress . . . a black patterned cushion . . . worn drawers . . . a shirt . . . a worn sewn garment . . . a worn blue garment . . . a carpet . . . a pitcher . . . a lamp. . . .

Grohmann, *AO*, xiv, pp. 185–186.

List of Palm Owners

In the name of God, the Merciful and the Compassionate.
Ibrāhīm ibn Maslama, one palm.
Mirt Aqīna, one palm.
Mirt ibn Luqmān, one palm.
Mūsā the watchman, one palm.
Abū Sahl, one palm.

Grohmann, *AO*, xii, pp. 5–6.

Certificate of Account (Tenth Century)

In the name of God, the Merciful and the Compassionate. Certificate of account of Aḥmad the ship's captain . . . half a dirham and a half a *dāniq* and a pound of cheese . . . sesame oil a half a *qīrāṭ* of spices and a pound . . . in his hand and. . . .

Grohmann, *AO*, xiv, p. 184.

[1] Payni 288 corresponds to May 26–June 24, 901.

47. Inscriptions from Egypt (882–913)

On Wood

In the name of God, the Merciful and the Compassionate. A blessing from God, good fortune, and prosperity. This shop with all its rights and limits, its ground floor and its upper floor, belongs to Ismāʿīl ibn Ramaḍān ibn Muḥammad al-Kinānī. He owns it [*mulk*] by the gracious sustenance and gift of God. In Rajab of the year 268 [February 882].

On a Piece of Linen

In the name of God, the Merciful and Compassionate. A blessing from God to the slave of God Aḥmad the Imam al-Muʿtamid ʿala' Allāh, the Commander of the Faithful, may God support him. This is what the Commander [of the Faithful] ordered in the workshop for brocade [*ṭirāz*] in the year 269 [882–883].

On Wood

In the name of God, the Merciful and the Compassionate. A blessing from God. To Muʿādh, called Abū Ṭālib, ibn ʿAtīq ibn ʿAbd al-Malik the cobbler, belong in this house with a shop twelve shares out of the twenty four shares held jointly and undivided with the whole of its rights and limits, its lower floor and its upper floor, and all rights belonging to it, pertaining thereto and deriving there from. . . . [300/912–913.]

On Wood

In the name of God, the Merciful and the Compassionate. A blessing from God, and bliss and felicity. This house with all its rights and limits, its lower floor and its upper floor, and all rights pertaining to it and deriving from it belong to Muḥammada, called Umm Ḥabīb, the daughter of Muḥammad ibn Ḥafṣ, and to her son ʿAlī ibn Marzūq conjointly and without division. [300/912–913.]

On Wood

In the name of God, the Merciful and the Compassionate. A blessing from God and bliss and felicity. This house with all its limits and its rights, its lower part and its upper part, its appurtenances, and its access, and all rights pertaining to it and deriving from it belong to Muḥammad ibn Ḥamdān ibn al-Ḥārith who owns it [*mulk*] by the grace and gift of God. . . .[300/912–913.]

RCEA, ii, nn. 696, 702, pp. 208, 212;
iii, nn. 925, 926, 934, pp. 72, 73, 78.

48. The Cultivation of Cotton in Spain and Sicily (Late Eleventh Century)

The way of doing this is that the earth should be prepared thoroughly to receive it, manured with thin, old dung or sheep's dung, then plowed in the month of January, then left for a little while, then plowed for a second and third time, up to ten times. This is the method known as the tenfold and is most used by the people of Sicily. After the completion of what we have described, it enters the ground, which is arranged in beds. It is best that at the time of sowing the earth should be moist. If it is not, it should be watered until it is moist and fragrant and then sown. Before sowing, the seed should be prepared in this way: The seed enters, what the ginner shakes out [?]; it is sprinkled with water, old, thin, sieved dung is thrown over it; and it is thoroughly rubbed by hand until the wool disappears, because if left alone, the seeds stick to one another. Alternatively, recourse may be had to sheep's dung; this should be thoroughly crumbled and the seed rubbed with it. It should then be sown in the same way as wheat [?],[1] except that it is thinned out in sowing so that there is a handsbreadth between each grain and the next. Then watering should be stopped until it grows to the length of a finger or about a handsbreadth. Then it should

[1] Reading uncertain.

be tended, pruned, straightened, and moved again and again, then watered, then singled and weeded, then watered, continuing this practice until the beginning of August. It should be watered every fifteen days. At the beginning of August watering should stop, for fear lest the plant go soft and turn in on itself, giving no produce. In the month of September picking begins. This is done in the morning, before the sun grows hot, because if it is picked in the heat of the sun the stalks break and get mixed with the wool and cannot be separated from it. If it is picked as we have described, it should be spread in the sun to reduce its moisture, because if it is gathered and stored before exposure to the sun, it spoils.

The most suitable soil for cotton in Spain is rough, dry soil, because in such soil it produces promptly, does not fall behind the times, and gives high yield. The Sicilians, on the other hand, choose rich soil for it, and so do the people of the coastal regions of Spain, and this suits it, please God.

Ibn Baṣṣāl, *Kitāb al-Filāḥa*, pp. 114–115.

49. A Singing Commercial (Ninth Century)

A merchant from Kūfa came to Medina with veils. He sold all but the black ones, which were left on his hands. He was a friend of al-Dārimī[1] and complained to him about this. At that time al-Dārimī had become an ascetic and had given up music and poetry. He said to the merchant, "Don't worry. I shall get rid of them for you; you will sell the whole lot." Then he composed these verses:

> Go ask the lovely one in the black veil
> What have you done to a devout monk?
> He had already girded up his garments for prayer
> Until you appeared to him by the door of the mosque.

He set it to music, and Sinān the scribe also set it to music, and it became popular. People said, "Al-Dārimī is at it again and has given up his asceticism," and there was not a lady of

[1] A poet and jurist who died in 869.

refinement in Medina who did not buy a black veil, and the Iraqi merchant sold all he had. When al-Dārimī heard this, he returned to his asceticism and again spent his time in the mosque.

Abu'l-Faraj al-Iṣfahānī, *Kitāb al-Aghānī,* iii, pp. 45–46.

50. A Clear Look at Trade (Ninth Century)

You have inquired, may God favor you, concerning the commodities that are prized in all countries, such as high-quality products, precious objects, and costly jewels, so that my answer may serve as an aid to those taught by experience and as a help to those trained in sundry trades and pursuits. I have therefore called it "A Clear Look." May God grant me success.

Certain men of experience among the ancients were of the opinion that whatever article is present is cheap because of its presence; it becomes dear because of its absence, when a need for it is felt.

The Byzantines say: If one of you cannot make a living in a country, let him move to another country.

The Indians say: Whatever becomes plentiful becomes cheap, except for good sense, which gains in value as it increases in quantity.

The Persians say: If you do not make a profit in a trade, leave it for another. If one of you does not make a living in a country, let him exchange it.

The Persians say: He who makes a profit in any market is he who sells that for which money is spent there.

The Arabs say: If you see a man whom fortune favors, then cling to him, for he attracts wealth.

A rich man was asked, "How did your wealth accumulate?" He replied, "I never sold on credit; I never refused a profit however small; I never acquired a dirham without using it in another deal."

It has been said, "Don't buy what you don't need, for you may have to sell what you can't do without."

A certain wise man claimed to have found this in a Persian

testament: "Man! There is no bond of kinship between you and the country where you live. The best country is that which suits you, the best time is that which makes you prosper, the best of men is he who is of use to you, the best water is that which quenches your thirst; the best mount is that which carries you; the best garment is that which clothes you; the best trade is that which profits you; the best knowledge is that which guides you; the best beauty is that which you like, even if it be ugly." It was also said, "The best craft is poplin, and the best trade is cloth."

On the Knowledge and Testing of Gold and Silver

The wise man said: Gold is loved, in ingots or otherwise, because it is like a lambent flame, massed rays, blood-red sulphur; its dominion endures because the test of the furnace does not reduce it nor the passing of time corrupt it. It is said that gold is precious because it suffers no changes, because its luster and beauty increase as it ages, and because all things diminish through touch and burial, save only gold which does not diminish at all.

The best dinars are the old ones, of greenish red. Some of the ancients claimed that a dinar could be tested by the way it stuck to the hair and the beard and by the difficulty of passing it through them. The bad dinar may be detected by its lightness.

It is said that the best gold is native and the best silver is virgin. The taste of pure silver is sweet, while the taste of debased coins is bitter and rusty. Counterfeit dirhams taste salty and ring like a [cracked?] bell, while silver has a pure, unmuted sound. It stills thirst if held in the mouth.

On Knowing Precious Stones and Their Value

It is said that you can distinguish between two groups of pearls by their taste; the sweet-tasting pearl comes from 'Umān, and the salty one, from the Red Sea. Both of them sink in water. The artificial pearl tastes bitter and greasy; it is light and floats in water.

It is said that when there is a worm inside the pearl, it feels hot when you suck or touch it. This is because of its soul sickness [?]. If there is no worm in it, it is cold to suck or touch. This is how it is tested.

Sailors say that the big pearls of changing color can be inserted in a slit, fresh, fat sheep tail, put inside a batter, and placed in an overheated oven. It will become clear and beautiful and recover its water. Likewise, when it is fumigated with camphor or treated with bone marrow and melon juice, it becomes clear.

The fleshy, substantial pearl is distinguished from the bony, nacreous pearl in that it is regular in shape, supple, and small, while the bony pearl is coarse and irregular.

The best pearl is the clear 'Umānī, regular in body, well-rounded, and balanced. Of two pearls equal in shape, appearance, color, and weight, the 'Umānī would be worth more. The 'Umānī pearl is more valuable and more prized than the Red Sea pearl, because the 'Umānī is sweet, pure, and clear, while the Red Sea pearl is somewhat salty with many defects.

If a pearl weighs half a *mithqāl*, it is called *durra*. An evenly rounded pearl weighing half a *mithqāl* can sometimes reach a price of 1000 *mithqāls* of gold; an egg-shaped pearl is of lower price. The price of pearls increases according to their weight and roundness. If their weight reaches two *mithqāls*, you can, if you wish, make its price 10,000, and if you wish 100,000. A round pearl of such weight and purity has no price; it is unique. The clearer and purer it is, the higher the price. The *durra yatīma* [orphan pearl] is a Red Sea pearl said to weigh three *mithqāls*. Small pearls are called *marjāna*.

The finest rubies are red. Then comes the rose-pink, then the yellow, then the sky-blue; the lowest is the white. The ruby comes from the mountain of Sarandīb in India. Real rubies can be distinguished from artificial rubies by three qualities: their weight in the scales, their coldness in the mouth when sucked, and the action of the file on them; for the ruby is a heavy stone, cold in the mouth, responding slowly to the file, while the artificial ruby is light in weight, hot to suck, and swift to file.

The best rubies are clear, pure, and luminous, whatever their color. Their price varies according to size. A clear red ruby weighing half a *mithqāl* can sometimes reach a price of 5000 dinars. The ring gem called al-Jabal[1] weighed two *mithqāls*. It was valued at 100,000 dinars and bought by Abū Jaʿfar al-Manṣūr for 40,000 dinars. A gem of sky-blue ruby can sometimes reach 200 dinars.

The best topaz are very green and of clear substance. The superior topaz can be distinguished from the artificial in the same way as with rubies: by weight, coldness of taste, and the slow action of the file. The artificial topaz is soft, light, hot to the taste, and quick to the file.

It is claimed that the best topaz are lustrous, clear, and pure. If such a piece weighs half a *mithqāl,* its price reaches 2000 *mithqāls* of gold. The price varies according to the size. The gem called Al-Baḥr weighed three *mithqāls;* Abū Jaʿfar al-Manṣūr bought it for 30,000 dinars, and it is now in the treasury of one of the Caliphs.

The best turquoises are milky-colored, bluish-green, clear, and old. The turquoise is a stone which the file cannot touch and which does not change in fire or hot water. The highest price of a turquoise gem weighing half a *mithqāl* is 20 dinars.

The best cornelian is from the Yemen, very red, with the appearance of lines on the surface. The clearer and more luminous it is, the better the price.

The best garnets are very red, with a color that flames like fire. The harder and bigger it is, the more precious and costly. The artificial stone is soft. To test its quality: if you put it near a feather, it picks it up. The more feathers it carries, the better its quality. The highest price for a superior garnet gem weighing half a *mithqāl* is 30 dinars. The precious stone owes its value to the extent of its luminosity and the range of its radiance at night.

Rock-crystal is chosen for its clearness and size. The best glass is that which is crystalline, clear, white and pure, and the superior *firʿawnī.*

The best diamonds are crystalline, clear, and white; then come the red ones. If one weighs half a *mithqāl,* its price reaches 100 dinars. The bigger and bulkier it is, the higher its price.

[1] "The Mountain." See vol. I, p. 40.

On the Knowledge of Perfumes, Essences, and Aromatics

It is claimed that the best aloes wood is Indian, from Mandal, unadulterated. The harder it is, the better. The quality is tested by the pungency of its fragrance and the potency of its smell. It is claimed that the best Indian aloes is the heavy kind that sinks in water, and the worst is the light kind that floats on the surface of the water. They regard the light kind as dead, without soul, and with a weak smell, while the heavy kind has a strong and penetrating odor.

The best musk is from Tibet, dry and fragrant; the worst is *buddī* [?]. Musk is adulterated with lead, castoreum, dragon's-blood, Syrian walnut gum. The lighter and more fragrant it is, the better.

They say that the best amber is the grey kind from Zābag; then the blue, then the yellow. The worst is . . . [thirty lines unreadable in manuscript].

On the Knowledge of Clothes and Their Quality

The best embroidered cloths are the Sābirī [Nīshābūrī ?], the ones from Kūfa, the silken, the gold-braided; then the Alexandrian pure linen, then the gold-braided linen, then the *Ghazalī* brocade, then the Yemeni, which has neither silk nor gold in it, being superior in this way to the *Ghazalī*. The silken linen cloths are not as costly as the Yemeni. A *Ghazalī* garment can sometimes cost 1,000 dinars.

The best squirrel is the ermine, then the back of this animal, then the Caspian squirrel, then the Khwarazmian, then that which is not adulterated with rabbit's down.

The best fox is the thick-haired black Caspian fox, not adulterated with dye; then the white fox, then the [dyed?] red, then the Caspian red, then the gray.

The best ermine is the one with the biggest tail. The best sable is the Chinese, then the Caspian, very white and very black, with long hair.

The best, most expensive, and finest draperies are the crimson and luminous Armenian *mirʿizzā;* then *raqm* poplin, then *qutūʿ* poplin, then Byzantine imperial brocade, then Maysānī brocaded poplin; then *Buzyūn*. The more gold is woven into these varieties, the better the quality and the higher the price. All other varieties can be woven with gold except the Armenian, the Maysānī, and the *Buzyūn*.

The best *Buzyūn* is the finely woven *miskī*, then the striped kind, then the kind adorned with circles, then the plain kind, then the one with squares, then with dots. A *ghifāra* in *miskī*, if it is of good workmanship and pure, can sometimes reach a price of fifty dinars.

Abū Qalamūn is a kind of crimson Byzantine imperial tapestry, with various violet stripes on red and green. They say that its color changes with the height of the day and the glare of the sun. Its price is very high.

The best woolen coverings [garments?] are Egyptian; then come the Persian ones from Khūzistān, the *mir'izzā* of Shīrāz, then the Iṣfahānī, the *mir'izzā* on silk from Fasā, then the ones from Ṭabaristān, then wool on wool.

The best shawls are from Rūyān in Ṭabaristān, then those from Āmul, then the Egyptian ones, then the ones from Qūmis. The best felts are Chinese, then the red ones from North Africa, then the white ones from Ṭālaqān, then those from Armenia, then those from Khurāsān.

The best leopard skins are from Berbera, spotted with bright white and deep black, with long spots like a starling. The finest skins are those with a small, clear black spot in the middle of the black part. If the black parts are joined to one another by a light black line, it is still finer. If the skin contains red with bright white and jet black, it is more beautiful and of higher price. The leopards of Berbera are small; one skin barely covers a single saddle. The highest price of a skin is fifty dinars. The North African and Indian skins are wider and bigger, but they do not fetch high prices and are not of good quality. The best leopard skins are spotted.

The best cotton is white, soft, . . . grained, and of pure and delicate whiteness.

It is said that crimson is a plant with a red worm in its root, which grows in three places in the world: in the West in the land of Andalus, in a district called Tārim, and in the land of

Fārs. The only people who know this plant and the places where it grows are a group of Jews who pick it every year in the month of February. The worm is dried and used to dye silk, wool, and so on. The place where they do the best dyeing is the land of Wāsiṭ.

They say that balsam is a tree in the land of Egypt. It is incised in the spring and exudes balsam oil, which is collected from it. It is not found anywhere except Egypt.

The earth almond [*Cyperus esculentus*] grows in the land of Shahrazūr. They say that it is a good aphrodisiac.

Qirmāz is a tree, called five-fingers [*panj angusht*] in Persian; it is nearly always found together with oleanders. It is a plant which seeks for the oleander, which grows with it and is called *fāzahr*. For this reason it is planted with it in a place where it grows. It is said that both plants were imported from the land of the Byzantines. It has a long and remarkable story.

On the Rare Commodities, Merchandise, Slave-Girls, Stones, and So Forth, Imported from Other Countries

Imported from India: tigers, leopards, elephants, leopard skins, red rubies, white sandalwood, ebony, and coconuts

From China: aromatics, silk, porcelain, paper, ink, peacocks, fiery horses, saddles, felts, cinnamon, and unmixed rhubarb [?]

From the Byzantines: silver and gold vessels, pure imperial dinars, simples, embroidered cloths, brocades, fiery horses, slave-girls, rare articles in red copper, strong locks, lyres, water engineers, specialists in plowing and cultivation, marble workers, and eunuchs

From Arabia: Arab horses, ostriches, thoroughbred she-camels, *qan* wood, and tanned hides

From Barbary and the regions of the Maghrib: leopards, acacia, felts, and black falcons

From the Yemen: cloaks, tanned hides, giraffes, breast plates [or buffalo?], cornelian, incense, indigo and turmeric

From Egypt: ambling donkeys, fine cloths, papyrus, balsam oil, and from its mines, high-grade topaz

From the Khazars: slaves, slave-women, armor, helmets, and hoods of mail

From the land of Khwārazm: musk, ermine, sable, squirrel, mink, and excellent sugarcane

From Samarqand: paper

From Balkh and its region: good grapes and mushrooms

From Būshanj: preserved capers

From Marw: barbiton players, high-grade barbitons, carpets, Marw cloth

From Jurjān: jujubes, pheasants, fine pomegranate seeds, soft woolen coats, and fine silks

From Amid: embroidered cloths, kerchieves, fine curtains, woolen head coverings

From Dabawand: arrowheads

From Rayy: plums, quicksilver, soft woolen coats, weapons, fine cloths, combs, royal head coverings, *Qass* linens, and pomegranates

From Iṣfahān: honeycombs, honey, quinces, Chinese pears, apples, salt, saffron, potash, white lead, antimony, bunks in tiers, fine cloths, and fruit drinks

From Qūmis: axes, saddlecoths, parasols, and woolen head coverings

From Kirmān: indigo and cumin

From Gor: electuaries and psyllium

From Bardha'a: fast mules

From Niṣībīn: lead

From Fārs: *tawwāzī* and *sābirī* linen clothes, rosewater, nenuphar oil, jasmine oil, and drinks

From Fasā: pistachios, various kinds of dried fruit, rare fruits, and glassware

From 'Umān and the seashore: pearls

From Maysān: rugs [or saddle cloths] and cushions

From Ahwāz and its districts: sugar, and silk brocades . . . castanet players and dancing girls . . . kinds of dates, grape molasses, and candy

From Sūs: citrons, violet oil, ocimum, horse cloths, and pack-saddles

From Mosul: curtains, thick felt, francolin, and quail

From Ḥulwān: pomegranates, figs, and pickles

From Armenia and Ādharbayjān: felts . . . pack saddles, carpets, fine mats, belts, and wool

On the Choicest Falcons, Peregrines, Sparrow Hawks, Sakers, and Other Birds of Prey

The best falcons are the white ones found between the Turkish land and Gīlān, then the black corvine ones from the lands of the Zanj to the Yemen and India, the bright red ones, then the dun-colored ones.

The best peregrines are the black, corvine ones from the sea and the white ones from Gurgān.

Likewise, among sparrowhawks the favorites are the black, corvine seabirds, then the white ones from India, then the red ones from the sea, with red bellies and white spotted breasts of brilliant color, with a large head, deep eyes without thinness, broad nostrils, with a wide and high breast, soft down, a long tail, green feet with the foot near the gauntlet, and heavy. When they reach a weight of 130, this is exactly right.

It is said that the merlin is the male of the saker, and the *afsī* is the male of the sparrowhawk. The male of the falcon is like a small merlin.

The Persians say: It hardly ever happens that a horse or a falcon has a fine appearance but lacks inner quality, or that they have fine qualities but lack appearance. If quality and appearance are combined, they are outstanding.

Another Chapter

With any stuff for clothing or drapery, the softer, gentler, and more lustrous, the better; with any jewel, pearl, or precious stone, the purer and more luminous, the finer; with any animal, wild or tame, the bigger and more docile, the more favored and esteemed; with any man, noble or humble, the wiser and easier, the better; with any woman, free or slave, the calmer, prettier, more abstemious, and more appreciative, the more virtuous; with any bird, of the plains or hills, the tamer, the more favored; with any possession, inherited or acquired, the more honest and more splendid, the more satisfying; with any enemy, small or great, the more intimate, the more hostile and envious. If a man's abode is not known, beware of his approach.

Fortune changes, and God's blessings are divided. Behave well in your pursuit, have pity on the poor and compassion for the weak, and you will be recompensed for it and requited. Fate is a carrier that brings things.

The best sleep is that which removes weariness and laziness.

The quality of things is perceived by the five senses: by sight, if it is beautiful and handsome, by the nose, if it is fragrant and scented; by taste, if it is sweet and tasty; by hearing, if it rings pure and clear; by touch, if it is soft and supple.

The Persians used to say: Heart and sight are two partners, taste and touch two allies, mind and memory two comrades, hearing and utterance two associates.

The best of men is easygoing, cheerful, and modest. The features by which the evil man can be recognized are that his face is frowning, not relaxed, his hue is pale and sickly without illness, he is fickle-hearted, hates and condemns fun and jest, and expresses himself uncouthly in conversation.

The features by which the virtuous man can be recognized are that he is easygoing and cheerful, of fine appearance and pleasant speech, with clear, unfrowning brow, not hasty, quarrelsome, or restless, not hostile to fun and jest, speaking well of those of whom he speaks, gentle in conversation, and modest.

Shāpūr the king said that there are seven kinds of man to whose words a wise man should not give weight: the drunkard, the jobber, the joker, the sick, the soothsayer, the slanderer, and the forgetful.

Al-Tabaṣṣur bi'l-tijāra, attributed to al-Jāḥiẓ.

51. The Markets of Seville (Twelfth Century)

Shopkeepers must be forbidden to reserve regular places for themselves in the forecourt of the great mosque or elsewhere, for this amounts to a usurpation of property rights and always gives rise to quarrels and trouble among them. Instead, whoever comes first should take his place.

The *muḥtasib* must arrange the crafts in order, putting like with like in fixed places. This is the best and most orderly way.

There must be no sellers of olive oil around the mosque, nor of dirty products, nor of anything from which an irremovable stain can be feared.

Rabbits and poultry should not be allowed around the mosque, but should have a fixed place. Partridges and slaughtered barnyard birds should only be sold with the crop plucked, so that the bad and rotten can be distinguished from the good ones. Rabbits should only be sold skinned, so that the bad ones may be seen. If they are left lying in their skins, they go bad.

Egg sellers must have bowls of water in front of them, so that bad eggs may be recognized.

Truffles should not be sold around the mosque, for this is a delicacy of the dissolute.[1]

Bread should only be sold by weight. Both the baking and the crumbs must be supervised, as it is often "dressed up." By this I mean that they take a small quantity of good dough and use it to "dress up" the front of the bread which is made with bad flour. A large loaf should not be made up out of the *poya*[2] rolls. These should be baked separately and as they are.

The glaziers must be forbidden to make fine goblets for wine; likewise the potters.

The *raṭl* weights for meat and fish and *ḥarīsa*[3] and fritters and bread should be made of iron only, with a visible seal on them. The *raṭl* weights of the shopkeepers should always be inspected, for they are bad people.

The cheese which comes from al-Madā'in[4] should not be sold, for it is the foul residue of the curds, of no value. If people saw how it is made, no one would ever eat it. Cheese should only be sold in small leather bottles, which can be washed and

[1] Apparently a common view. A Spanish Arabic proverb includes the large consumption of truffles among the signs by which the dissolute may be recognized.

[2] A roll given to the baker as payment for baking bread in his oven. In modern Spanish the word denotes the money paid to the baker for this service.

[3] See above, p. 126.

[4] A term applied to the fertile islands in the lower Guadalquivir, below Seville.

cleaned every day. That which is in bowls cannot be secured from worms and mold.

Mixed meats should not be sold on one stall, nor should fat and lean meat be sold on one stall. Tripe should only be sold dry on boards, for water both spoils it and increases its weight. The entrails of sheep must be taken out, so that they should not be sold with the meat and at the same price, which would be a fraud. The heads of sheep should not be skinned, except for the young. The guts must always be removed from the bodies of animals, except lambs, and should not be left there, for this too would be an occasion for fraud.

No slaughtering should take place in the market, except in the closed slaughterhouses, and the blood and refuse should be taken outside the market. Animals should be slaughtered only with a long knife. All slaughtering knives should be of this kind. No animal which is good for field work may be slaughtered, and a trustworthy and incorruptible commissioner should go to the slaughterhouse every day to make sure of this; the only exception is an animal with a defect. Nor should a female still capable of producing young be slaughtered. No animal should be sold in the market which has been brought already slaughtered, until its owner establishes that it is not stolen. The entrails should not be sold together with the meat and at the same price. A lamb weighing six *raṭls* with its offal shall not be sold at the same price as a lamb the meat of which alone is of that weight.

Fish, whether salt or fresh, shall not be washed in water for this makes it go bad. Nor should salted fish be soaked in water, for this also spoils and rots it.

[Word missing in text] should only be sold cut into small pieces and with the bones removed. Jerked meat should not be sold, for it is prepared with bad and rotten meat. There is no goodness in it, and it is a deadly poison.

Left-over and rotten fish should not be sold.

Sausages and grilled rissoles should only be made with fresh meat and not with meat coming from a sick animal and bought for its cheapness.

Flour should not be mixed with the cheese used for fritters. This is fraud, and the *muḥtasib* must watch out for it.

The cream must always be pure and not mixed with cheese. The leftovers of the cooks and fryers should not be sold.

Vinegar should only be bought from a trustworthy merchant, for it can be mixed with much water, which is a fraud. The vinegar maker should be ordered not to use too much water when he makes vinegar for someone, for this spoils it.

The copper pots used by the *ḥarīsa* makers, as also the spans of the fritter makers and the fryers, should be lined with tin only, since copper with oil is poisonous.

Women should be forbidden to do their washing in the gardens, for these are dens for fornication.

Grapes in large quantities should not be sold to anyone of whom it is known that he would press them to make wine. This is a matter for supervision.

Fruit must not be sold before it is ripe for this is bad, except only for grapes, which are good for pregnant women and for the sick. Large cucumbers which can be counted should not be sold by weight [?].[6]

Grocery products which have wastage in the form of liquid, powder, or a kernel should only be sold with an allowance for wastage determined by the merchants and generally agreed.

Groceries which are purchased by the shopkeepers by measure of capacity should only be sold by measure of capacity.

Wild figs may only be sold in pairs.

The seller of grapes should have baskets and nets in which to arrange them, as this is the best protection for them.

Cakes should be properly baked and should only be made wide, as thin ones are good only for the sick.

If someone assays gold or silver coins for a person, and later it emerges that there is base metal in them, the assayer must make good, for he deceived and betrayed the owner of the coins, who placed his trust in him. Swindlers when detected must be denounced in all crafts, but above all in assaying coin, for in this case the swindler can only be a person who is expert in matters of coin.

[5] *Ruṣāṣ*, usually lead, occasionally tin. The latter meaning is more likely here.

[6] The meaning of this passage is uncertain.

Women should not sit by the river bank in the summer if men appear there.

No barber may remain alone with a woman in his booth. He should work in the open market in a place where he can be seen and observed.

The cupper. He should only let blood into a special jar with graduation marks, so that he can see how much blood he has let. He should not let blood at his discretion, for this can lead to sickness and death.

The water wheel. Most of the holes for the spindles should be wedged, as this is best for its working.

No one may be allowed to claim knowledge of a matter in which he is not competent, especially in the craft of medicine, for this can lead to loss of life. The error of a physician is hidden by the earth. Likewise a joiner. Each should keep to his own trade and not claim any skill of which he is not an acknowledged master—especially with women, since ignorance and error are greater among them.

Only a skilled physician should sell potions and electuaries and mix drugs. These things should not be bought from the grocer or the apothecary whose only concern is to take money without knowledge; they spoil the prescriptions and kill the sick, for they mix medicines which are unknown and of contrary effect.

The sale of tame pigeons must be prohibited, for they are used only by thieves and people of no religion. The sale of cats should also be banned. Any broker who is known to be treacherous and dishonest should be excluded from the market, for he is a thief. He must be watched and not employed.

The lime stores and [other] empty places must be forbidden, because men go there to be alone with women.

Only good and trustworthy men, known as such among people, may be allowed to have dealings with women in buying and in selling. The tradespeople must watch over this carefully. The women who weave brocades must be banned from the market, for they are nothing but harlots.

On festival days men and women shall not walk on the same path when they go to cross the river.

The tax farm on . . . must be suppressed.[7]

Cargo ships must be known, and their holds should not be overloaded, especially when there are storms, as we have said.[8] The owners and captains of ships carrying wheat, charcoal, and other goods must be instructed to lighten their loads and not endanger the Muslims.

The heads of sheep, the meat of which is brought to the market, must be washed clean of blood. Otherwise, in narrow or crowded places it would not be possible to secure passersby from pollution by the blood. The ends of the stalls which protrude from the shops must be sawn off, since the meat hanging there would soil the clothes of passersby and make the way narrow.

The bakers must be ordered to wash their pans every day and to scrape and polish their boards to prevent vermin from entering them. They must not make large loaves with the dough for *poya* rolls. These must be cooked separately and sold by weight.

Graves should be slightly lengthened and widened. I saw a corpse which was exhumed from the grave three times; graves should allow for this. I saw another which had to be forced into the grave. The first concern of the *muḥtasib* should be to demolish buildings erected in the cemetery and to watch over this for reasons I have already explained above.[9]

Paper should be of somewhat larger format, with more glazing.

Raw bricks should be thicker and smoother.

The basins in the public baths should be covered. If they are left uncovered, they cannot be protected from pollution, yet this is a place of purity. The bath attendant, the masseur, and the barber should not walk about in the baths without a loincloth or drawers.

A Muslim must not massage a Jew or a Christian nor throw

[7] Reading uncertain.

[8] A whole section of the book from which this reading is excerpted is devoted to the river and river traffic.

[9] This matter is discussed in detail in the section on cemeteries in the book from which this reading is excerpted.

away his refuse nor clean his latrines. The Jew and the Christian are better fitted for such trades, since they are the trades of those who are vile. A Muslim should not attend to the animal of a Jew or of a Christian, nor serve him as a muleteer, nor hold his stirrup. If any Muslim is known to do this, he should be denounced.

Muslim women shall be prevented from entering their abominable churches, for the priests are evil-doers, fornicators, and sodomites. Frankish[10] women must be forbidden to enter the church except on days of religious services or festivals, for it is their habit to eat and drink and fornicate with the priests, among whom there is not one who has not two or more women with whom he sleeps. This has become a custom among them, for they have permitted what is forbidden and forbidden what is permitted. The priests should be ordered to marry, as they do in the eastern lands. If they wanted to, they would.

No women may be allowed in the house of a priest, neither an old woman nor any other, if he refuses marriage. They should be compelled to submit to circumcision, as was done to them by al-Muʿtaḍid ʿAbbād.[11] They claim to follow the rules of Jesus, may God bless and save him. Now Jesus was circumcised, and they celebrate the day of his circumcision as a festival, yet they themselves do not practice this.

The contractor[12] of the bathhouse should not sit there with the women, for this is an occasion for license and fornication. The contractor of hostelries for traders and travelers should not be a woman, for this is indeed fornication. The broker of houses shall not be a young man, but a chaste old man of known good character.

Clothes must not be cleaned with beetles. Laundry men should be forbidden to do this, as it is harmful to the clothes.

[10] That is, Christians from outside Spain and from those parts of Spain not under Muslim rule.

[11] Ruler of Seville, 1040–1069. This story is not confirmed by the chroniclers.

[12] That is, the tax farmer who operates or controls the establishment.

A Jew must not slaughter meat for a Muslim.[13] The Jews should be ordered to arrange their own butcher's stalls.

The qāḍī must order the people of the villages to appoint a keeper in every village to guard private property from encroachment, for the peasants regard the property of the people of the city as licit to them. No riding animal or cattle should be turned loose without a halter. In the words of the proverb, "In the keeper is the protection of the State."

The property of the people and of the Muslims must be protected at the time of the harvest and other times from any kind of injury whatsoever. When the ears of the grain begin to form, it must be forbidden to cut and sell them. This is done only to avoid paying the tithe.

The curriers and silk dyers must be ordered to ply their trades outside the city only.

The felt makers should be ordered to improve their work. They make the felts slack, with little wool, and useless. The wool must be shaken free of lime.

The furriers must be advised not to use pigeons' dung to disguise worn out furs. This is a deceit which they practice.

Dyers must be forbidden to dye green with passerine or to dye light blue with brazilwood. This is fraudulent, since these dyes lose their color quickly. Some grocers use lycium leaf to make the henna green. This gives the henna a bright and fine green color. This is fraud.

A garment belonging to a sick man,[14] a Jew, or a Christian must not be sold without indicating its origin; likewise, the garment of a debauchee. Dough must not be taken from a sick man for baking his bread. Neither eggs nor chickens nor milk nor any other foodstuff should be bought from him. They should only buy and sell among themselves.

The sewer men must be forbidden to dig holes in the streets, as this harms them and causes injury to people, except when they are cleaning the entire street.

[13] Some Muslim jurists allow Muslims to eat meat from animals killed by Jews, whose dietary code in part coincides with that of Islam. Animals killed by Christians, who have no dietary laws, are always forbidden.

[14] Probably lepers are meant.

Itinerant fortune-tellers must be forbidden to go from house to house, as they are thieves and fornicators.

A drunkard must not be flogged until he is sober again.

Prostitutes must be forbidden to stand bareheaded outside the houses. Decent women must not bedeck themselves to resemble them. They must be stopped from coquetry and party making among themselves, even if they have been permitted to do this [by their husbands]. Dancing girls must be forbidden to bare their heads.

No contractor, policeman, Jew, or Christian may be allowed to dress in the costume of people of position, of a jurist, or of a worthy man. They must on the contrary be abhorred and shunned and should not be greeted with the formula, "Peace be with you," for the devil has gained mastery over them and has made them forget the name of God. They are the devil's party, "and indeed the devil's party are the losers" [Qur'ān, lvii, 22]. They must have a distinguishing sign by which they are recognized to their shame.

Catamites must be driven out of the city and punished wherever any one of them is found. They should not be allowed to move around among the Muslims nor to participate in festivities, for they are debauchees accursed by God and man alike.

When fruit or other foodstuffs are found in the possession of thieves, they should be distributed in prisons and given to the poor. If the owner comes to claim his goods and is recognized, they should be returned to him.

Ibn 'Abdūn, pp. 43–51.

52. An Invitation to Merchants (ca. 1280–1290)

In writing *amāns* for the people of Islam, one begins the *amān* with the word *rusima,* in the same way as one begins short rescripts and edicts; this is a strange practice.

This is a copy of an *amān* in this form, cited by Muḥammad ibn al-Mukarram, one of the secretaries in the Bureau of Correspondence of [Sultan] al-Manṣūr Qalawun,[1] in his memorandum

[1] Sultan of Egypt, reigned 1280–1290.

entitled "The Memorandum of the Wise," written on behalf of the above-mentioned al-Manṣūr Qalawun to the merchants who came to Egypt from China, India, Sind, Yemen, Iraq, and Asia Minor, as composed by the master Fatḥ al-Dīn ibn 'Abd al-Ẓāhir, head of the Bureau of Correspondence in the government offices in Egypt. It reads as follows:

> A decree has been issued, may God exalt the Sultan's exalted command, and may his [the Sultan's] justice keep the subjects in assured protection. He requests the prayers of the people of both east and west for his thriving reign, and let all of them be sincere. He offers a genuine welcome to those who come to his realm, as to the garden of Eden, by whatever gate they may choose to enter, from Iraq, from Persia, from Asia Minor, from the Ḥijāz, from India, and from China. Whoever wishes to set forth—the distinguished merchants, the men of great affairs, and the small traders, from the countries enumerated and also those which have not been enumerated—and whoever wishes to enter our realms may sojourn or travel at will and to come to our country of broad lands and leafy shades, then let him, like those whom God has destined for this, make firm resolve on this worthy and beneficial act, and let him come to a country whose inhabitants have no need either of supplies or reserves of food, for it is an earthly paradise for those who dwell in it, and a consolation for those who are far from their own homes, a delight of which the eye does not weary, a place from which one is never driven by excessive cold, for one lives there in perpetual spring and permanent well-being. It is enough to say that one of its descriptions is that it is God's beauty spot on His earth. God's blessing accrues in the baggage of whoever does a good deed by lending or receives a good deed by borrowing. Another of its features is that anyone who comes there hoping for anything, gets what he wants, for it is a land of Islam, with armies whose swords are beyond reproach. For justice has made its lands prosper and has multiplied its inhabitants. The buildings have increased so that it is a land of great cities. The needy is at ease there, and does not fear the violence of the creditors, for demands there are not exacting and deferments easily obtained. The rest of the people and all the merchants have no fear there of any oppression, for justice protects.
>
> Whoever becomes aware of this our decree, among the merchants who live in Yemen and India and China and Sind and

elsewhere, let them prepare to travel and come to our country, where they will find the reality better than the word and will see a beneficence beyond the mere fulfillment of their promises and will sojourn in "a fair land under a forgiving Lord" [Qur'ān, xxxv, 15] and in comfort deserving of gratitude (for only the grateful is rewarded) and in security of person and property, and felicity which illuminates their circumstances and fulfills their hopes. They will receive from us all the justice that they expect. Our justice responds to those who call on it, has procedures which will be praised by their way of life, will leave their property to their descendants, and will protect and preserve them so that they will take shelter under its shadow and be protected. Whoever brings merchandise with him, such as spices and other articles imported by the Kārimī[2] merchants, will suffer no unjust impost nor be subjected to any burdensome demand, for [our] justice will leave with them what is desirable and remove what is burdensome. If anyone brings [white] male slaves [mamlūk] or slave-girls, he will find their sale price beyond his expectations and [will be accorded] the tolerance in fixing a profitable price which is customarily accorded to those who import such slaves from near and all the more from distant lands; for our desire is directed toward the increase of our troops, and those who import mamlūks have gained a title to our generosity. Let whoever can do so increase his import of mamlūks, and let him know that the purpose in demanding them is to increase the armies of Islam. For thanks to them, Islam today is in glory with flag unfurled and the Sultan al-Manṣūr [Qalawun]. The mamlūk who is thus imported is removed from darkness to light. Yesterday he was blamed for unbelief; today he is praised for faith and fights for Islam against his own tribe and people.

This is our decree for all traveling merchants to whose knowledge it comes, 'They seek the bounty of God, while others fight in the cause of God.' [Qur'ān, lxxiii, 20] Let them read in it the orders which will ease their task; let them be guided by its star, nourished by its wisdom. Let them mount the neck of the hope which impels them to leave their homes and stretch out their hands in prayer for him who wishes people to come to his country, so that they may benefit from his generosity in all clarity and in all beneficence; and let them take advantage

2 An association of merchants in Egypt and Arabia, engaged in the eastern trade.

of the occasions for profit, for they are ripe for picking. These true promises are sent to them to confirm their high hopes and reaffirm to them that the noble rescript is valid, by the command of God, in accordance with what the pens have written, and [God is] the best Guarantor.

Al-Qalqashandī, *Ṣubḥ al-a'shā*, xiii, pp. 339–342.

53. On Prices in Cities (Fourteenth Century)

Know that in all markets there are to be found all the needs of mankind. Some of these are necessities, that is, foodstuffs, like wheat and barley; or similar foods, such as beans, chick peas, peas, and other edible seeds, greenstuffs which give flavor, such as onions, garlic, and the like. Others are luxuries and superfluities, such as spices, fruits, clothes, tools, riding animals, and various manufactures and constructions.

If a city is large and populous, the prices of necessities such as foodstuffs are cheap, and the prices of luxuries such as spices, and fruits, and the like are high. If a city has few inhabitants and a low material level, the opposite occurs.

The reason for this is that cereals are necessary foods, and the demand for them is therefore great. No one neglects to provide food for himself and for his household for a month or for a year. The demand for food is, therefore, common to all, or at least to most of the inhabitants, both in the city and in its surroundings, and this cannot be otherwise. Everyone who procures food has, beyond his own needs and those of his household, a large surplus which would suffice to satisfy the needs of many people in that city. The food is thus assuredly more plentiful than the needs of the inhabitants of the city require, and food prices are therefore generally low, except in those years when natural disasters strike them. If people did not withhold food as a safeguard against such disasters, it could be distributed free without cost or counterpart, because it becomes more plentiful as prosperity increases.

Other commodities, such as spices and fruit, and the like, are not general necessities, and their procurement does not involve the work of all or even of most of the inhabitants of the city.

If the city is large and thriving and needs many luxuries, there is a great desire to acquire and accumulate such commodities, each according to his relative position. The supply is therefore very much less than the demand. While purchasers [in urgent need] are many, the goods themselves are few. Those who want them jostle for them, and the people of luxury and ease are willing to pay extravagant prices for them, since they need them more than others. This raises the prices of these commodities, as can be seen.

The same applies to manufactures and services, which are also expensive in thriving cities. There are three reasons for the high cost of these things: first, the great demand, because of the important place given to luxuries in a large and populous city, second, the high value that the craftsmen set on their work and on their specialized services, because their livelihood is easy in a city in which food is plentiful; third, the many people of luxury and their many needs requiring the specialized services of others and the employment of craftsmen. They therefore pay the craftsmen more than the value of their work, in competition for their services. The workers, craftsmen, and artisans become proud, their work becomes expensive, and the townspeople spend much money for their services.

But in small towns with small populations there are few foodstuffs, since there is little work and since the inhabitants are afraid of a shortage of food because the town is small. Therefore, they grab and hoard whatever food comes their way. Food therefore becomes scarce, and its price rises because of the demand for it. The other nonvital commodities are not required because of the small numbers of the population and their low standard. There is little trade, and these commodities are sold at low prices. Sometimes the price of foodstuffs is augmented by taxes and tolls imposed upon them by the ruler in the markets and at the city gates and by the payments which the tax collectors levy for their own benefit from sales. For this reason prices in the cities are higher than in the country, because while taxes and tolls and imposts are few in the country, or absent entirely, they are numerous in cities, especially toward the end of the period of rule of a dynasty.

The cost of agricultural work also enters into the cost of foodstuffs, and their prices reflect this. This has happened in Spain in our time. The Christians have seized the good lands and fertile soil and driven the Muslims to the coastal zone where the country is rugged and the soil poor and unfertile. The Muslims in Spain are therefore obliged to devote much effort to their lands and fields so as to make them fit for growing grain. This preparation involves costly labor and requires materials, such as manure and the like, which also involve expenditure. Work on the land among them involves certain expenses which they take into account in fixing the price of their produce. Therefore, the cost of living in Spain is high, since the Christians expelled the Muslims and drove them to the Muslim coastal zones in which they now live. Because of this, when people hear of the high prices in their country, they think it is due to a shortage of food and grain in their country, but it is not so. On the contrary, they have, as far as we know, the most flourishing and best tended agriculture in the inhabited world. There are few of them—Sultan or subject—who have no lands or fields or farms, except for a small number of craftsmen and artisans and newcomers to the country, such as volunteers for the Holy War, in whose pay the Sultan includes a special allocation of food and fodder. The real reason for the high price of grain there is what we have said.

The opposite is true in Barbary, where agriculture flourishes, the land is fertile and they incur no extra expense for cultivation, which is extensive and general. This is the reason for the low cost of food in their country.

Ibn Khaldūn, *Al-Muqaddima*, pp. 362–364.

54. An Experiment with Paper Money in Persia (1294)

The Introduction of the Unhallowed Chao *and the Harm that Resulted Therefrom in the Land.*

Ṣadr al-Dīn and some of the amirs sometimes talked and thought about the *chao* [paper money], which is current in China, and the possibility of putting it into circulation in this country. They raised this matter at court, and Gaykhātū[1] ordered Pulad Chingsang to inquire into the matter. He reported that *chao* was paper which bore the stamp of the king and was current in all China in place of minted coins. The hard money there is *balish,* which comes into the state treasury.

Now Gaykhātū was an extremely generous king, who bestowed excessive bounty, and the money in the world was not enough for him. He therefore approved this scheme. Ṣadr al-Dīn wanted to do something which no one else had ever done and for that reason made great efforts in this matter.

Shiktur Noyon, who was the wisest of the amirs, maintained that *chao* would ruin the country and would lead to the dishonoring of the king and the dispersal of the peasants and the soldiers. Ṣadr al-Dīn said to Gaykhātū in reply that Shiktur Noyon was a great lover of gold, and that was why he was trying to make nothing of *chao.* A decree was issued, which they prepared in haste.

On Friday, 27 Sha'bān [693/July 27, 1294], Akbuka, Togachar, Ṣadr al-Dīn, and Tamachi-Inak went to Tabrīz to launch the *chao.* They arrived there on 19 Ramaḍān [August 13], promulgated the decree, and prepared a great quantity of *chao.* On Saturday, 19 Shawwāl 693 [September 12, 1294], in the city of Tabrīz, they put the *chao* into circulation. The decree laid down that any person who refused to accept it would be summarily executed. For one week, in fear of the sword, they accepted it, but they gave very little in return. Most of the people of Tabrīz perforce chose to leave, taking the textiles and foodstuffs from the bazaars with them, so that nothing was available, and people who wanted to eat fruit went secretly to the orchards. The city, which had been so populous, was completely emptied of people. Vagabonds and ruffians looted whatever they found in the streets. Caravans ceased to go there. At night vagabonds lay in ambush on the roads through the orchards, and if some poor wretch tried to get an ass-load of grain or a basket of fruit by stealth and take it home, they took it away from him,

[1] Mongol Il-Khan of Persia, reigned 1291–1295.

and if he tried to stop them, they said, "Sell it, and take its price in this blessed *chao*, and show where you bought it!" In brief, the people were struck by disaster, and the poor wretches stretched out their hands in prayer.

One day by chance Gaykhātū passed through the bazaar. He saw that the shops were empty and asked why. Ṣadr al-Dīn said, "Sharaf al-Dīn Lākūshī, the headman of this place, has died, and it is the custom of the Tabrīzīs, in mourning their chiefs, to stay away from the bazaars." On Friday the people in the cathedral mosque made such a great clamor before Qutb al-Dīn that they obtained permission and sold food for gold in the backstreets, and they killed some people because of this. Normal commercial transactions and the taxes on them ceased. One day a dervish in the bazaar seized Ṣadr al-Dīn's reins and said,

> The smell of burnt liver has pervaded the world.
> Can't you smell it with that nose of yours?

Ṣadr al-Dīn, affected by these words, and with the assent of the retainers after this ruination, obtained a decree authorizing the sale of foodstuffs for gold. Because of this people became bold and transacted business openly in gold, and the absent returned to the city, and within a short time it was flourishing again. In the end, the attempt to introduce *chao* did not succeed. It was abandoned, and the people were saved from this trouble.

Rashīd al-Dīn, *Jāmiʿ al-tawārīkh*, iii, pp. 239–241.

5 Poets, Scholars, and Physicians

The following excerpts are chosen to exemplify the place of literature and science in the life of medieval Islam. The first two, from the writings of a ninth century scholar, explain both the literary esthetic and the social function of Arabic poetry. The third, an autobiographic fragment by the great Avicenna, depicts his education and development as a scientist and philosopher. The three remaining texts, two of them translated from the Hebrew, reveal the familiar figure of the Jewish doctor, here represented by a tract on medieval practice and ethics, a short biography of Maimonides by a Muslim historian, and an extract from a letter by Maimonides describing his own life and work.

55. An Arabic Definition of Poetry (Ninth Century)

Poetry is the mine of knowledge of the Arabs, the book of their wisdom, the muster roll of their history, the repository of their great days, the rampart protecting their heritage, the trench defending their glories, the truthful witness on the day of dispute, the final proof at the time of argument. Whoever among them can bring no verse to confirm his own nobility and the generous qualities and honored deeds which he claims for his forebears, his endeavors are lost though they be famous, effaced by the passage of time though they be mighty. But he who binds them with rhymed verses, knots them with scansion, and makes them famous through a rare line, a phrase grown proverbial, a well-turned thought, has made them eternal against time, preserved them from negation, averted the plot of the enemy, and lowered the eye of the envious.

Ibn Qutayba, *'Uyūn al-Akhbār*, ii, p. 185.

56. Introduction to the Book of Poetry and Poets (Ninth Century)

This is a book which I have written about poets. In it I have spoken of poets, their times, their merits, the circumstances which gave rise to their verses, their tribes and the names of their ancestors, of those among them who are known by a byname or by a patronymic, of that which is praiseworthy in a man's story and admirable in his verses, and also of the errors and defects which scholars have criticized in their expression and in their meaning, and of that which the ancients said first and the moderns borrowed from them. I have spoken also of the divisions and categories of poetry, of the criteria by which a poem is chosen and found beautiful, and of some other matters which I have included in this first part.

My chief concern has been with famous poets who are known to most men of letters and whose verses are proof-texts for rare words, grammar, and the interpretation of the book of God, may He be exalted, and the traditions of the Prophet of God, may God bless and save him. As to those whose names are obscure, whose fame is slight, whose verses are unused, and who are known only to some specialists, I have named very few of this class, for I know only a few of them, and on these few I have no information—and I am aware that you have no need for me to list names for you, without illustrating them by a narrative, a date, a pedigree, an anecdote, or some strange or beautiful verse.

You may perhaps think, God have pity on you, that it is the duty of one who compiles a book such as this to leave no poet, ancient or modern, without mentioning him and presenting him to you. You may suppose that poets are in the same position as the relaters of traditions or historical narratives, of kings and nobles, who are few enough to be counted and enumerated. But the poets who are known for their poetry in their clans and in their tribes in the time of heathendom and in the time of Islam are too numerous to be encompassed or for anyone to embrace them all, even if he spent his life in investigating them and exhausted all his efforts in search and inquiry. I do not think that any one of our scholars has mastered the poetry of a single tribe to the point where there was no poet in the tribe whom he did not know and no ode which he had not recited.

Sahl ibn Muḥammad informed us, on the authority of al-Aṣma'ī, on the authority of Kirdīn ibn Misma', who said: some young men called on Abu Ḍamḍam after nightfall: "What brings you here, scoundrels?" he asked. "We came to talk with you," they said. "You lie," he said. "You said to yourselves, "The shaykh has grown old; let's go and have some fun with him. Perhaps we may catch him out." Then he recited to them the verses of a hundred different poets (another time he said eighty) who are all called 'Amr. Al-Aṣma'ī added, "Khalaf al-Aḥmar and I counted and we could only reach thirty." That is what Abū Ḍamḍam remembered, and he was not the most copious of transmitters. And it is likely that there were other poets called 'Amr whom he did not know and who were more numerous than those he did know. And that is apart from the tribal poets whose verses are lost and have not been handed down to us by scholars and transmitters.

Abū Ḥātim informed us, on the authority of al-Aṣma'ī, who said: There were three brothers of the Banū Sa'd who never came to the cities and whose verses in the *rajaz* meter are lost. They were called Mundhir, Nudhayr, and Muntadhir, and it is said that Muntadhir was the author of an ode attributed to Ru'ba which begins, "Dark depths, desolate passages . . ."

In this book I have not dealt with those whose primary concern was something other than poetry. We have seen an author who wrote a book of this kind in which he mentioned among the poets some persons who are not known for their verses and who composed only a few fragments, such as the qāḍī Ibn Shubruma and the traditionist Sulaymān ibn Qaṭṭa al-Taymī. If we tried to include such as these among the poets, we would include most of mankind, for there is hardly anyone with the slightest tincture of letters and the smallest natural gift who has not composed some verse. We would have to include the Companions of the Prophet of God, may God bless and save him, most of the followers of the next generation, and a great host of scholars, caliphs, and nobles and place them all among the ranks of the poets.

I have not followed, in my choice of the verses I have cited from each poet, the practice of the conformists who find beautiful that which others have already found beautiful. I do not regard an ancient poet with awe because he is ancient or a modern with disdain because he is modern, but have looked at both with the eye of equity. I have given each his part and have accorded him his full due. I know one of our scholars who extols a stupid poem because its author is ancient and puts it in his anthology and despises a fine poem which has no other fault in his eyes than that of having been composed in his own time or by someone he had seen.

God did not confine scholarship, poetry, and eloquence to one period and withhold it from others, nor did He endow one group of people and not others. He made this a common good, shared among His worshippers in every age. He has so ordered it that every ancient was modern in his own time, and every nobleman was at first an upstart. Jarīr, Farazdaq, al-Akhtal, and their like were counted as moderns in their time. Abū ʿAmr ibn al-ʿAlāʾ said, "There is more of this modern poetry, and it is getting better; I am thinking of becoming a transmitter of this poetry." Then we began to see these poets as ancients, as they became remote from us in time. The same will happen when our successors look at their successors—such as al-Khuraymī, al-ʿAttābī, al-Ḥasan ibn Hāniʾ, and others.

For every poet who has achieved something fine by word or deed, we have mentioned his achievement and have praised him for it. This achievement has not been diminished in our eyes by the recent date or youthful years of its author or actor. Likewise, when we have encountered something bad in an ancient or a noble poet, it is not raised up in our eyes by the nobility or antiquity of its author.

It would have been right to include in this book stories about the mighty power and immense importance of poetry, about those whom God has raised up by praise and those whom He has humbled by satire, about all that the Arabs have preserved by way of useful stories, authentic genealogies, wisdom resembling the wisdom of the philosophers, the science of horses, the science of the stars and the lunar mansions and the art of conducting oneself by them, the winds which herald rain and which do not, the lightning flashes and which are rainless and which truly promise rain, the clouds and which bear rain and which only glower; and about the verses by which the miser is urged to generosity, the coward to combat, the base to greatness. But I considered that what I said about these things in the *Book of the Arabs* is plentiful and adequate, and I did not desire to prolong what I have to say here by repeating it. Whoever wishes to be introduced by this means to the sweetness and bitterness of poetry may refer to that book, if it pleases Almighty God.

Ibn Qutayba, *Kitāb al-Shi'r wa'l-Shu'arā'*, pp. 2–6.

57. The Autobiography of Avicenna (Tenth–Eleventh Centuries)

My father was from Balkh and moved from there to Bukhārā during the reign of Nūḥ ibn Manṣūr.[1] He was employed as an official and administered a village called Kharmaythān, a dependency of Bukhārā and an administrative center. Nearby was a village called Afshana, where he married my mother, who came from there, and settled down. I was born to her there, as was my brother. Later we all moved to Bukhārā, where I was given teachers of Qur'ān and polite letters [*adab*]. By the time I was ten years old, I had mastered the Qur'ān and so much of polite letters as to provoke wonderment.

My father was one of those who had responded to propaganda for the Egyptians[2] and was counted among the Ismā'īlīs. He had accepted their teachings on the soul and the mind, as had my brother. They often discussed it with one another. I listened to them and understood what they said, and they tried to win me over to this doctrine. Sometimes they also used to discuss

[1] A Samanid ruler, reigned 977–997.
[2] The Fatimid Caliphs in Cairo.

philosophy, geometry, and Indian arithmetic,[3] and my father decided to send me to a certain grocer who knew Indian arithmetic so that I could learn it from him.

Then Abū 'Abdallāh al-Nātilī, who claimed to be a philosopher, came to Bukhārā. My father lodged him in our house in the hope that I would learn something from him. Before he came, I was studying jurisprudence under Ismā'īl al-Zāhid [the Hermit], and I was one of his best pupils. I became proficient in the different methods of questioning and of objection to the respondent, in accordance with the customary procedures. Then, under the guidance of al-Nātilī, I began to read the *Isagoge*.[4] When he told me the definition of *genus,* that is, that which is said of a number of things which differ in species in answer to the question "What is it?" I began to give greater precision to this definition in a way the like of which he had never heard before. He was full of admiration for me and persuaded my father to let me devote myself entirely to learning. Whatever problem he put to me, I resolved better than he could himself. Thus I learned from him the broad principles of logic, but he knew nothing of the subtleties. Then I began to read books and study commentaries on my own until I mastered logic. I also read the geometry of Euclid, from the beginning to the fifth or sixth figure under the guidance of al-Nātilī, and was then able to cope with the rest of the book on my own. Then I passed to the Almagest.[5] When I had finished with the preliminaries and came to the geometrical figures al-Nātilī said to me, "Read it on your own and solve the problems yourself, and then explain to me what you have read so that I may show you what is right and what is wrong." The man was not capable of handling this book himself. I therefore began to explain the book by myself. There were many difficult problems which al-Nātilī had not known until the time when I explained them to him and made him understand them.

[3] Arithmetic with the zero and positional notation. The Muslims learned this system in India and introduced it to Europe. Hence, the common but inaccurate term "Arabic numerals."

[4] An introduction to Aristotle's *Categories* by the neoplatonist Greek philosopher Porphyrius.

[5] An astronomical treatise by Ptolemy.

Eventually al-Nātilī left me and went to Gurganj. For my part, I busied myself with the study of the *Fuṣūṣ al-Ḥikam*[6] and other commentaries on physics and metaphysics, and the doors of knowledge opened before me. Then I took up medicine and began to read books written on this subject. Medicine is not one of the difficult sciences, and in a very short time I undoubtedly excelled in it, so that physicians of merit studied under me. I also attended the sick, and the doors of medical treatments based on experience opened before me to an extent that cannot be described. At the same time I carried on debates and controversies in jurisprudence. At this point I was sixteen years old.

Then, for a year and a half, I devoted myself to study. I resumed the study of logic and all parts of philosophy. During this time I never slept a whole night through and did nothing but study all day long. I acquired great knowledge. For every problem which I considered, I established firmly the premises of its syllogisms and arranged them in accordance with this knowledge. Then I considered what might be deduced from these premises, and I observed their conditions until the true solution of the problem was demonstrated. Whenever I was puzzled by a problem or was unable to establish the middle term of a syllogism, I would go to the mosque, pray, and beg the Creator of All to reveal to me that which was hidden from me and to make easy for me that which was difficult. Then at night I would return home, put a lamp in front of me, and set to work reading and writing. Whenever sleep overcame me or when I felt myself exhausted, I would drink a modest cup to restore my strength and then go on reading. When I dozed, I would dream of the same problem, so that for many problems the solution appeared to me in my sleep. I went on like this until I was firmly grounded in all sciences and mastered them as far as was humanly possible. What I learned then is what I know now, and I have not added to it to this day. Thus I mastered logic, physics, and mathematics.

Then I returned to the study of the divine science. I read

[6] A treatise by the Muslim philosopher al-Fārābī. He died in 950.

the book called *Metaphysics*,[7] but could not understand it, the aim of its author remaining obscure for me. I read the book forty times, until I knew it by heart, but I still could not understand its meaning or its purpose. I despaired of understanding it on my own and said to myself, "There is no way to understand this book." Then one afternoon I happened to be in the market of the booksellers, and a crier was holding a volume in his hand and shouting the price. He offered it to me, and I rejected it impatiently, believing that there was no profit in this science. He persisted and said, "Buy this book from me, it is cheap. I will sell it to you for three dirhams because its owner needs the money." I bought it and found that it was Abu'l-Naṣr al-Fārābī's book, explaining the meaning of the *Metaphysics*.[8] I returned to my house and made haste to read it. Immediately the purposes of this book became clear to me because I already knew it by heart. I was very happy at this, and the next day I gave much alms to the poor in thanksgiving to Almighty God.

The Sultan of Bukhārā at that time was Nūḥ ibn Manṣūr. He was stricken by an illness which baffled the physicians. My name was well-known among them because of the extent of my studies. They mentioned me to the Sultan and asked him to summon me. I appeared before him and joined them in treating him and distinguished myself in his service.

One day I asked his permission to go into their library, look at their books, and read the medical ones. He gave me permission, and I went into a palace of many rooms, each with trunks full of books, back-to-back. In one room there were books on Arabic and poetry, in another books on jurisprudence, and similarly in each room books on a single subject. I read the catalogue of books of the ancients and asked for those I needed. Among these books I saw some the very names of which many people do not know, books which I had never seen before and never saw again.

I therefore read these books, made use of them, and thus knew the rank of every author in his own subject. When I reached

[7] That is, of Aristotle.

[8] A reference to al-Fārābī's *Kitāb al-Ḥurūf*, a commentary on Aristotle's *Metaphysics*.

the age of eighteen, I had completed the study of all these sciences. At that point my memory was better, whereas today my learning is riper. Otherwise, my knowledge is the same and nothing has been added.

In my neighborhood there lived a man called Abu'l-Ḥasan al-'Arūḍī who asked me to write him an encyclopedic work on science. I compiled the *Majmū'* for him and named it after him. In it I dealt with all sciences other than mathematics. I was then twenty-one years old. There was another man in my neighborhood who was called Abū Bakr al-Baraqī and was born in Khwārazm. He was unique in jurisprudence, Qur'ānic exegesis, and asceticism, with an inclination toward these sciences. He asked me to explain books on these sciences for him, and I therefore wrote for him a book called *Al-Ḥāṣil wa'l-Maḥṣūl* in about twenty sections. I also wrote him a book on ethics, which I called *Kitāb al-Birr wa'l-Ithm*. These two books are only to be found with him, since he did not lend them to anyone to make copies.

Then my father died, and my situation was transformed. I had to enter the service of the Sultan, and necessity obliged me to leave Bukhārā and move to Gurganj, where Abu'l-Ḥusayn al-Suhaylī, a lover of these sciences, was the vizier.[9] I was presented to the ruler 'Alī ibn al-Ma'mūn. I was then wearing the costume of a jurist—a hood [*ṭaylasān*] and a chin-flap. They assigned me a monthly salary suited to one such as myself. Then necessity obliged me to move to Fasā, thence to Bāvard, thence to Ṭūs, to Shaqqān, to Samanqān, to Jājarm the frontier of Khurāsān, and thence to Gurgān. My objective was the amir Qābūs,[10] but it happened that at this time Qābūs was captured and imprisoned in a fortress where he died. I therefore went toward Dihistān, where I was taken seriously ill and later returned to Gurgān, where Abū 'Ubayd al-Jūzjānī joined me. I composed an ode on my situation, of which here is a verse:

When I grew great no city could contain me,
When my price rose I lacked a buyer.

Ibn al-Qifṭī, *Ta'rīkh al-ḥukamā'*, pp. 413–417.

[9] A vizier of the Khwārazm-Shah. He died in 1027.
[10] Qābūs ibn Vashmgīr, ruler of Gurgān and Ṭabaristān, died 1012.

58. A Guide for Physicians (Ninth–Tenth Centuries)

1. Since it is the nature of living creatures to seek their sustenance and to concern themselves with those things that maintain their being; so, too, is man, whose image is the image of God, necessarily bound to strive and to concern himself with those things whereby are maintained his being, his existence, and his survival before concerning himself with other knowledge and occupations in which others than he participate, for man is nearest to himself. Therefore, the usefulness of the practice of medicine is very great indeed, and man is always bound and obliged to put it in the forefront of his studies.
2. Since the science of medicine is very vast and the life of man too short to reach its end, therefore expert physicians must be distinguished and separated from the fools. They busy themselves constantly with the study of books and pore over them by night and day, and devote themselves to this above other men who do not join them in this work.[1]
3. Speed or slowness or hesitation in the work of a craftsman depends on the weight or lightness or triviality of that on which he works. He who is engaged in boring crystal must be careful and attentive, lest by haste he mar the beauty of his work. This is not so with one whose work is with the dirt in the street. It therefore befits one whose concern is the healing of human bodies, the noblest of the creations in this world, to consider and examine his patients very meticulously, to do his work and deliberation and care, lest he make mistakes which he cannot remedy. The sage said, "If you see a physician who hastens to answer questions you put to him about an illness and who boasts of his healing, consider him a fool." The Prince of Physicians[2] said, "I have never given a man a purgative without being anxious and

[1] The text of the second half of this paragraph is obscure. The translation is conjectural.

[2] Galen.

lying sleepless four nights before and after administering it."

4. Just as a physician, as I have said, must not be precipitate in his work, so equally he must not be lazy or dilatory, for most illnesses will not wait for him. He should be midway between the extremes, neither hasty and precipitate nor lazy and hesistant. But with acute and urgent diseases he must think and act quickly, for they will press him.
5. If you look into the books of the ancient physicians you will find things there which appear confusing and others which you will find difficult to accept, so that it may occur to you to deny them. You have no right to speak against them or dispute with them in view of the great authority which they enjoy among men. Had you lived in their day, you could have answered them and debated with them on these matters. But now you must busy yourself and seek various interpretations for them, or amend the texts, for often you may consider that these sentences are not as the author meant them, or perhaps even that the author himself was in error, for there is no man that does not err. The books in which this may occur to you most frequently are those composed and compiled without arguments or evidence, in the form of aphorisms, like the books of Hippocrates.
6. The best of physicians is he who occupies himself and reads and studies constantly in the books of the ancient physicians and especially in the books of the Prince of Physicians, Galen, who speaks at great length and deals most thoroughly with the treatment of illnesses. They are wrong who say, "Do not go to a physician but to an empiric." The ignoramus does not know what he is doing, and he kills a thousand before he cures one. If he say, "Rely on me, for I have practical experience," do not listen to him, for life is too short to know a single disease or the nature of a single plant by practical experience. One should therefore busy oneself with the experience of the ancients in the course of millennia, which in the generosity of their hearts and their pity for us they wrote down, preserving their experience for us.
7. If the knowledge and wisdom of a physician were seen and visible on his face and in his appearance, then most men

would not err in recognizing them and in assessing the extent of their knowledge. But most of the common people do not look with discernment, but judge physicians by their talk and chatter and self-praise, by their height and the size of their bellies and the length of their beards. Hence the saying, "The fool looks to the outward appearance, the wise man to the heart."[3]

8. If the physician comes from a far land and speaks in a strange and unintelligible language, the common people think him clever, gather around him, and seek his advice.
9. Because of the sins and transgressions of this profession, every fool and ignoramus joins it and bears its name, and none protests. Yet all its affairs are obscure, profound, and very difficult, even for those who have wisdom and understanding.
10. Most of the ignorant physicians will sometimes be of service to you, for they will ruin and destroy, and you will be called upon to mend what they have marred.
11. The physician does not work the cure. He does but prepare and clear the path for nature, the real healer.
12. In most long illnesses, men lose their judgment and despair of recovery and say that the physician cannot cure them, for cure, to them, means the sudden removal of disease. They do not know that when the humors are numbed or dried, as when the climax is delayed in a quartan fever, then the months or years of that long disease are but as the days of a tertian fever.
13. Since the object of the practice of medicine is the possible and not the necessary, and since death is ordained and inevitable, there can be no physician who is good and praiseworthy in the eyes of all men.
14. Just as you must read all the books written on the practice of medicine, so too must you know the relevant principles of natural science, of which medicine is a branch. You must also be proficient in the methods of logic so that you may be able effectively to refute the fools who pass as physicians, to confound them, and to make them respect you.
15. There is less need of a physician to preserve health than to

[3] Cf. I Samuel, xvi, 7.

remove disease, what though it is better for a man not to be sick than to be sick and recover.[4]

16. A physician should not decide, on the basis of a cure of a patient by another physician, that he is a competent practitioner unless he also applies the other tests that I have mentioned. For in most cases nature cures without a physician.
17. The physician who promises to remove a sickness sins grievously, for he changes the nature of possibility and turns it into a necessity.
18. If you can feed the patient on food similar to his diet when in health, do so. Try also to feed him at his usual mealtimes. By this you will strengthen his nature.
19. Try as far as possible to make the medicines and various potions agreeable to the palate of the patient, for then the limbs will draw them to themselves and benefit from them. For this reason sugar and honey are prescribed and mixed with medicine.
20. The better you know and understand the temperament and characteristics of the patient when he is healthy, and the more you feel his pulse and examine his urine, the more easily will you cure him.
21. If you can carry out your treatment effectively with diet or with healing foods, then do not use drugs, for most of them are enemies and antagonists of nature, especially the purgatives.
22. If a man consults many physicians, then, unless they all visit him at once and reach a joint agreement, he endangers his life. For if each comes alone, the second will try to alter or add to the instructions of the first.
23. Try always in your treatment to use simple drugs, for it is easier for you to know their power than to know that of the compound drugs.
24. Do not despise any cure of which you hear, for often results may be achieved by simple means which you could not accomplish with a multiplicity of prescriptions and medicines.

[4] The text of this sentence is obscure and probably corrupt. The translation is tentative.

25. Do not rely in your treatment on specifics, for most of them are foolishness and superstition.
26. Do not hasten to treat minor ailments by a change of temperament or by evacuation. For most of these nature alone, with a good diet, is sufficient.
27. It is one of the attributes of a physician that he should be satisfied in his own diet with moderate quantities of wholesome foods and that he should be neither a glutton nor a drunkard. It is shameful and disgraceful for him to suffer a long illness, for the common people would say, "If a man cannot heal himself, how can he heal others?"
28. Stop your mouth from uttering prophecies or pronouncing decrees. Let most of your remarks be conditional.
29. Do not let your mouth sin because of what happens to any other physician, for every man has his hour. Let your deeds alone praise you, and do not seek glory in the shame of a colleague.
30. Be most diligent in visiting and healing poor and needy patients, for there is no greater charity than this.
31. Reassure and encourage the patient with the prospect of recovery, even if you are not sure of it, for thus you will strengthen his nature.
32. Do not trust in apothecaries and in makers of compound drugs, for sometimes they give less because of the high price or use old and weakened ingredients and spoil your treatment. Therefore, make sparing use in your treatment of the compound drugs which they sell.
33. There are illnesses which are healed merely by your preventing the patient from pursuing his evil habits. Such patients also ask the physician to do something active. If he does not, they consider it a shortcoming on his part.
34. [Gap in the manuscript].
35. The urine indicates only the state of the liver and the urinal channels and then only if all its conditions are taken into account. The ignoramuses of our time seek to prophesy, without even examining the patient, and to say what illness he has, whether he will live or die, and such other foolishness.
36. It is the prime duty of the physician to come to the patient

during the growth and crisis of the illness but not in the period of rest and recovery. Then people will be pleased with him and praise his work.

37. The physician should avoid devoting himself to the treatment of hopeless diseases, for they cannot be cured or else the patients grow weary of the trouble and expense and then look askance at his treatment.
38. If a patient does not follow your instructions, if his servants and his household do not attend speedily to your orders, and if they do not accord you proper respect, give up the case.
39. Fix your fee with the patient when his illness is at its worst, for when he gets better he will forget what you have done for him.
40. The more you charge for your work and the more costly is your treatment, the more will your work be respected by men. Only those for whom you work for nothing will think lightly of your skill.
41. The physician cannot devote his thoughts and attentions to the treatment of a patient for nothing. His legs will not carry him to the house, and his treatments will be of no avail.
42. Do not visit the patient too often nor sit with him too long unless the treatment of his disease requires it, for it is new faces that give pleasure.
43. Visiting too many illnesses disturbs the judgment of a physician and confuses his actions.
44. Most of the ignorant will seek your advice on how you would treat an illness, so that you should tell them whether the patient will live or die with this disease. Imagining themselves to be clever, they think to themselves that if he is to live, he will not need a physician, while if death is in store for him, the physician cannot avert it. The fools do not realize that when you say that he will live, it is on condition that he gets proper treatment and diet.
45. Most ignorant physicians deal with every illness by bloodletting and purge, even if its cause is emptiness and lack of heat. They tell those who consult them that had their humors remained in the body, they would have stifled them, and

they tell them, in order to frighten and terrify them, that the white mucous on the surface of the blood is pus and that they are full of foulness, and they order further bloodletting until they dry up all their humors. May God return their recompense on their head, may their strength dry up like a potsherd, may their moisture turn into the drought of summer, selah.[5]

46. Be diligent in the treatment of princes and of the great ones among the people, for they will help you with their wealth, will always praise you, and will love you after their recovery. But the low and mean will hate you after their recovery when they remember the fee you took from them, "for as he thinketh in his heart, so is he."[6]

47. It is a widespread custom and a notorious foolishness for men to gather together and come to have their blood let, even if they do not need it. They tell one another that such and such a day is auspicious for bloodletting, and whoever has his blood let on that day will be safeguarded against such and such an illness. So they gather in hundreds in the house of the bloodletter who after letting their blood tells them, in order to be able to exploit them further, that he sees in the blood that they will need a further bloodletting; and the fools return to have their blood let again, until their blood overflows his vessels, and he "sets aside that which is full."[7]

48. There is another foolishness widespread among the common people. They regard themselves as physicians for certain ailments and believe that a man with an internal inflammation must not eat anything, not even very light food, because they think that food stops up the windpipe and prevents the cough. Thus they enfeeble his nature and sap his strength. They also believe that they should not give the patient anything to drink with this sickness. Some of them withhold bread from anyone with a fever. In this very country I have

[5] Cf. Joel, iv, 4; Psalms, xxii, 15, and xxxii, 4.
[6] Proverbs, xxxiii, 7.
[7] II Kings, iv, 4.

seen a case where the physician ordered a clyster for a patient, in order to soften his nature, and then the patient stood up to walk with it, and he fainted and died, and from that day onward all the people of the city avoided using a clyster for any patient because they thought that it was as deadly as a sword, and they made it a law, and no physician may use a clyster there. There are notions about medicine which they regard as true and right, though they are clearly false. Thus they think that young male chicks are colder than females, that vinegar, since it arises from wine, must not be included in the diet of a patient. They also believe that women are hotter than men and that the sneeze is the end of the disease. Because they see that when they go barefoot and get cold out of doors in the cold air, their stomachs are loosened because of the cold and the recoil of the loose matter in the body and bowels, they think that all things cold are aperients according to the degree of their coldness and many other such absurdities.

49. The expert physician has no need to choose times for blood-letting or purging or other treatments. To test [horoscopes][8] is vain and the disease presses.

50. Excessive toil and effort wither the strength of the physician and prevent him from always considering and attending to every patient, hoping for his recovery and praying for him, as he would do for his own "kin that is near to him."[9]

Isaac Israeli, *Sefer Musar Rōf'im.*

59. Musā ibn Maymūn (Twelfth Century)

The Israelite, the Andalusian. This man was one of the people of Andalus, a Jew by religion. He studied philosophy in Andalus, was expert in mathematics, and devoted attention to some of the logical sciences. He studied medicine there and excelled in it. But he lacked courage in action. 'Abd al-Mu'min ibn 'Alī

[8] This appears to be the meaning of this phrase.
[9] Lev., xxi, 2.

al-Kūmī the Berber,[1] who gained possession of the Maghrib, proclaimed in all the lands which he ruled that Jews and Christians were to be expelled from them. He appointed a time limit and stipulated that whoever adopted Islam could remain in his place and continue to earn his livelihood, on the same terms and with the same obligations as the Muslims, but whoever remained in the religion of his community was to leave by the appointed time. If he remained beyond that date under the jurisdiction of the Sultan, then his life and property were forfeit. When this order was put into effect, he whose possessions weighed lightly on him departed, and he whose wealth was great or who was attached to his household and his property remained, making a show of Islam and concealing his unbelief. Mūsā ibn Maymūn was one of those who did this in his country, and he stayed there. And when he showed the outward signs of Islam, he also complied with its details, such as reading the Qur'ān and prayer. He did this until he found an opportunity to travel. After assembling his possessions in the time that was needed for this, he left Andalus and went to Egypt, accompanied by his family. He settled in the town of Fusṭāṭ, among its Jews, and practiced his religion openly. He lived in a district called al-Maṣīṣa and made a living by trading in jewels and suchlike. Some people studied philosophy under him. This was in the last days of the Egyptian 'Alid dynasty.[2] They wanted to employ him with the rest of the physicians and to send him out to the king of the Franks[3] in Ascalon, who had requested a physician of them. They chose him, but he refused to perform this service or become involved in this affair, and so he remained. When the Turks ruled Egypt and the 'Alid dynasty collapsed, the qāḍī al-Fāḍil 'Abd al-Raḥīm ibn 'Alī al Baysānī took him under his protection, favored him, and assigned him a stipend. He went to join the other physicians and did not differ from them in his opinion because of his lack of experience [?]. He was not gentle [?] in healing and treatment.

[1] A Berber chief who succeeded Ibn Tūmart, the first leader of the Almohad reformist movement. He reigned from 1133 to 1163.

[2] The Fatimid Caliphate.

[3] Probably Amalric, king of Jerusalem. He went to Egypt in 1164 and 1167.

He married in Cairo the sister of a Jewish scribe called Abu'l-Ma'ālī, the secretary of the mother of Nūr al-Dīn 'Alī, known as al-Afḍal, the son of Ṣalāḥ al-Dīn Yūsuf ibn Ayyūb, and he had a son by her who today is a physician in Cairo after his father. Abu'l-Ma'ālī married Mūsā's sister, and had several children by her, one of whom is Abu'l-Riḍā, a calm, intelligent physician who attends the family of Qilij Arslan[4] in the land of Rūm.

Mūsā ibn Maymūn died in Cairo in the year 605 [1208–9].[5] He ordered his heirs to carry his body, when the smell had ceased, to Lake Tiberias and bury him there, seeking to be among the graves of the ancient Israelites and their great jurists, which are there. This was done.

He was learned in the law and secrets of the Jews and compiled a commentary on the Talmud, which is a commentary and explanation of the Torah; some of the Jews approve of it. Philosophic doctrines overcame him, and he compiled a treatise denying the canonical resurrection. The leaders of the Jews held this against him, so he concealed it except from those who shared his opinion in this. He compiled an abridgement of twenty-one books of Galen, with many additions, in sixteen books. It came out very abridged and quite useless; nothing can be done with it. He edited the *Kitāb al-Istikmāl* [*Book of Perfection*] of Ibn Aflaḥ al-Andalusī, on astronomy, and improved it, for there was some confusion in the original. He also edited the *Kitāb al-Istikmāl* of Ibn Hūd, on mathematics. This is a fine, comprehensive book, needing some correction. He corrected and improved it and had it read to him.[6]

In the latter part of his life he was troubled by a man from Andalus, a jurist [*faqīh*] called Abu'l-'Arab ibn Ma'īsha, who came to Fusṭāṭ and met him. He charged him with having been a Muslim in Andalus, accused him [of apostasy] and wanted to have him punished.[7] 'Abd al-Raḥīm ibn 'Alī al-Fāḍil

[4] The Seljuqid Sultan of Konya.
[5] In fact he died in 1204.
[6] The normal technique of publication. A disciple wrote the book down from dictation or lectures and then read it to the master, who gave a certificate of approval.
[7] The penalty for apostasy was death.

prevented this, and said to him, "If a man is converted by force, his Islam is not legally valid."

Ibn al-Qifṭī, *Ta'rīkh al-ḥukamā'*, pp. 317–319.

60. A Day in the Life of a Court Physician

I live in Fusṭāṭ, and the king lives in Cairo, and between the two places there is a distance of two Sabbath day's journey [about 1 1/2 miles]. With the king I have a very heavy program. It is impossible for me not to see him first thing every day. If he suffers any indisposition, or if any of his sons or concubines falls sick, I cannot leave Cairo, and I spend most of my day in the palace. It may also happen that one or two of his officers fall sick, and I must attend to them. In short, I go to Cairo early every morning, and if there is no mishap and nothing new, I return to Fusṭāṭ in the afternoon, and certainly not before then. By then I am hungry, and I find the anterooms all filled with people: Gentiles and Jews, great and small, judges and bailiffs, friends and enemies, a mixed multitude, who await the moment of my return. I dismount from my beast and wash my hands and go to them to soothe them and placate them and beg them to excuse me and wait while I eat a quick meal, my only one in the whole day. Then I go out to treat them and write prescriptions and instructions for their illnesses. They come and go without a break until night, and sometimes, I swear by my faith in the Torah, until two hours of the night or more. I talk to them and instruct them and converse with them, lying on my back from exhaustion. By nightfall I am so worn out that I cannot speak. In fine, no Jew can speak to me or keep company with me or have private conversation with me except on the Sabbath. Then all or most of the congregation come to me after prayers, and I instruct the community on what they should do throughout the week, and they read for a while until noon, and then they go their way; some of them return and read again between the afternoon and evening prayers.

This is how I spend the day.

Moses ben Maimon, Letter to Samuel ibn Tibbon,
Qōveṣ teshūvōt ha-Rambam ve-Igrōtav, iii, p. 28.

6 Race, Creed, and Condition of Servitude

8
Social Principles

In principle the Islamic Caliphate was a theocracy, a single universal state of which God was the ultimate sovereign and in which all Muslims were brothers. In fact, of course, it was an empire created by conquest, in which before long the inevitable inequalities between conquerors and conquered appeared. The conquerors were Muslims; they were also—and primarily—Arabs and showed a normal human unwillingness to concede equality to aliens and inferiors, even when these adopted the dominant faith and thus claimed membership of the ruling community. At first, Arab and Muslim were almost synonymous terms, to the point that non-Arab converts became adoptive members of the Arab tribes. These converts were known as mawālī *(singular* mawlā*), a word combining the notions of freedman and client and thus indicating the light in which they were regarded. Growing both in numbers and in self-confidence, the* mawālī *played an increasing role in the life of the Islamic Empire, and their ultimately successful struggle for equal status is a major theme of early Islamic history. A parallel theme, at first of even greater importance, was the rise of the half-breeds—those whose fathers were Arabs but whose mothers were slave-women taken from among the conquered peoples. These, too, were for a while subject to disabilities and were not admitted to equality with the full-blooded Arab conquistadores.*

Many of the subject peoples were in due course assimilated and became part of Arabic-speaking Islam. Others, notably the Persians, preserved a strong sense of separate identity and in time created a new culture of their own within Islam. The advent and Islamization of the Turks added the third major component of Islamic civilization in the Middle East.

All these groups were Muslims and could claim the equal status accorded to them by the Islamic dispensation. The position of non-Muslims was quite different. For polytheists, idolators, and free-thinkers there could be no tolerance, and the law gave them the choice between Islam and the sword. For followers of what Islam recognized as revealed religions, that is, chiefly, Jews and Christians, there was a third choice, the dhimma. *This was a kind of covenant whereby, in return for the acceptance of certain restrictions and disabilities and the payment of certain additional taxes, the non-Muslim communities were accorded religious and personal security and a large measure of autonomy in the conduct of their communal affairs.*

One other important group was subject to legal and social disabilities—the slaves. Medieval Islam never developed a slave-based economy like that of the Roman Empire. It did, however, import and employ vast numbers of slaves, sometimes for economic use, more commonly for either military or domestic purposes. Their status was elaborately regulated by the Holy Law.

Some extracts from the Qur'ān, from the hadīth, *and from a geographical writer may serve to illustrate the notions current in early Islam on these problems.*

61. From the Qur'ān

Among God's signs are the creation of the heavens and of the earth and the diversity of your languages and of your colors. In this, indeed, are signs for those who know.

xxx, 21/22.

We have revealed to you an Arabic scripture [*Qur'ān*],[1] so that you may warn the Mother of Cities[2] and those around

[1] Literally a reading, from *qara'*, to read (or read aloud). Cf. the Hebrew *miqrā*, a term for the Pentateuch.

[2] *Umm al-qurā*, usually taken to mean Mecca. The expression would appear to be a translation of the Greek *metropolis*, mother-city.

her, and give warning of the Day of Reunion, of which there is no doubt, a party in Paradise and a party in Hellfire.

If God had wished, he would have made them all one community [*umma*], but He causes those whom He pleases to enter into His mercy, while the unjust have no patron and no helper.

xlii, 5–6/7–8.

We have created you from a male and a female, and We have made you into peoples and tribes so that you may come to know one another. The noblest among you in the eyes of God is the most pious, for God is omniscient and well-informed.

xlix, 13.

Fight against those who do not believe in God or in the Last Day, who do not forbid what God and His Prophet have forbidden or practice the true religion, among those who have been given the Book,[3] until they pay the *jizya* from their hand, they being humbled.[4]

ix, 29.

62. Sayings Ascribed to the Prophet

Love the Arabs and desire their survival, for their survival is a light in Islam, and their passing is a darkness in Islam.

Those who revile the Arabs are polytheists.

Love the Arabs for three reasons: because I am an Arab, because the Qur'ān is in Arabic, and because the inhabitants of Paradise speak Arabic.

If the Arabs are humbled, Islam is humbled.

To love the Arabs is faith; to hate them is unbelief. Who loves the Arabs loves me; who hates the Arabs hates me.

[3] That is, those possessing a revealed religion.
[4] This passage has been variously explained. The above is the most generally accepted interpretation.

O people! The Lord is one Lord; the father is one father; the religion is one religion. Arabic is neither father nor mother to any of you, but is a language. Whoever speaks Arabic is an Arab.

O Arabs! Give praise to God who relieved you of tithes.

There are seventy parts of wickedness. The Berbers have sixty-nine, and mankind and the Jinns have one.

The best of mankind are the Arabs; the best of the Arabs are Quraysh; the best of Quraysh are the Banū Hāshim. The best of the non-Arabs are the Persians; the best of the blacks are the Nubians; the best of pigments is safflower; the best of property is real estate; and the best of dyes is henna.

If God intends something gentle, He reveals it to the ministering angels in courtly Persian; if He intends something severe, He reveals it in clarion Arabic.

The people with the greatest share in Islam are the Persians.

If faith were hung on the Pleiades, the Arabs would not reach it, but the men of Persia would.

If knowledge were in the Pleiades, the men of Persia would reach it.

Who speaks Persian gains in love and loses in manhood.

When Persians adopt Islam, they become members of Quraysh and are our brothers and our kin.

The ruin of the Arabs will come when the sons of the daughters of Persia grow up.

May God curse both lots of foreigners, the Persians and the Byzantines [Rūm].

I see nations that are dragged to heaven in chains.

al-Muttaqī, *Kanz al-'Ummāl,* vi, pp. 66, 203–204, 207, 214–215.

Leave the Ethiopians alone as long as they leave you alone, and keep away from the Turks as long as they keep away from you.

The Prophet said, when his finger was bandaged because of a scorpion bite: You say that there is no enemy. But you will go on fighting against enemies until you fight Gog and Magog, who are the people with broad faces, small eyes, and reddish hair. They will multiply on every side, and their faces are like hammered shields.

Al-Muttaqī, *Kanz al-'Ummāl,* vii, p. 204.

When the Prophet was speaking of the conditions of the Last Hour and the Troubles at the end of Time and the coming of the Oghuz Turks, he said: Learn the language of the Turks, for their dominion will be long.

I have an army whom I called Turks and settled in the East. When I am angry with a people, I set the Turks in authority over them.

Al-Kāshgharī, *Dīwān Lughāt al-Turk,* i, pp. 293–294.

Do not marry women for their beauty, which may destroy them, nor for their money, which may corrupt them, but for religion. A slit-nosed black slavewoman, if pious, is preferable.

Ibn Māja, *Sunan,* i, p. 597.

Marry like with like and match like with like. Choose carefully for your offspring, and beware of the Zanjī, for he is a distorted creature.

Arabs are the equals of Arabs [in marriageability], and *mawālī* are the equal of *mawālī,* except for weavers and cuppers.

O *mawālī!* The wrongdoers among you are those who intermarry with Arabs. O Arabs! The wrongdoers among you are those who intermarry with *mawālī.*

Al-Muttaqī, *Kanz al-'Ummāl,* viii, pp. 24–28.

When captives were brought, the Prophet, may God bless and save him, used to allocate a family together, not wishing to separate them.

The Prophet of God, may God bless and save him, cursed anyone who separated a mother and her child, a brother and his brother.

A slave came to the Prophet and swore allegiance to him for the Hijra, and the Prophet, may God bless and save him, did not know that he was a slave. Then his master came looking for him, and the Prophet said, "Sell him to me," and he bought him for two black slaves. Thereafter he accepted no man's allegiance without first asking him whether he was a slave.

Ibn Māja, *Sunan,* ii, pp. 755, 756, 958.

63. The Classes of Mankind (ca. 902–903)

Al-Faḍl ibn Yaḥyā said, "Men are divided into four classes: kings, raised up by their right to rule; viziers, distinguished by understanding and judgment; upper classes, raised up by affluence; and middle classes, linked with them by education. The rest of mankind are vanishing scum,[1] floating refuse, vile men and women bound to meanness, whose only concern is to eat and to sleep."

Ibn al-Faqīh, p. 1.

[1] Cf. Qur'ān, xiii, 18.

9
Ethnic Groups

The following extracts illustrate Arab and other ethnic attitudes, the resurgence of Persian pride and self-awareness, and the Turkish sense of imperial mission.

64. Al-Ma'mūn and the Arabs (Early Ninth Century)

A man came to al-Ma'mūn in Syria several times and said to him, "O Commander of the Faithful, look upon the Arabs of Syria as you look upon the Persians of Khurāsān!" Al-Ma'mūn replied, "You ask too much, O brother of the people of Syria. By God, I cannot dismount a Qaysī from his horse without finding that not a single dirham remains in my treasury. As for Yemen, by God, I do not like them, and they have never liked me. As for Quḍā'a, their leaders await the Sufyānī and his rebellion so as to join his supporters. As for Rabī'a, they have a grudge against God for sending His Prophet from Muḍar; of any two of them, one is a Kharijite rebel. Let me be, may God strike you!"

Al-Ṭabarī, iii, p. 1142.

65. Arabs, Non-Arabs, and Freedmen (Early Ninth Century)

This is the point which the non-Arabs have reached with the doctrine of the Shu'ūbiyya,[1] as also the *mawālī* with their

[1] A faction of non-Arab Muslims, mostly Persian, who protested against Arab privilege and superiority in the Islamic Empire and claimed that the non-Arab Muslims were at least the equals of the Arabs. See *EI*[1], s.v.

boast of superiority over both the Arabs and the non-Arabs. A new school had arisen among these *mawālī*, a new group of upstarts emerged, who claim that the *mawlā*, by virtue of his clientage [*walā'*], has become an Arab, since the Prophet, may God bless and save him, said, "The *mawlā* of a tribe belongs to it," and "Clientage is a form of kinship like descent. It can be neither sold nor given."

We know that when Kingdom and Prophethood belonged to the non-Arabs, they were nobler than the Arabs. When God transferred these to the Arabs, they in turn became nobler than the non-Arabs.

They say, "We *mawālī*, as non-Arabs in the past, are nobler than the Arabs, and as Arabs in the present we are nobler than the non-Arabs. The non-Arabs have a past but no present, the Arabs have a present but no past, while we have both, and he who has two qualities is better than he who has only one. God turned the *mawlā* from a non-Arab into an Arab by clientage, as He made the Arab ally of Quraysh a Qurayshī by alliance[2] and made Ismā'īl[3] an Arab from a non-Arab. Had not the Prophet, may God bless and save him, said that Ismā'īl was an Arab, we could not regard him as anything but a non-Arab, because the non-Arab cannot become an Arab, as the Arab cannot become a non-Arab, and we know that God made Ismā'īl an Arab after he had been a non-Arab because the Prophet, may God bless and save him, said so. The same applies to his sayings, 'The *mawlā* of a tribe belong to it,' and 'Clientage is a form of kinship.' "

They also say: God made Abraham, peace be upon him, the father of men whom he did not engender as well as of those whom he did engender. He made the wives of the Prophet the mothers of the believers, though they had no children, and made the guardian the father of someone whom he did not engender. They said many other things, which we cited in their proper place.

Nothing is more conducive to evil and corruption than boast-

[2] On the Arabian practice of alliance see *EI*², "Ḥilf."

[3] The Biblical Ishmael. On his role in Muslim scripture and tradition, see *EI*², "Ismā'īl."

ing matches, and all but a few of mankind are boasters. What can be more galling than that your slave should claim to be nobler than you are, while admitting that he became noble because you freed him?

Al-Jāḥiẓ, *Rasā'il* (1933), pp. 299–300.

66. The Shu'ūbiyya (Ninth–Tenth Centuries)

One of the arguments of the Shu'ūbiyya against the Arabs was as follows: We went toward justice and equalization, and all men came from one substance and from the seed of one man, and we adduce the words of the Apostle of God (upon him blessings and peace) who said, "The believers are brothers and their blood is equal, and the least of them can conclude a *dhimma* for them, and they are one body as against all others." And he also said during the farewell pilgrimage, in the sermon in which he bade farewell to his community and put the seal on his prophetic mission, "O people! God has removed from you the pride of the age of ignorance [*jāhiliyya*] and its boasting of ancestry. All of you are from Adam, and Adam was of clay. The Arab has no advantage over the non-Arab, save only through piety." This saying of the Prophet (upon him blessings and peace) accords with the words of Almighty God, "The noblest among you before God are the most pious" (Qur'ān, xlix, 13]. But you have persisted in your boasting and you say, "They are not equal to us, even if they preceded us in Islam and even if they prayed until they are bent like bows and fasted until they are like bowstrings."

We forgive and consent that you boast about your ancestors, although your Prophet (may God bless and save him), has forbidden you to do so, if you persist, but we answer you, following the Prophet's utterance and command, and we rebut the argument you use in boasting against us, and we say: Tell us how you answer what the non-Arabs say to you. Do you reckon pride of ancestry to lie entirely in kingship and prophethood? If you claim that it is kingship, the non-Arabs say to you: Ours are the kings of all the earth, the Pharaohs, the Nimrods, the Amalekites, the Chosroes, and the Caesars! Can anyone have kingship like that of Solomon, who ruled over mankind and the Jinns and the birds and the winds, and he was one of us! Or has anyone had kingship like that of Alexander, who ruled over all the world and reached to the places where the sun rises and sets and built a rampart of iron joining two peaks and imprisoned behind it a multitude of people more numerous than all the people in the world. Almighty God said, "Until Gog and Magog are conquered, and they slide down every slope" [Qur'ān xxi, 96]. There is nothing more indicative of their numbers than this, and none of the children of Adam has left monuments like his in the world. If he had no other monument than the lighthouse of Alexandria, which he founded on the bed of the sea and put a mirror on top of it in which the whole sea is reflected, it would have sufficed! Ours, too, are the kings of India, one of whom wrote to 'Umar ibn 'Abd al-'Azīz as follows:

> From the king of kings, who is the son of a thousand kings, and whose wife is the daughter of a thousand kings, and in whose stables are a thousand elephants, and who has two rivers which produce aloes and madder and walnuts and camphor whose fragrance reaches twelve miles, to the king of the Arabs, who does not assign any partners to God, as follows: I wish you to send me a man to teach me Islam and acquaint me with its rules. Farewell.

If, on the other hand, you claim that pride of ancestry rests only on prophethood, then all the prophets and apostles from Adam onward are ours, save only four, Hūd, Ṣāliḥ, Ismā'īl, and Muḥammad. Ours are the two chosen ones in the world, Adam and Noah, who are the two original stocks from which all mankind derive. We are thus the roots and you are the branches—indeed, you are but one of our twigs.

Say what you please after this, and make your claims. The fact remains that non-Arab nations in every part of the world have kings who unite them, cities which gather them, laws which they obey, philosophy which they produce, and wonders which they devise by way of tools and crafts, such as the making of brocade, which is the most wonderful of handicrafts, or chess, which is the noblest of games, or the steelyard, which can weigh one *raṭl* or a hundred *raṭls*, or like the natural philosophy of the Greeks, with the armillary sphere, the astronomical table, and the astrolabe with which the positions of the stars can be determined and knowledge of distances and the revolutions of the heavenly spheres and the science of eclipses can be attained.

The Arabs, on the other hand, never had a king who could unite their main part, draw in their outlying parts, subdue their wrong-doers, and control their fools. They achieved nothing at all in the arts and crafts and made no mark in philosophy. Their only achievement is in poetry, and this is shared by the non-Arabs. The Greeks indeed have remarkable poetry, with proper meter and scansion. Of what then can the Arabs boast against the non-Arabs? They are like ravening wolves and pouncing wild beasts, eating one another and attacking another. Their men are bound in shackles, and their women are carried off captive, slung across the cruppers of camels. If they manage to utter a cry for help, they are not rescued till evening, by which time they have been trampled[1] like a paved road. . . .

The Arabs in the time of ignorance used to take each other's women in their raids, without ceremony of marriage or concern for *istibrā'*,[2] so how can any of them know who is his father?

Those with a strong feeling of loyalty among the Arabs reply: Even if we had done nothing for our *mawlā* but enfranchise him and conferred no other benefaction on him than to rescue him from unbelief and remove him from the house of polytheism to the house of the true faith, it would have been much. As it says in the tradition, "They are people who are dragged to their share of bliss in iron collars," and also, "God himself marvels at people who are led to Paradise in chains."

And that is not all. We have risked our lives for them, and who confers a greater boon on you than he who suffers death for your sake? God commanded us to fight you and enjoined

[1] A euphemism for sexual intercourse.

[2] The investigation required by law to ascertain whether the womb of a newly acquired slave-woman is empty. Her acquirer may not cohabit with her until this is established. See *EI*[2], s.v.

us to wage holy war against you and inclined us to allow you to buy your freedom.

Nāfi' ibn Jubayr ibn Muṭ'im gave precedence to a *mawlā* to lead him in prayer. People spoke to him about this, and he said, "I wished to be humble before God in praying behind him."

The same Nāfi' ibn Jubayr, when a funeral passed by, used to ask who it was. If they said, "A Qurashī," he would say, "Alas for his kinsfolk!" If they said, "An Arab," he would say, "Alas for his countrymen!" If they said, "A *mawlā*, he would say, "He is the property of God, Who takes what He pleases and leaves what He pleases."

They used to say that only three things interrupt prayer: a donkey, a dog, and a *mawlā*. The *mawālī* did not use the *kunya* but were addressed only by their personal names and bynames. People did not walk side by side with them, nor allow them precedence in processions. If they were present at a meal, they stood while the others sat, and if a *mawlā*, because of his age, his merit, his learning, was given food, he was seated at the end of the table, lest anyone should fail to see that he was not an Arab. They did not allow a *mawlā* to pray at funerals if an Arab was present, even if the only Arab present was an inexperienced youth. The suitor for a *mawlā* woman did not address himself to her father or brother, but to her patron, who gave her in marriage or refused, as he pleased. If her father or brother gave her in marriage without the patron's approval, the marriage was invalid and, if consummated, was fornication, not wedlock.

Ziyād said: Mu'āwiya called al-Aḥnaf ibn Qays and Samura ibn Jundub and said to them, "I have seen these red[3] people grow numerous, and I see that they have begun to revile the early Muslim leaders, and I foresee that they will attack the Arabs and try to seize power. I think that I shall kill part of them and leave part of them to supply the markets and maintain the roads. What do you think?"

Al-Aḥnaf said, "I don't think I like it. These people are my half-

[3] A term frequently applied to the Persians, sometimes also to other non-Arabs.

brother, my mother's brother, my *mawlā*, they and we have ancestors in common. I would rather be killed myself defending them!" And he bowed his head in silence.

Samura ibn Jundub said, "Leave them to me, O Commander, and I will deal with them and finish the business." Mu'āwiya said, "Go now, while I look into this matter." Al-Aḥnaf said, "We left him, and I was afraid and went home to my people feeling sad, but next day he sent me a message, and I learned that he had adopted my opinion and rejected Samura's opinion."

It is related that 'Āmir ibn 'Abd al-Qays, known for his piety, asceticism, austerity, and humility, was addressed in the presence of 'Abdallāh ibn 'Āmir the governor of Iraq, by Ḥumrān, the *mawlā* of the Caliph 'Uthmān ibn 'Affān. Ḥumrān accused 'Āmir of reviling and abusing the Caliph. 'Āmir denied this, and Ḥumrān said to him, "May God not multiply your kind among us!" To this 'Āmir replied, "But may God multiply your kind among us!"

'Āmir was asked, "Does he curse you and do you bless him?" "Yes," he replied, "for they sweep our roads, sew our boots, and weave our clothes!"

'Abdallāh ibn 'Āmir, who was leaning, sat bolt upright and said, "I didn't think that you, with your virtue and your asceticism, knew about these things." To which 'Āmir replied, "I know more than you think I know."

They said that when Umayya ibn Khālid b. 'Abdallāh sent his brother 'Abd al-'Azīz to fight the Azraqīs, they defeated him and killed his friend Muqātil ibn Misma' and captured his wife Umm Ḥafṣ the daughter of al-Mundhir ibn al-Jārūd of the tribe of 'Abd al-Qays. They set her up in the market, unveiled and with her charms exposed, and they inspected her and looked her over. She was one of the most perfect and beautiful of beings. The Arabs and the *mawālī* were bidding against one another, and the Arabs raised the bidding out of ethnic loyalty [*'aṣabiyya*] and the *mawālī* raised the bidding out of clientage [*walā'*] until the Arabs brought it to 20,000. The bidding continued until the price reached 90,000. Then a Khārijī Arab of the tribe of 'Abd al-Qays came up behind her and struck off her head with his sword. They seized him and brought him before Qaṭarrī ibn al-Fujā'a, and said, "O Commander of the Faithful, this man has destroyed treasury property to the value of 90,000 and has killed a slave-girl belonging to the believers." Qaṭarrī asked the man, "What do you say?," He replied, "O Commander of the Faithful, I saw these Arabs and Persians quarreling about her, until voices were raised and eyes became bloodshot and it only remained to clash swords. I thought that 90,000 was a trifle by the side of the discord between Muslims which I feared."

Qaṭarrī said, "Let him go! One of God's eyes has marked her." They said, "Allow talion against him!" and Qaṭarrī answered, "I shall not allow talion against one whom God incited."

Later this man of 'Abd al-Qays went to Basra, where he called on al-Nu'man ibn al-Jārūd to ask for a reward for his action. He gave him one and treated him generously.

Ibn 'Abd Rabbih *Al-'Iqd al-Farīd*,
iii, pp. 317–319, 325, 326–328.

67. A Persian Rebel (Ninth Century)

I am the son of noblemen of the line of Jam[1]
and heir to the inheritance of the Persian kings.
I revive their glory which had faded
and was effaced by the length of time.
I claim their vengeance before the world,
though others may sleep, heedless of their rights, I do not sleep.
Men are concerned with their pleasures,
but my concern is to pursue my purposes,
To that which is of high import,
vast scope, and exalted nature.
I hope Almighty God will grant
I reach my goal through the best of men.
With me is the banner of Kaviyan[2]

[1] Jam or Jamshid, the mythical founder of the line of kings of Iran.

[2] The imperial standard of the Sasanids, the last Iranian dynasty before the Arab conquest.

by which I hope to prevail over the nations.
Say to the sons of Hāshim, all of them:
Make haste to abdicate, before you are sorry!
We have mastered you by force,
with the thrust of lances and the blows of sharp swords.
Our fathers gave you kingship,
but you have shown no gratitude for their bounty.
Go back to your own country in the Ḥijāz
to eat lizards and tend sheep
While I shall ascend the throne of kings
by the edge of the sword and the point of the pen.

Ibrāhīm ibn Mamshādh, in Yāqūt,
Irshād, i, pp. 322–323.

68. Persian Pride (Eleventh Century)

My people made fate their henchman
and strode across the peaks of epochs.
They swathed their heads with the sun
and built their houses with the stars.
My forebear was Chosroes, of the towering palace—
who among men has a forebear like mine?
The ancient power of royalty is mine,
even above the honor of Islam and of culture.
I drew glory from the best of forebears
and religion from the best of Prophets.
I based my pride on both sides,
the majesty of the Persians and the religion of the Arabs.

Mihyār al-Daylamī, *Dīwān,* i, p. 64.

69. The Empire of the Turks (Eleventh Century)

I have seen that God caused the sun of empire to rise in the mansions of the Turks, and turned the heavenly spheres around their dominion, and named them Turk, and gave them sovereignty, and made them kings of the age, and placed the reins of the people of this time in their hands, and ordained them over mankind, and sustained them in the right, and strengthened those who join them and strive for them and attain fulfilment through them and are saved from the ignominy of the vile and lowly. It is incumbent on every man of sense to rally to them so as to safeguard himself from their arrows, and there is no better way to approach them than by speaking their language.

Al-Kāshgharī, *Dīwān lughāt al-Turk*, p. 2.

70. Abū Ḥanīfa and the Turks (Early Thirteenth Century)

My mother's father, Muḥammad ibn 'Alī ibn Aḥmad al-Rāwandī, related of the great Imam, the greatest of qāḍīs, Ẓahīr al-Dīn al-Astarābādī, may God have mercy on him, that he said: I heard through a chain of trustworthy authorities that when the great Imam Abū Ḥanīfa of Kūfa, may God be pleased with him, was on his final pilgrimage, he grasped the ring of the Ka'ba and said, "O God, if my reasoning [*ijtihād*] is correct and my doctrine [*madhhab*] is true, give it help. For I have established the Holy Law for Thy sake, O God!"

A ghostly voice replied from the Ka'ba, "You have spoken truth, and your doctrine will remain as long as the sword is in the hand of the Turks."

God be praised, the support of Islam is strong, the followers of Abū Ḥanīfa are happy and of good cheer and clear-eyed. In the lands of the Arabs, the Persians, the Romans, and the Russians, the sword is in the hands of the Turks and the fear of their swords is rooted in men's hearts. The Sultans of the line of Seljuq, may God have mercy on those of them who are passed and prolong the lives of those who are living, have so fostered scholars of the school of Abū Ḥanīfa that the marks of their affection are on the hearts of everyone, young and old.

Al-Rāwandī, *Rāḥat al-Ṣudūr*, pp. 17–18.

10
Black and White

The Arab expansion in Africa and the growth of the slave trade brought large numbers of black Africans into the Middle East, and a new sense of color differences developed. The first of the following three excerpts asserts the superiority of the Middle Eastern complexion over the excessive whiteness and blackness of the northern and southern peoples; the second presents a common explanation of why blacks are black; the third offers a defense, at least partly satirical, of the blacks against their detractors.

71. Black, White, and Brown (ca. 902–903)

A man of discernment said: The people of Iraq have sound minds, commendable passions, balanced natures, and high proficiency in every art, together with well-proportioned limbs, well-compounded humors, and a pale brown color, which is the most apt and proper color. They are the ones who are done to a turn in the womb. They do not come out with something between blond, buff, blanched, and leprous coloring, such as the infants dropped from the wombs of the women of the Slavs and others of similar light complexion; nor are they overdone in the womb until they are burned, so that the child comes out something between black, murky, malodorous, stinking, and crinkly-haired, with uneven limbs, deficient minds, and depraved passions, such as the Zanj, the Ethiopians, and other blacks who resemble them. The Iraqis are neither half-baked dough nor burned crust, but between the two.

Ibn al-Faqih, p. 162.

72. The Curse of Ḥām (Ninth Century)

Wahb ibn Munabbih said: Ḥām the son of Noah was a white man, with a handsome face and a fine figure, and Almighty God changed his color and the color of his descendants in response to his father's curse. He went away, followed by his sons, and they settled by the shore, where God increased and multiplied them. They are the blacks. Their food was fish, and they sharpened their teeth like needles, as the fish stuck to them. Some of his children went to the West [Maghrib]. Ḥām begat Kūsh ibn Ḥām, Kan'ān ibn Ḥām, and Fūṭ ibn Ḥām. Fūṭ settled in India and Sind and their inhabitants are his descendants. Kūsh and Kan'ān's descendants are the various races of blacks: Nubians, Zanj, Qarān, Zaghāwa, Ethiopians, Copts, and Berbers.

Ibn Qutayba, *Kitāb Al-Ma'ārif*, p. 26.

73. In Defense of the Blacks against the Whites (Ninth Century)

They [the blacks] say: Men are agreed that there is no people on earth among whom generosity is more general and more frequent than the Zanj, and these two qualities [that is, courage and generosity] are only found among those who are noble.

They are the aptest of creatures for measured, rhythmic dancing, for beating the drum to a regular rhythm, and this without training or instruction.

No people on earth has better voices than they, nor is there any language on earth that is lighter to the tongue than theirs, nor is there any race on earth more nimble of tongue or less addicted to dragging their words.

There is no people on earth among whom you do not find stammerers and stutterers, save them. One of them can hold forth in the presence of the king of the Zanj from sunrise till sunset and has no need of gesture or pause until he finishes what he has to say.

There is no people on earth among whom bodily strength or vigor are more general than they. One man can lift a heavy stone which a whole group of Arabs or others could not. They are brave, physically strong, and generous. These are honorable qualities.

With his fine character and inoffensiveness, you never see the Zanjī other than cheerful, laughing, and trustful, and this is honorable.

People say that they are generous because of their weakness of mind, their lack of discernment, their ignorance of consequences. We answer them: This is poor commendation that you give to generosity and unselfishness! By this reasoning those who have the greatest wisdom and the widest knowledge should be the meanest of men and the least inclined to do good. Yet we see that the Slavs are meaner than the Greeks, who are superior to them in discernment and intelligence, while according to your reasoning the Slavs ought to be more generous and more liberal. Likewise, we see that women have less sense than men and children have less sense than women, but are meaner than they are. If more sense meant greater meanness, then the child should be the most generous of all. Yet, in fact, we know nothing on earth that is worse than a boy, for he is the most untruthful of mankind, the most calumnious, the nastiest, and the meanest, the least inclined to do good, and the most ruthless. Only gradually does the boy leave these qualities as he gains in sense and gains in good deeds.

How then can the lack of sense be the cause of generosity in the Zanj? You have admitted that they are generous, and then you make assertions which are untenable, and we have already shown you the fallacy of your argument according to true reasoning. This opinion would mean that the coward is wiser than the brave man, the treacherous wiser than the loyal, and that the worrier is wiser than the patient man. This is something for which you have no proof. These qualities in men are a gift of God. Sense is a gift, and good character is a gift, and generosity and courage likewise.

The Zanj say to the Arabs: It is part of your ignorance that in the time of heathendom you regarded us as good enough to marry your women, yet when the justice of Islam came, you considered this no longer valid, and you found us distasteful, though the desert was full of our people who married your women, who were rulers and leaders, who defended your honor and saved you from your enemies . . .

. . . .

They said: The Prophet, may God bless and save him said: I was sent to the red and the black.

Now you know that the Zanj, the Ethiopians, and the Nubians are not called white or red and that they have no name but black. We also know that God, may He be glorified and exalted, sent His Prophet to all mankind, to both the Arabs and the non-Arabs. Since the Prophet said that he was sent to the red and the black, and since we are neither red nor white, it follows that he was sent to us, and that by black he meant only us. These two names embrace all mankind. If the Arabs count as red, then they come together with the Greeks, Slavs, Persians, and Khurāsānīs; if they count as black, then they derived this name from our name and are called black, though they are tawny and brown, and are included with us, as the Arabs in their grammar use the masculine to cover both masculine and feminine.

Since the Prophet, may God bless and save him, was aware that the Zanj, the Ethiopians, and the Nubians are neither red nor white, but black and since God, may He be exalted, sent him to the "black and the red," it follows that He made us and the Arabs equal.

. . . .

They say: You have never seen the genuine Zanj. You have only seen captives who came from the coasts and forests and valleys of Qanbuluh, from our menials, our lower orders, and our slaves. The people of Qanbaluh have neither beauty nor intelligence. (Qanbaluh is the name of the place by which your ships anchor.) The Zanj are of two kinds, Qanbaluh and Lanjuya, just as the Arabs are of two kinds, Qaḥṭān and ʿAdnān. You have never seen any of the people of Lanjuya, neither from the coast nor from the interior, and if you saw them you would forget beauty and perfection.

If you say: "How is it that we have never seen a Zanjī who had the intelligence even of a child or of a woman?" we would answer you, "When you have seen, among the captives from Sind and India, people of intelligence and knowledge, education and character, that you expect these qualities in the Zanj who fall into your hands? Yet you know how much there is in India of mathematics, astronomy, medical science, turnery and woodwork, painting, and many other wonderful crafts. How does it happen that among the many Indian captives you have made there has never been one of this quality, or even a tenth of this quality?"

If you say, "People of standing, intelligence and knowledge only live in the center, near the seat of government; these are hangers-on, uncouth types, peasants, people of the coasts and swamps and forests and islands, plowmen and fishermen," we answer you, "The same is true of those whom you see and those you do not see of us. Our answer to you is as your answer to us."

They say: If a Zanjī and a Zanjī woman marry and their children remain after puberty in Iraq, they come to rule the roost thanks to their numbers, endurance, knowledge, and efficiency. On the other hand, the child of an Indian and an Indian woman, or of a Greek and a Greek woman, or of a Khurāsānī and a Khurāsānī woman remain among you and in your country in the same condition as their fathers and mothers. The child of two Zanjī parents does not remain thus after puberty, so that we do not find, among ten thousand, one who does what we said, except when a Zanjī mates with a non-Zanjī woman or a Zanjī woman with a non-Zanjī man. Were it not for the fact that neither the Zanjī man nor the Zanjī woman has much desire for people of other races, we would see an abundant progeny for Zanjī men, while Zanjī women hardly respond to non-Zanjī men.

They say: Likewise, you whites are not very active in seeking progeny from Zanjī women, and the Zanjī woman falls pregnant more swiftly to a Zanjī than to a white man.

They say: It hardly ever happens among you that a man

has a hundred children sprung from his loins, unless it is a Caliph, and then it is because of the large number of his women. You don't find this among the rest of you. Among the Zanj so large a progeny would not be considered remarkable, for there are many such in their country. A Zanjī woman bears about fifty times in about fifty years, each birth being twins, so that there are more than ninety. For it is said that women do not bear children when they reach sixty, except for what is told of the women of Quraysh in particular.

The Zanj are the most eager of all God's creatures for their women, and so also their women for them. They are also better than other women.

. . . .

They say: If white men look on black women without desire, so too do black men look on white women without desire, for passions are habits and mostly convention. Thus, for the people of Basra, the most desirable women are Indians, the daughters of Indian women and Ghūrīs; for the Yemenīs the most desirable women are Ethiopians and the daughters of Ethiopian women; for the Syrians the most desirable women are Greeks and the daughters of Greek women. Each people has a taste for the women whom they import as slaves and captives, apart from the exceptions, and no inferences can be drawn from exceptions.

. . . .

They say: The blacks are more numerous than the whites. The whites at most consist of the people of Persia, Jibāl, and Khurāsān, the Greeks, Slavs, Franks, and Avars, and some few others, not very numerous; the blacks include the Zanj, Ethiopians, the people of Fazzān, the Berbers, Copts, and Nubians, the people of Zaghāwa, Marw, Sind and India, Qamār and Dabīlā, China, and Māṣīn. There is more sea than land, and the islands of the sea between China and Africa are full of blacks, such as Ceylon, Kalah, Amal, Zābij, and their islands as far as India, China, Kābul, and those shores.

They say: Al-Ishtiyām the blind man used to say: There

are more blacks than whites, more rocks than mud, more sand than soil, more saltwater than sweet water.

They say: The Arabs belong with us and not with the whites, because their color is nearer to ours. The Indians are more bronzed than the Arabs, and they belong to the blacks. For the Prophet, God bless and save him, said, "I was sent to the red and the black," and everyone knows that the Arabs are not red, as we have already stated above.

He said: This advantage belongs to us and to the Arabs, as against the whites, if the Arabs want it. If they do not want it, then the advantage is ours alone against all the rest.

. . . .

To those who despise the color black, we would reply that the excessively lanky, thin, and reddish hair of the Franks, Greeks, and Slavs, the redness of their locks and beards, the whiteness of their eyebrows and eyelashes, are uglier and more loathsome. There are no albinos among blacks, but only among you.

. . . .

They say: We have knowledge of philosophy and theory; we are the cleverest of people and have reasons for blackness [?]. We say: God, may he be exalted, did not make us black to disfigure us, but the land did this to us. The proof of this is that there are black tribes among the Arabs, such as the Banū Sulaym ibn Manṣūr, and all who settle in the hot country, besides the Banū Sulaym, are all black. They have slaves to pasture and water their flocks, and as menials and servants from the Spaniards [?], and their women are Greeks, and in three generations the heat makes them the same color as the Banū Sulaym. The effect of this heat is such that the gazelles, ostriches, reptiles, jackals, foxes, sheep, donkeys, horses, and birds which are there are all black. Blackness and whiteness are determined only by the character of the country, and the water and soil which God has given it, by the nearness or remoteness of the sun, the strength or mildness of the heat; they have nothing to do with deformity or punishment, disfigurement or shortcoming.

It is with the country of the Banū Sulaym as with the country of the Turks. Anyone who sees their camels and horses and all that they have which is Turkish sees that it is one and the same—everything they have looks Turkish. Probably the frontiersmen on the border marches see their sheep mixed with the Byzantine sheep, but can distinguish them from one another, because they recognize the Byzantine type. We see the offspring of Arabs and Arab women settled in Khurāsān, and we would not doubt that they are native villagers. This exists in all things. Thus we see that locusts and worms on plants are green, and we see that the louse is black on a young man's head, white if his hair whitens, red if it is dyed.

Our blackness, O people of the Zanj, is not different from the blackness of the Banū Sulaym and other Arab tribes we have mentioned.

Al-Jāḥiẓ, *Rasā'il* (1965), i, pp. 195–197, 210–213, 215–217, 219–220.

11
The Status of Non-Muslims

The dhimma *on the whole worked well. The non-Muslims managed to thrive under Muslim rule, and even to make a significant contribution to Islamic civilization. The restrictions were not onerous and were usually less severe in practice than in theory. As long as the non-Muslim communities accepted and conformed to the status of tolerated subordination assigned to them, they were not troubled. The rare outbreaks of repression or violence directed against them are almost always the consequence of a feeling that they have failed to keep their place and honor their part of the covenant. The usual cause was the undue success of Christians or Jews in penetrating to positions of power and influence which Muslims regarded as rightly theirs. The position of the non-Muslims deteriorated during and after the Crusades and the Mongol invasions, partly because of the general heightening of religious loyalties and rivalries, partly because of the often well-grounded suspicion that they were collaborating with the enemies of Islam.*

The following excerpts consist of legal texts, caliphal decrees, and passages from chronicles dealing with the treatment of non-Muslims.

74. The Pact of ʿUmar (Seventh Century?)

We heard from ʿAbd al-Raḥmān ibn Ghanam [died 78/697] as follows: When ʿUmar ibn al-Khaṭṭāb, may God be pleased with him, accorded a peace to the Christians of Syria, we wrote to him as follows:

> In the name of God, the Merciful and Compassionate.
> This is a letter to the servant of God ʿUmar [ibn al-Khaṭṭāb],

Commander of the Faithful, from the Christians of such-and-such a city. When you came against us, we asked you for safe-conduct (*amān*) for ourselves, our descendants, our property, and the people of our community, and we undertook the following obligations toward you:

We shall not build, in our cities or in their neighborhood, new monasteries, churches, convents, or monks' cells, nor shall we repair, by day or by night, such of them as fall in ruins or are situated in the quarters of the Muslims.

We shall keep our gates wide open for passersby and travelers. We shall give board and lodging to all Muslims who pass our way for three days.

We shall not give shelter in our churches or in our dwellings to any spy, nor hide him from the Muslims.

We shall not teach the Qur'ān to our children.

We shall not manifest our religion publicly nor convert anyone to it. We shall not prevent any of our kin from entering Islam if they wish it.

We shall show respect toward the Muslims, and we shall rise from our seats when they wish to sit.

We shall not seek to resemble the Muslims by imitating any of their garments, the *qalansuwa*, the turban, footwear, or the parting of the hair. We shall not speak as they do, nor shall we adopt their *kunyas*.

We shall not mount on saddles, nor shall we gird swords nor bear any kind of arms nor carry them on our persons.

We shall not engrave Arabic inscriptions on our seals.

We shall not sell fermented drinks.

We shall clip the fronts of our heads.

We shall always dress in the same way wherever we may be, and we shall bind the *zunnār* round our waists.

We shall not display our crosses or our books in the roads or markets of the Muslims. We shall only use clappers in our churches very softly. We shall not raise our voices in our church services or in the presence of Muslims, nor shall we raise our voices when following our dead. We shall not show lights on any of the roads of the Muslims or in their markets. We shall not bury our dead near the Muslims.

We shall not take slaves who have been allotted to the Muslims.

We shall not build houses overtopping the houses of the Muslims.

(When I brought the letter to 'Umar, may God be pleased with him, he added, "We shall not strike any Muslim.")

> We accept these conditions for ourselves and for the people of our community, and in return we receive safe-conduct.
>
> If we in any way violate these undertakings for which we ourselves stand surety, we forfeit our covenant [*dhimma*], and we become liable to the penalties for contumacy and sedition.

'Umar ibn al-Khaṭṭāb replied: Sign what they ask, but add two clauses and impose them in addition to those which they have undertaken. They are: "They shall not buy anyone made prisoner by the Muslims," and "Whoever strikes a Muslim with deliberate intent shall forfeit the protection of this pact."

Al-Ṭurṭūshī, *Sirāj al-Mulūk*, pp. 229–230.

75. The Pact to Be Accorded to Non-Muslim Subjects (Eighth–Ninth Centuries)

If the Imam wishes to write a document for the poll tax (*jizya*) of non-Muslims, he should write:

In the name of God, the Merciful and the Compassionate.

This is a document written by the servant of God so-and-so, Commander of the Faithful, on the 2d of the month of Rabī' I, in the year such-and-such, to so-and-so son of so-and-so, the Christian, of the descendants of such-and-such, of the people of the city of so-and-so.

I accord to you and to the Christians of the city of so-and-so that which is accorded to the *dhimmīs*, in conformity with what you have given to me and the conditions I have laid down concerning what is due to you and to them, and I have agreed to your request and accorded to you and to them, on behalf of myself and of all the Muslims, safe-conduct [*amān*], for as long as you and they maintain all that we have required of you, namely:

You will be subject to the authority of Islam and to no contrary authority. You will not refuse to carry out any obligation which we think fit to impose upon you by virtue of this authority.

If any one of you speaks improperly of Muḥammad, may God bless and save him, the Book of God, or of His religion, he forfeits the protection [*dhimma*] of God, of the Commander of the Faithful, and of all the Muslims; he has contravened the conditions upon which he was given his safe-conduct; his property and his life are at the disposal of the Commander of the Faithful, like the property and lives of the people of the house of war [*dār al-ḥarb*].

If one of them commits fornication with a Muslim woman or goes through a form of marriage with her or robs a Muslim on the highway or subverts a Muslim from his religion or gives aid to those who made war against the Muslims by fighting with them or by showing them the weak points of the Muslims, or by harboring their spies, he has contravened his pact [*'ahd*], and his life and his property are at the disposal of the Muslims.

If he commits some lesser offense against the property or the honor of a Muslim or against an infidel under Muslim protection, with a pact or safe-conduct, he shall be punished.

We shall supervise all your dealings with Muslims. If there is anything in which you are engaged which is not lawful for a Muslim, we shall reject it and punish you for it. If you sell a Muslim something we hold forbidden, such as wine, pig, blood, or carrion, and the like, we shall annul the sale, confiscate the price if it has been paid, and not return the thing to you if it still exists, but pour it out if it is wine or blood and burn it if it is carrion; if the purchaser has already consumed it, we shall not oblige him to pay for it, but we shall punish you for it.

You shall not give a Muslim anything to eat or drink which is forbidden, nor marry him in the presence of witnesses chosen from among you nor by wedding rites we hold to be invalid.

We shall not supervise transactions between you and your coreligionists or other unbelievers nor inquire into them as long as you are content. If the buyer or the seller among you desires the annulment of a sale and comes to us to ask for this, we shall annul it or uphold it in accordance with the provisions of our law. But if payment has been made and the purchase consumed, we shall not order restitution, for this would count as a completed sale between polytheists.

If one of you or any other unbeliever applies to us for judgment, we shall adjudicate according to the law of Islam. But if he does not come to us, we shall not intervene among you.

If you commit manslaughter against a Muslim or a protected person [*mu'āhad*], whether protected by you or by others, your clan is liable for the blood price as with the Muslims. Your clan consists of your paternal kinsmen. If the offender is one of you who has no kin, he himself is liable for the blood price with his own property. If he kills with intent, he is subject to retaliation unless the heirs are content to receive the blood price, in which case they must get it at once.

If any of you steals and the victim takes him before a judge, his hand shall be cut off if his crime is punishable by this penalty, and he shall make restitution.

If anyone commits slander and a legal penalty [*ḥadd*] is due, it shall be inflicted on him; if there is no legal penalty, he shall be punished at discretion so that the laws of Islam may be applied among you in these matters, both specified and unspecified.

You may not display crosses in Muslim cities, nor proclaim polytheism, nor build churches or meeting places for your prayers, nor strike clappers, nor proclaim your polytheistic beliefs on the subject of Jesus, son of Miriam, or any other to a Muslim.

You shall wear the girdle [*zunnār*] over all your garments, your cloaks and the rest, so that the girdles are not hidden. You shall differentiate yourselves by your saddles and your mounts, and you shall distinguish your and their headgear [*qalansuwa*] by a mark which you shall place on your headgear. You shall not occupy the middle of the road or the seats in the market, obstructing Muslims.

Every free adult male of sound mind among you shall have to pay a poll tax [*jizya*] of one dinar, in good coin, at the beginning of each year. He shall not be able to leave his city until he pays his poll tax or appoints someone to pay it on his behalf, with no further liability until the beginning of the year. The poor among you is liable for the poll tax, which should be paid for him. Poverty does not free you from any obligation, nor does it abrogate your pact [*dhimma*]. . . . You are subject to no taxes on your money other than the poll tax as long as you stay in your country or travel around in the lands of the Muslims otherwise than as a merchant. You may in no circumstances enter Mecca. If you travel for trade, you shall pay to the Muslims a tenth part of all your merchandise. You may go wherever you wish in the lands of the Muslims, except Mecca, and reside wherever you wish in the lands of the Muslims, except the Ḥijāz, where you may only stay for three days in any city, after which you must leave.

Whoever has hair under his garments, has attained puberty, or has completed his fifteenth year before this, is subject to these conditions if he accepts them. If he does not accept them, he has no covenant.

Your children under age, boys below puberty, persons of unsound mind, and slaves are not liable for the poll tax. But if the madman recovers his reason, the child attains puberty, or the slave is emancipated and follows your religion, they are all liable for the poll tax.

These conditions are binding on you and on those who have accepted them. Those who reject them we cast out.

We owe you protection, for yourselves and for property which it is lawful for you to hold according to our laws, against anybody, Muslim or other, who seeks to wrong you, as we would protect our own persons and property, and we administer justice to you in matters under our jurisdiction as we do with our own property. But no one among you can ask us to protect any forbidden thing which you own, such as blood, carrion, wine, or pigs, as we would protect lawful property. We shall not prevent you from having them, but we shall not allow you to display them in the cities of the Muslims. If a Muslim or any other buys such merchandise, we shall not compel him to pay the price, because these are forbidden things and therefore have no price which could be legally enforced. But we shall restrain him from troubling you in this, and if he persists he shall be punished, though not by enforcing payment for what he took from you.

You must observe all the conditions which we have imposed.

You may not deceive a Muslim nor give aid to their enemies by word or deed.

This is the pact and covenant of God, and the greatest obligation to respect this covenant which God has ever imposed on any of His creatures. You have the pact and covenant of God, the protection [*dhimma*] of so-and-so, Commander of the Faithful, and the protection of the Muslims to carry out their obligations toward you.

Those of your children who reach the age of puberty are in the same position as you are, in regard to what we have given to you and in the obligation to observe all the conditions which we have laid down for you.

If you change or modify anything, then the protection of God, of so-and-so the Commander of the Faithful, and of the Muslims shall be withdrawn from you. If anyone of those to whom we gave this was not present when we wrote it, and hears of it and accepts it, the conditions stated in it are binding on him and on us. If he does not accept it, we cast him out.

Witnesses.

Al-Shāfi'ī, *Kitāb al-Umm,* iv. pp. 118–119.

76. The Tax on the Unbelievers (Mid-Seventh Century)

'Umar wrote to Abū 'Ubayda: . . . Leave these lands which God has granted you as booty in the hands of their inhabitants and impose on them a poll tax [*jizya*] to the extent that they can bear and divide the proceeds among the Muslims. Let them till the soil, for they know more about it and are better at it than we are. Neither you nor the Muslims who are with you should treat the unbelievers as booty and share them out, because of the peace established between you and them and because you take poll tax from them according to their capacity. God made this clear to us and to you when He said in His book, "Fight against those who do not believe in God nor in the Last Day, who do not hold forbidden what God and His

Apostle have forbidden, who do not practice the religion of truth but are of those to whom a Book has been given, until they pay the poll tax from their hand, they being humbled" [Qur'ān, ix, 29]. If you take the poll tax from them, you have no claim on them or rights over them. Have you considered, if we take them [as slaves] and share them out, what will be left for the Muslims who come after us? By God, the Muslims would not find a man to talk to and profit from his labors. The Muslims of our day will eat [from the work of] these people as long as they live, and when we and they die, our sons will eat their sons forever, as long as they remain, for they are slaves to the people of the religion of Islam as long as the religion of Islam shall prevail. Therefore, place a poll tax upon them and do not enslave them and do not let the Muslims oppress them or harm them or devour their property except as permitted, but faithfully observe the conditions which you have accorded to them and all that you have allowed to them.

Abū Yūsuf, *Kitāb al-Kharāj*, pp. 140–141.

77. Al-Mutawakkil and the *Dhimmīs* (850)

In the year [235/850], al-Mutawakkil gave orders that the Christians and the *dhimmīs* in general be required to wear honey-colored hoods [*ṭaylasān*] and girdles [*zunnār*]; to ride on saddles with wooden stirrups and with two balls attached to the rear; to attach two buttons to the conical caps [*qalansuwa*] of those who wear them and to wear caps of a different color from those worn by the Muslims; to attach two patches to their slaves' clothing, of a different color from that of the garment to which they are attached, one in front on the chest, the other at the back, each patch four fingers in length, and both of them honey-colored. Those of them who wear turbans were to wear honey-colored turbans. If their women went out and appeared in public, they were only to appear with honey-colored head scarves. He gave orders that their slaves were to wear girdles, and he forbade them to wear belts [*minṭaqa*]. He gave orders to destroy their churches which were newly built and to take the tenth part of their houses. If the place was large enough, it was to be made into a mosque; if it was not suitable for a mosque, it was to be made an open space. He ordered that wooden images of devils should be nailed to the doors of their houses to distinguish them from the houses of the Muslims. He forbade their employment in government offices and on official business where they would have authority over the Muslims. He forbade that their children attend Muslim schools or that any Muslim should teach them. He forbade the display of crosses on their Palm Sundays and Jewish rites in the streets. He ordered that their graves be made level with the ground so that they should not resemble the graves of the Muslims.

Al-Ṭabarī, iii, pp. 1389–1390.

78. From a Decree of the Caliph al-Mutawakkil (850)

It has become known to the Commander of the Faithful that men without judgment or discernment are seeking the help of *dhimmīs* in their work, adopting them as confidants in preference to Muslims, and giving them authority over the subjects. And they oppress them and stretch out their hands against them in tyranny, deceit, and enmity. The Commander of the Faithful, attaching great importance to this, has condemned it and disavowed it. Wishing to find favor with God by preventing and forbidding this, he has decided to write to his officers in the provinces and the cities and to the governors of the frontier towns and districts that they should cease to employ *dhimmīs* in any of their work and affairs or to adopt them as associates in the trust and authority conferred on them by the Commander of the Faithful and committed to their charge, since [God] gave the Muslims faith in religion, confidence in their brothers the believers, and ability and competence to discharge the duties entrusted to them and the tasks imposed on them, thus removing the need to seek the help of polytheists, instead of God's help, and of those who give the lie to His Apostles, who deny His miracles, and who place another god beside Him, whereas, in fact, there is no God but He alone and He has no partner. The Commander of the Faithful asks of God, Who inspired him in this and put it into his heart, generous reward and honorable recompense in the hereafter.

May God help the Commander of the Faithful to achieve his purpose, to glorify Islam and its people, and to humble polytheism and its henchmen.

Know, therefore, the decision of the Commander of the Faithful, and do not seek help from any of the polytheists and reduce the people of the protected religions to the station which God has assigned to them. Cause the letter of the Commander of the Faithful to be read aloud to the inhabitants of your district and proclaim it among them, and let it not become known to the Commander of the Faithful that you or any of your officials or helpers are employing anybody of the protected religions in the business of Islam.

Al-Qalqashandī, *Ṣubḥ al-aʿshā*, xiii, p. 368.

79. On Jewish and Christian Officials in Egypt (Tenth–Eleventh Centuries)

It is said that [the Fatimid Caliph al-ʿAzīz] appointed ʿĪsā ibn Nasṭūrus the Christian as his secretary and delegated a Jew called Menasseh as deputy in Syria. The Christians and the Jews felt strong because of these two, and they plagued the Muslims. The people of Fusṭāṭ set to work and wrote a complaint and put it in the hands of a doll, which they made of paper. It said, "By God who raised up the Jews through Menasseh and the Christians through ʿĪsā ibn Nasṭūrus and humbled the Muslims through you, will you redress my wrong?" And they placed this doll with the note in its hand in the path of al-ʿAzīz. When he saw it he gave orders to pick it up, and when he read what was in it and saw the paper doll, he understood what was meant. Then he arrested them both, took 300,000 dinars from ʿĪsā, and also took much money from the Jew.

Ibn al-Athīr, ix, p. 81.

80. More of the Same

The vizier of al-'Azīz was Abu'l-Faraj Ya'qūb ibn Yūsuf ibn Killis who was a Jew and was later converted to Islam. The Caliph put him in charge of the affairs of his whole realm. Ibn Zawlāq said that he was the first to serve as vizier to the 'Ubaydī [Fatimid] dynasty in the land of Egypt and that before that he was one of the secretaries of Kāfūr. When he died, al-'Azīz grieved for him very deeply and closed the *dīwān* for several days in his honor. His death occurred in the year 380 [991]. After him, he appointed as vizier a Christian called 'Īsā ibn Nasṭūrus and then arrested him. The vizier of al-Ẓāhir was Abu'l-Qāsim 'Alī ibn Aḥmad al-Jarjarā'ī, who served from the year 418 [1027] until his death in the reign of al-Mustanṣīr in the year 436 [1045]. After him, Abū Naṣr Ṣadaqa ibn Yūsuf al-Falāḥī served as vizier; he was a Jew and became a Muslim. With him was Abū Sa'd al-Tustārī the Jew, who conducted the affairs of the state for him. A poet said:

> The Jews of this time have attained their uttermost
> hopes, and have come to rule.
> Glory is upon them, money is with them, and from among them
> come the counsellor and the ruler.
> O people of Egypt, I advise you, turn Jew, for the
> heavens have turned Jew!

al-Suyūṭī, *Ḥusn al-Muḥādara*, ii, p. 129.

81. The Tolerance of al-Ẓāhir (Early Eleventh Century)

Al-Ẓāhir issued a rescript . . . which was read before the people, expressing his good intentions toward all and reaffirming that all persons entrusted with authority in the service of the state and in the administration of justice must base themselves on what is right, pursue justice in all that comes before them and concerns them, defend the peaceful and upright, and pursue wrong-doers and troublemakers. He also said that he had heard of a fear among the people of the protected religions, the Christians and Jews, that they would be compelled to pass to the religion of Islam and of their resentment at this, since there should be no constraint in religion [Qur'ān, ii, 256]. He said that they should remove these imaginary fears from their hearts and be assured that they would enjoy protection and care and retain their position as protected communities. Whoever among them wishes to enter the religion of Islam by the choice of his own heart and by the grace of God, and not for the purpose of self-advancement and aggrandizement, may do so and be both welcome and blessed; whoever prefers to remain in his religion, but not the backslider, has protection and safeguard, and it is the duty of all members of the [Muslim] community to guard and protect him.

Yaḥyā al-Antākī, pp. 235–236.

82. On Deporting Non-Muslims (Twelfth Century)

If the Imam wishes to move the people of the protected religions [*ahl al-dhimma*] from their land, it is not lawful for him to do so without justification, but it is lawful if there is justification. The justification in our time is that the Imam may fear for the safety of the people of the protected religions at the hands of the infidel enemy [*ahl al-ḥarb*], since they are helpless and have little strength, or he may fear for the safety of the Muslims at their hands, lest they inform the enemy of the points of weakness of the Muslims.

Qāḍīkhān, *Fatāwī,* iii, p. 616.

83. Question and Answer (Thirteenth Century)

Question: A Jew has been appointed inspector of coins in the treasury of the Muslims, to weigh the dirhams that come and go and to test them, and his word is relied upon in this. Is his appointment permissible under the Holy Law, or not? Will God reward the ruler if he dismisses him and replaces him with a competent Muslim? Will anyone who helps to procure his dismissal also be rewarded by God?

Answer: It is not permissible to appoint the Jew to such a post, it is not permitted to leave him in it, and it is not permissible to rely on his word in any matter relating to this. The ruler, may God grant him success, will be rewarded for dismissing him and replacing him with a competent Muslim, and anyone who helps to procure his dismissal will also be rewarded. God said, "O you who believe, do not take intimates from among those who are not of your own people, for they will spare no pains to corrupt you; what they desire is what makes you suffer; their hatred appears in their mouths, but that which is hidden in their breasts is greater. We have made the signs clear to you, if you can understand" [Qur'ān, iii, 114]. The meaning of this is that you should not adopt outsiders, that is, the unbelievers, and allow them to penetrate to your innermost affairs. "They will spare no pains to corrupt you." This means that they will not refrain from anything which is in their power to cause you harm, damage, or injury. "Their hatred appears in their mouths," for they say, "We are your enemies."

Al-Nawawī, *Al-Manthūrāt, in RÉJ*, xxviii, p. 94.

84. Incident in Cairo (1301)

In the month of Rajab [700/March–April 1301] a misfortune befell the people of the protected religions [*ahl al-dhimma*]. This happened because they lived a life of increasing luxury in Cairo and Fusṭāṭ and indulged in such things as riding on fine horses and splendid mules with magnificent trappings and wore sumptuous clothes and received high positions. It happened that the vizier of the king of the Maghrib came on his way to the Pilgrimage and foregathered with the Sultan and the amirs at a time when he was under the Citadel, and suddenly a man passed by on horseback, surrounded by a number of people walking on foot by his stirrup and begging him and beseeching him and kissing his feet, while he turned his back on them and took no notice of them—or rather, rebuffed them and called on his henchmen to drive them away. The Maghribī was told that this rider was a Christian. This disturbed him greatly. He met two of the amirs, Baybars and Salār, and told them what he had seen and condemned this and wept greatly and denounced the business of the Christian and said, "How can you hope for victory when the Christians ride among you on horseback, wear white turbans, humiliate the Muslims, and have them run in their service?" So he went on in his denunciation and spoke of the duty of rulers to humble the *dhimmīs* and to moderate their dress. His words influenced the amirs, and a decree was issued convening a meeting in the presence of the judges. Qāḍīs and jurists were invited and the patriarch of the Christians was summoned, and a decree of the Sultan was issued, requiring the *dhimmīs* to conform to the prescriptions of the law of Muḥammad. The qāḍīs assembled in the Ṣāliḥī *madrasa* situated in the Bayn al-Qaṣrayn quarter, and the chief qāḍī Shams al-Dīn Aḥmad al-Surūjī al-Ḥanafī was appointed to act for them in this matter. The patriarch of the Christians was summoned with a group of their bishops, the leading priests among them, and the notables of their community, and likewise the *dayyān*[1] of the Jews and the chiefs of their community. They were asked about the pact which was fixed with them in the Caliphate of the Commander of the Faithful 'Umar ibn al-Khaṭṭāb, may God be pleased with him, and they gave no answer to this. The discussion with them went on a long time until it was settled that the Christians should be distinguished by wearing blue turbans and the Jews by wearing yellow turbans; that they be forbidden to ride horses or mules or to do any of the things which they were forbidden to do by the Lawgiver, may God bless and save him; and that they be bound to fulfill the conditions which the Commander of the Faithful 'Umar ibn al-Khaṭṭāb, may God be pleased with him, had imposed on them. They pledged themselves to this, and the patriarch testified that he forbade all Christians to break these rules or to disregard

[1] A Hebrew word meaning judge (in Rabbinic law).

them. The chief of the Jews and their *dayyān*, said, "I have made this known to all the Jews that they may not break these rules or disregard them." The meeting was dissolved, and the Sultan and the amirs were informed of what had happened, and letters were sent to the provinces of Egypt and Syria concerning this.

On Maundy Thursday, which fell on 20 Rajab [March 30, 1301], the Christians and the Jews were called together in Cairo, Fusṭāṭ, and their surroundings, and it was decreed that no one of them should be employed in the office of the Sultan or in the offices of the amirs, that they should not ride horses or mules, and that they should observe all the conditions imposed upon them. Proclamation to this effect was made by criers in Cairo and Fusṭāṭ, and warning given that if anyone disobeyed this, his blood would be shed. The Christians felt constrained by this and tried with money to procure its abrogation, but the amir Baybars, the Taster, who had taken a praiseworthy stance in the execution of the decree, pursued it with increased persistence, and the Christians were compelled to conform. The *amīn al-mulk* 'Abdallāh ibn al-Ghannām, the chief accountant attached to the Sultan's person, and many others became Muslims because they desired to remain in their positions of authority and disdained to wear blue turbans and ride on donkeys. Couriers were sent by the postal service [*barīd*] to impose on the Christians and the Jews from Dongola in Nubia to the Euphrates that which has already been mentioned.

The common people laid their hands on the synagogues of the Jews and the churches of the Christians and destroyed them in accordance with a *fatwā* of the jurist Shaykh Najm al-Dīn Aḥmad ibn Muḥammad ibn al-Rif'a. The amirs convened the qāḍīs and jurists to examine the case of the synagogues and churches. Ibn al-Rif'a declared that it was a duty to destroy them, but the chief qāḍī Taqī al-Dīn Muḥammad ibn Daqīq al-'Īd disagreed and argued that if there was proof that they had been built after the advent of Islam they should be destroyed, but if not, they should not be touched. The others concurred and they dispersed. When the decree of the Sultan concerning the *dhimmīs* became known to the people of Alexandria, they turned on the Christians and destroyed two of their churches. They also destroyed Jewish and Christian houses that overtopped the houses of their Muslim neighbors. They lowered the benches of their shops until they were lower than the benches of the Muslim shops. Two churches were also destroyed in Fayyūm.

The decree concerning the *dhimmīs* reached Damascus by courier on Monday, 7 Sha'bān [April 17, 1301]. The qāḍīs and notables met at the house of the amir Aqqush al-Afram, and the Sultan's decree to this effect was read to them. On the 15th of the month [April 25] criers proclaimed that the Christians were to wear blue turbans, the Jews yellow turbans, and the Samaritans red turbans, with threats of punishment for disobedience. The Christians and Jews in all the realm of Egypt and Syria had to do as they were ordered and dyed their turbans, except for the people of Kerak, for the amir Jamāl al-Dīn Aqqush al-Afram al-Ashrafī who was governor saw fit to leave them as they were, with the excuse that most of the people of Kerak were Christians. The Christians in Kerak and Shawbak did not therefore change their white turbans.

The churches in the land of Egypt remained closed for a year until the envoys of al-Ashkarī, the king of the Franks [sic],[2] came and interceded for their reopening, whereupon the Mu'allaqa church in Fusṭāṭ and the Melchite church of Michael were opened. Then envoys came from other kings, and the church in the Zuwayla quarter and the Church of Nicholas were opened.

Al-Maqrīzī, *Sulūk*, i, pp. 909–913.

85. Another Incident in Cairo (1309–1310)

The qāḍī Jamāl al-Dīn ibn al-Qalānisī informed me of the details of this audience, of the respect and honor shown to him, and the gratitude and praise given to him by the Sultan [Muḥammad ibn Qalawun] and the amirs who were present. The chief qāḍī, Manṣūr al-Dīn al-Ḥanafī, also told me about it, but Ibn

[2] Probably an error. Elsewhere in this work al-Ashkarī is called king of the Romans (that is, Byzantines). The name no doubt derives from Lascaris.

al-Qalānisī's account is more detailed, he being at that time the qāḍī of the army. Both of them were present at this audience.

I was told that when Shaykh Taqī al-Dīn Ibn Taymiyya appeared before him, the Sultan rose to his feet as soon as he saw him and walked to the far end of the chamber, where the two of them embraced for a while. Then he went with him to a bench by a window overlooking a garden, where they sat for a while talking together. Then they came, the shaykh's hand in the Sultan's hand, and the Sultan sat down with Ibn Jamā'a the qāḍī of Egypt on his right, Ibn al-Khalīlī the vizier on his left, and Ibn Ṣaṣrā, followed by Ṣadr al-Dīn 'Alī al-Ḥanafī, below him. Shaykh Taqī al-Dīn sat next to the Sultan at the edge of his sofa.

The vizier spoke about the desire of the *dhimmīs* to return to wearing white turbans with emblems and said that they would undertake to pay the *dīwān* 700,000 dinars every year, in addition to their regular poll tax. Those present were silent, among them the qāḍīs of Egypt and Syria and the great Egyptian and Syrian ulema, including Ibn al-Zamlakānī.

Ibn al-Qalānisī said, "I was at the Sultan's audience, next to Ibn al-Zamlakānī, and not one of the ulema or the qāḍīs spoke." The Sultan asked them, "What do you say?" seeking a ruling from them, and not one of them spoke.

Then Shaykh Taqī al-Dīn knelt on his knees and spoke harshly to this Sultan about this and strongly rejected what the vizier had said. He raised his voice, and the Sultan tried to quiet him gently, unhurriedly, and respectfully. But the shaykh spoke vehemently, saying things which no one else could equal or approach. He vigorously denounced anyone who would agree to this and said to the Sultan, "God forbid that at the first audience you hold in the majesty of kingship, you should help the *dhimmīs* for the sake of the vanities of this mortal world. Remember God's grace to you when He restored your dominion to you, crushing your enemy and giving you victory over your foes."

The Sultan said that it was the Chief Taster who had introduced this for them and the shaykh said, "What the Chief Taster did was by your orders, for he was only your deputy."

The Sultan was astonished by this.

Ibn Kathīr, *Al-Bidāya wa'l-nihāya*, xiv, pp. 53–54.

86. A Decree of Al-Malik al-Ṣāliḥ (1354)

A noble decree, to the effect that all the communities of Jews, Christians, and Samaritans in the Egyptian lands and the God-guarded realms of Islam and their dependencies must conform to the covenant accorded by the Commander of the Faithful ʻUmar ibn al-Khaṭṭāb, may God be pleased with him, to the members of these communities in bygone times, as follows: That they shall not build any new convent or church or hermitage in the lands of Islam, nor rebuild any such building which is destroyed; that they shall not harbor spies nor any who are suspect to the Muslims, nor shall they deceitfully plot against the Muslims; that they shall not teach their children the Qur'ān; that they shall not make public display of polytheism; that they shall not obstruct any of their relatives who wish to accept Islam; that they shall not dress like the Muslims, but shall wear blue and yellow distinguishing dress; that their women shall be prevented from dressing like Muslim women; that they shall not ride with stirrups nor gird a sword, nor ride on a horse or mule but only on donkeys, side-seat on litters; that they shall not sell intoxicating drinks; that they shall keep to their special dress wherever they are; that they shall wear girdles not made of silk around their waists; that the Christian woman who appears in public shall wear a cotton veil, dyed blue, and the Jewess a yellow veil; that none of them shall enter the bath except wearing a sign around his neck which distinguishes him from the Muslims, such as a ring made of iron or lead or some other material; that they shall not build themselves houses higher than the houses of the Muslims, nor equal to them, but only lower; that they shall knock lightly with their clappers and not raise their voices in their churches; that they shall not work in the service of our exalted state, may God strengthen its foundations, nor in the service of any of the amirs, may Almighty God strengthen them, nor shall any of them hold a position which would give him authority over any of the Muslims; that jurisdiction over the estates of the dead among them shall be according to the noble Muḥammadan Holy Law and that the rules of administrative confiscation will be applied to them equally as to the Muslim dead; that the women of the protected communities shall not enter public bathouses together with the Muslim women, but that separate bathhouses shall be made for them, into which they shall enter. All this is in accordance with the rulings of the doctors of the Holy Law, as has been explained.

Al-Qalqashandī, xiii, pp. 378–379.

12
Slaves

The following passages consist of a document, on papyrus, certifying the manumission of a slave, a description from a Persian political treatise of the training of Turkish military mamlūks, and excerpts from a legal work, a handbook for buyers of slaves, and a late medieval Egyptian literary delectus.

87. A Letter of Deferred Manumission for a Slave (916)

In the name of God, the Merciful and the Compassionate.

This is a letter from Yaḥyā ibn Nasr the goldsmith, the freedman of Hārūn ibn Mūsā ibn Muḥammad, for his black slave, mature, hairless, and wide-eyed, who is called Mubārak. He wrote it for him and acknowledged and attested its contents, being in good health and legally responsible, voluntarily and not under constraint, as follows:

I manumit you so that you remain in my service as long as I live, but if I die and you, Mubārak, still live, then you are free for the sake of God and the afterlife, and there is no claim on you other than that of clientage [*walā*], and your clientage is to me and to my heirs.

I have written this document for you, O Mubārak, granting you deferred manumission [*tadbīr*], I being in sound health, so that it may serve as proof and document in your hand at all times.

The following attested the acknowledgement of Yaḥyā ibn Naṣr the goldsmith and his *mudabbar* slave Mubārak in this letter, they being in good health and legal responsibility, voluntarily and not constrained, on Tuesday, the 19 Muḥarram of the year 304 [July 23, 916]. [List of witnesses follows.]

Papyrus, in Grohmann, *Der Islam,* pp. 19–24.

88. The Slaves in the Palace (Tenth Century)

This was the rule followed at the court of the Samanids.

Slaves were promoted in stages, in accordance with their service, skill, and merit. Thus when they bought a new slave they made him serve for one year on foot. He walked by the stirrup and wore a Zandānī coat. During this year, such slaves were not allowed to mount on horseback, either in public or in private, and if one was detected, he was punished. When one year of service was completed, the tent commander informed the chamberlain, who arranged for him to be given a Turkish horse with a cord in its mouth and a plain bit and strap. When he had served for one year with a horse and whip, they gave him a long sword to gird round his waist. In the fifth year they gave him a better saddle, a bridle adorned with a star, a Dārā'ī cloak, and a club which he hung from a ring [on his saddle]. In the sixth year they gave him parade dress, and in the seventh year they gave him a tent with one pole and sixteen pegs and assigned three [new] slaves to him. They gave him the title of tent commander and dressed him in a black felt hat adorned with silver and a Ganja cloak. Each year they increased his status, dignity, retinue, and rank until he became a troop commander and eventually a chamberlain. If his capacity and skill became generally known, if he accomplished some great deed and was manly and loyal to his sovereign, they would make him an amir and appoint him governor of a province, but not before he reached the age of thirty-five.

Niẓām al-Mulk, *Siyāsat-nāma,* pp. 94–95.

89. Laws Regarding Slaves (Early Eleventh Century)

On the Status of Concubine-Mother.

When a slave woman bear her master a child, she becomes for him an *umm walad* [concubine-mother]. He may not sell her nor transfer ownership in her to any other. He may, however, cohabit with her, require her to serve him, rent her services to others, or marry her.

The legitimate paternity of her child is only established if her master recognizes it. But if thereafter she bears another child, the paternity of the master shall be established without any further declaration by him. If, however, he denies it, a simple declaration suffices.

If he marries her and she bears him a child, the child shall follow the condition of his mother. If the master dies, she shall be emancipated at the expense of the estate, and she shall not be subject to claims by creditors for any debts he may have incurred.

If a man cohabits in marriage with someone else's slave-woman and she bears him a child, and if he subsequently becomes her master, she shall become his *umm walad.*

If a father cohabits with a slave-woman belonging to his son and she bears a child which the father claims, his paternity is established, and this slave-woman becomes his *umm walad.* He then owes her value, but he does not have to pay the *'uqr*[1] for her nor the value of her child.

If the father's father cohabits with her, the father being alive, the paternity is not established. But if the father is dead, the paternity is established in relation to the grandfather in the same way as to the father.

If the slave-woman belongs to two co-owners and gives birth to a child which one of the two claims, his paternity is established and she becomes his *umm walad.* He owes the other co-

[1] Indemnity for illicit sexual relations with a slave-woman.

owner half of the *'uqr* on her and half of her value but no part of the value of her child. If the two co-owners both claim the child, the paternity of both shall be established, and she shall become an *umm walad* to both of them. Each shall owe the other half of the *'uqr,* the two debts cancelling one another. The child shall inherit from both as if he were exclusively his child, and they shall inherit from him as would a single father.

. . . .

The Runaway Slave

If a slave runs away and a man restores him to his master from a distance of three days journey or more, the finder can claim a reward of forty dirhams from the owner. If he restores him from a shorter distance, the amount shall be reduced proportionately. If the value of the slave is less than forty dirhams, the finder shall receive as reward the amount of his estimated value less one dirham. If the slave runs away from the finder, the latter is not liable. It is proper that the finder should declare, when he takes possession of him, that he does so in order to restore him.

If the runaway slave has been given as pledge for a debt, the reward is due from the pledge holder.

The Slave Authorized to Engage in Trade (Ma'dhūn)

If the master grants general permission to his slave, the slave may lawfully engage in all kinds of trade and may buy and sell and give and receive pledges. If the master specifically authorizes him to practice one kind of trade, the slave is deemed to be authorized to practice all trades. If the master authorizes the slave to carry out a single specified transaction, the slave shall not be deemed an authorized slave.

The authorized slave may lawfully admit liability for his debts and usurpations. He may not marry, join his slaves in marriage, emancipate slaves by contract [*mukātaba*] or for payment, or make gifts with or without counterpart, except that he may give a small quantity of food or return hospitality received.

His debts fall on his own person. He may be sold to pay the creditors, unless his master redeems him, and his price shall be shared among the creditors in proportion. If anything remains owing, it may be claimed from him after he has become free.

If the master interdicts him [that is, annuls his authorization], this interdiction only becomes valid when it is known to his fellow traders. If the master dies, goes mad, or becomes an apostate and joins the House of War, the authorized slave shall be interdicted.

If the authorized slave runs away, he shall be interdicted. When he is interdicted, he may lawfully recognize a debt on assets which he still holds, according to Abū Ḥanīfa. If he has incurred debts which absorb his assets and his own person, his master cannot dispose of the said assets in his possession. If, therefore, the master emancipates the slaves of the authorized slave, their emancipation is not valid, according to Abū Ḥanīfa. But according to Abū Yūsuf and Muḥammad, the master is the owner of the authorized slave's assets.

If the authorized slave [who has contracted a debt] sells something to his master for its value, the sale is lawful. But if he sells it to him at a loss, it is not lawful. If the master sells something to the slave for its value or less, the sale is lawful. If the master hands it to the authorized slave before having received its price, this price shall be cancelled. If the master retains possession of it until the price is paid, this is lawful.

If the master emancipates his authorized slave while the latter is indebted, this emancipation is lawful and the master stands surety against the creditors to the amount of the slave's value. For the remainder of the debt the emancipated slave is liable.

If a female authorized slave gives birth to a child belonging to her master, this interdicts her.

If the guardian of a minor authorizes him to engage in trade, the position of this minor in buying and selling is like that of an authorized slave, provided that he understands what selling means.

On Emancipation ('Itq)

Emancipation is performed by one who is free, of age, and of sound mind on a slave who is his property [*mulk*]. If the master says to his slave or slave-woman "You are free," or "emancipated," or "freed," or "I have freed you," or "I have emancipated you," then the slave is emancipated whether the master intended to emancipate him or not. The same applies if he says, "Your head is free," or "your face" or "your neck" or "your body," or if he says to his slave-woman, "Your vulva is free." If he says, "I have no ownership [*mulk*] over you," intending by this to grant freedom, the slave shall be emancipated, even without explicit emancipation. The same applies to other indirect expressions of emancipation. But if he says, "I have no authority [*sulṭān*] over you," intending by this to emancipate him, the slave shall not be emancipated.

If he says, "This is my son" and he confirms this, or if he says, "This is my freedman [*mawlā*]" or addresses his slave as "my freedman," the slave shall be emancipated. If he merely addresses his slave as "my son" or "my brother," the slave shall not be emancipated.

If he says to a young slave who physically could not be his son, "This is my son," the slave shall be emancipated, according to Abū Ḥanīfa.

If the master says to his slave-woman, "You are divorced," intending by these words to grant freedom, the slave-woman shall not be emancipated.

If a master says to his slave, "You are like a freeman," he shall not be emancipated, but if he says "You are nothing but free," he shall be emancipated.

When someone becomes owner of a slave who is his relative within the prohibited degrees, this slave shall be emancipated.

When the master emancipates a part of his slave, this part alone shall be emancipated, and the slave shall have to work for his master for the remainder of his value. This is according to Abū Ḥanīfa. According to Abū Yūsuf and Muḥammad he shall be emancipated in his entirety.

If the slave belongs to two co-owners and one of them emancipates his share, this emancipation shall be valid. If the emancipator has adequate means, then his partner may choose as he wishes between the following: to emancipate or to obtain indemnity from his partner for the value of his part or to make the slave work for him. If the emancipator lacks means, then his partner may choose, as he wishes, either to emancipate the slave or to make him work for him. But according to Abū Yūsuf and Muḥammad the second partner can only claim indemnity when the emancipator has means and can only make the slave work when the emancipator lacks means.

If two men buy the son of one of them, the father's share is emancipated without indemnity. The same applies if they both inherit the son. The father's partner shall have the choice either to emancipate his part or to make the slave work for him.

If each of two co-owners bears witness that the other has emancipated his share, the slave is emancipated in his entirety. The slave shall work for each of two co-owners up to the value of his share, whether they be well off or poor, according to Abū Ḥanīfa. But Abū Yūsuf and Muḥammad say that if they are well off, the slave shall not have to work for them, that if they are poor he shall have to work for them, and if one of them is well off and the other poor, he shall work for the one who is well off and shall not work for the one who is poor [sic].

If anyone emancipates his slave "for the love of God" or for the Devil or for an idol, the slave shall be emancipated.

Emancipation given under constraint or drunkenness is valid.

If the emancipator makes the emancipation subject to the acquisition of ownership or the fulfilment of a condition, this shall be valid, as for divorce.

If a slave leaves the House of War and comes among us as a Muslim, he shall be emancipated.

If a master emancipates a pregnant slave-woman, her fetus is emancipated with her. If he specifically emancipates the fetus, then it shall be emancipated but not the mother.

If a master emancipates his slave in return for a sum of money, and the slave accepts this, he shall be emancipated and held liable for the debt. If the master says, "If you pay me 1,000 you will be free," this stipulation shall be valid and the slave shall become *ma'dhūn* [authorized to trade]. If the slave brings the stipulated amount, the judge shall compel the master to accept it, and the slave shall be emancipated.

The child of a slave-woman born to her master is free. Her child born to her husband is the slave of her master. The child of a free woman born to a slave is free.

Al-Qudūrī, *Mukhtaṣar*, pp. 180–185, 220–243.

90. On Buying Slaves (Eleventh Century)

Useful advice when buying slaves, according to the sayings of the wise men and philosophers; ten pieces of advice, of which four apply equally to male and female slaves, viz:

1. Their injunction that the shopper should make a careful examination before buying and should not decide at first glance. They said: one who shops for a thing should not be in dire need of it, for the hungry man approves any food that appeases his hunger, and the naked man finds suitable any rag that warms and covers him. Accordingly they said: a lecher should not shop for slave-girls, for the tumescent has no judgment since he decides at first glance, and there is magic in the first glance and charm in the new and strange. If he feels an urgent need, he will make a choice at first glance which his senses will later belie when the need is no more. Therefore, it is said: Repeated looking wears out novelty, and constant examination reveals artifice and exposes deceit.
2. The warning of the ancients before purchase. They said: beware of buying slaves at fairs and festivals, for it is at such markets that the slave-dealers perfect their cunning tricks. How often has a scraggy girl been sold as plump, a dirty brown as a golden blond, an aging man as a full-bottomed boy, a bulging paunch as a trim, flat waist, a stinking mouth as perfumed breath. How often do they dye blemishes in the eyes and leprous sores on the body, and make light blue eyes dark blue. How often do they dye yellow cheeks red,

make thin cheeks fat, enlarge small orifices, remove hair from cheeks, stain fair hair jet black, curl lanky hair, whiten brown faces, make splindly legs rounded, thicken falling hair, and gild pockmarks, tattoo marks, freckles, and scabies . . . How often has a sick slave been sold as healthy, and a boy as a girl. All this in addition to the slave-merchants' practice of encouraging the slave-girls in shameless flirtation with passing young men who regard carrion as lawful meat, as well as their bedecking themselves with rouge and henna and soft, dyed garments. We have heard a slave-dealer say, "A quarter of a dirham's worth of henna raises the price of a slave-girl by 100 silver dirhams." . . .

3. Their injunction not to decide at the first hearing of male and female slaves. They said: Do not decide at the first sight of a slave or slave-girl . . . but be more inclined to doubt than to trust. It is safer to be suspicious.
4. A special warning for the great. They said: Let the great—anyone with an enemy who he fears may seek to murder him or to penetrate his secrets—beware of buying a eunuch or a slave-girl, especially if she can write and has come out of a ruler's household, without thoroughly investigating her; also beware of buying a mulatto slave-girl from a merchant or broker, for this is a trick by which many kings and great ones have perished.

Three pieces of advice relating especially to the purchase of male slaves, viz:

1. Their warning to the purchaser against buying a slave accustomed to beating and argument. They said: do not buy a slave whose master used to beat him very much, and do not omit to inquire about the previous owner and his reason for selling the slave, and find out about this before you buy him from the slave himself and from others, for there is great benefit in such an inquiry, either in binding him to you or in leaving him.
2. [Is the cause] the boldness of the slave in blaming his master and belittling him or the master's resentment at his slave's complaints and disrespect for him? Is the cause of the selling in the master or in the slave?
3. Their advice on what to do before employing him. They said: The slave's character will be determined by your treatment

of him from the moment when he first enters your house. If you embolden him, he will be bold; if you train him, he will be obedient; if he associates with bad slaves or other bad people, he will be bad.

Two pieces of advice relating to female slaves, viz:

1. How to make sure that slave-girls are free from pregnancy before purchase. They said: Be careful to ascertain that female slaves are free from pregnancy before taking possession of them, and beware of their spurious discharge and lying claims. Many of them insert other girls' blood in their private parts. The one to ascertain this is a woman who would not wish you to have another man's child foisted on you. Order her to examine her breasts and feel her stomach. You can also know this from the pallor of her complexion and her desire for salty food, for this is a craving due to pregnancy.
2. On taking care after purchase of tricks to become pregnant against the owner's will. They said: Be careful on two points. If you buy a slave-girl who has not yet reached puberty, it often happens that she reaches puberty while in your possession without your knowledge, concealing this from you because she desires motherhood.

Beware of Lesbian [?] slave-girls who fancy that they are barren and that they dislike pregnancy, for often they will deceive you in this.

One piece of advice which concerns the seller, not the buyer.

They said: never send a slave-girl from your house to the slave-dealer, except during the menstrual flow. Otherwise she is likely to become pregnant in the slave-quarters and claim that it is yours.

We have indeed seen one in our time who bled during pregnancy, but this is rare.

On the Different Kinds of Slaves, According to Their Countries and Origins

We shall report what we have found out, what is well-known, what we have gathered from books, and what we have learned by inquiry from travelers, concerning the various races of slaves and the differences between them in body and in character, so that we may satisfy the inquirer in this matter with the fruit of experience and trial. Twenty-five sections, as follows:

The first section contains the explanation of terms, the meanings of which the reader needs to know.

If you hear me say "Fārisiyya," know that I mean a woman who is born in Fārs. Both parents may be Fārisī, but the father alone suffices. If the offspring of a Negress mate with whites for three successive generations, thereafter black gives way to white, a flat nose gives way to a long nose, the limbs become dainty, and the character changes accordingly. The same usage is to be understood with reference to all races.

If you hear me speak of a slave-girl as a "fiver," by this I mean that her height is five spans.

If I say *shahwāriyya,* this is not the name of a race but is a Persian word derived from [the Arabic] *shahwa* [passion] and means "perfect passion."

If I say Manṣūriyya, I am referring to al-Manṣūra which is beyond the river [Indus], that is, to Multān, and not to al-Manṣūra of the Arabs.

Then come four sections, relating to the four points of the compass.

The first concerns the eastern lands. The color of the people of these lands is white tinged with red. Their bodies are fertile, their voice clear, their sicknesses few, their faces handsome, their characters noble, their sheep plentiful, their trees tall. There is no anger in them and no courage because of their equitable dispositions; they are a people of calm and of meek temper. All this is because of the temperate sun in that region, their temperate food, and their clear water.

The second concerns the western lands. These are almost the exact opposite of what we have described in the eastern lands, since the sun does not rise over them in the mornings.

The third concerns the northern lands. These are the ones whose inhabitants live under the signs of the Bear and the Goat, such as the Slavs. These are broad-chested and brave, of portly build to conserve heat, but with thin legs because the heat escapes from the extremities. They live long because of their excellent digestion, but their women are barren because they are never clean from menstrual blood.

The fourth concerns the southern lands. These are the ones whose people live under the southern Pole [sic], such as the Ethiopians, and their condition is the opposite of that of the people of the northern lands. Their color is black, their waters are brackish and turbid, their stomachs cold, and their digestion bad. Their natures are calm, their lives short, and their bellies soft because of bad digestion.

Then follow twenty sections dealing with the countries, one by one.

The Indian women are in the southeast. They have good stature, brown color, and a plentiful share of beauty, with pallor, a clear skin, fragrant breath, softness, and grace, but old age comes quickly upon them. They are faithful and affectionate, very reliable, deep, sharp-tongued, and of fine character. They cannot support humiliation but endure pain without complaint until they are killed. They can master great things when compelled or provoked. Their women are good for childbirth, their men, for the protection of persons and property and for delicate handicrafts. They catch cold easily.

The women of Sind are between the east and the south. They closely resemble the Indians whose country adjoins theirs, except that their women are distinguished by their slender waists and long hair.

The women of Medina are brown in color, and of upright stature. They combine sweetness of speech and grace of body with charm, roguishness, and beauty of form and flesh. These women are not jealous of men, are content with little, do not grow angry, and do not scold. There are negresses among them, and they are suitable for training as singing girls.

The women of Ṭā'if are golden brown and shapely. They are the most cheerful of all God's creatures, the funniest, and the merriest. They are not good as mothers of children, for they are slow to pregnancy and die at childbirth. Their men are the most active of mankind in courtship, the most assiduous in company, and the most excellent in song.

The Berber women are from the island of Barbara [sic], which is between the west and the south. Their color is mostly black, though some pale ones can be found among them. If you can find one whose mother is of Kutāma, whose father is of Ṣanhāja, and whose origin is Masmūda, then you will find her naturally inclined to obedience and loyalty in all matters, active in service, suited both to motherhood and to pleasure, for they are the most solicitous in caring for their children. Abū ʻUthmān the slave-dealer says, "If it happens that a Berber girl with her racial excellence is imported at the age of nine, spends three years in Medina and three years in Mecca, comes to Iraq at the age of fifteen and is educated in Iraq, and is bought at the age of twenty-five, then she adds to the excellence of her race the roguishness of the Medinans, the languor of the Meccans, and the culture of the women of Iraq. Then she is worthy to be hidden in the eyelid and placed in the eye."

The Yemeni women are of the same race as the Egyptians, with the body of the Berbers, the roguishness of the Medinans, and the languor of the Meccans. They are the mothers of handsome children somewhat resembling the Bedouin Arabs.

The Zaranjī women are from a country called Zaranj. Ibn Khurradādhbeh says that from this place to the city of Multān is a journey of two months, and Multān is in the middle of India. A peculiarity of this race is that during sexual intercourse they sweat a liquid like musk, but they are not good for motherhood.

The Zanj women have many bad qualities. The blacker they are, the uglier their faces, the more pointed their teeth, the less use they are and the more likely to do some harm. For the most part, they are of bad character, and they frequently run away. It is not in their nature to worry. Dancing and rhythm are innate and ingrained in them. Since their utterance is obscure, they have been compensated with music and dance. It is said that if a Zanjī were to fall from heaven to earth, he would beat time as he fell. They have the cleanest teeth of mankind because they have much saliva, and they have much saliva because they have bad digestion. They can endure hard work. If the Zanjī has had enough to eat, you can chastise him heavily and he will not complain. There is no pleasure to be got from their women because of their stench and the coarseness of their bodies.

The Ethiopian women. Most of them have gracious, soft, and weak bodies. They are subject to phthisis and hectic fever and are no good for singing or dancing. They are delicate and do not thrive in any country other than that in which they were born. They are good, obliging, tractable, and trustworthy, and are distinguished by strength of character and weakness of body, just as the Nubians are distinguished by strength of body despite their slenderness and also by weakness of character and shortness of life because of their bad digestion.

The women of Mecca are languorous, feminine, with supple wrists and of a white color tinged with brown. Their figures are beautiful, their bodies lissom, their mouths clean and cool, their hair curly, their eyes sickly and languid.

The women of Zaghāwa are of vicious character and full of grumbles. Their ill nature and evil disposition lead them to do terrible things. They are worse than the Zanj and than all the black races. Their women are useless for pleasure, and their men are useless for service.

The Bujja women are between the south and the west in the country which lies between Ethiopia and Nubia. They are golden in color, with beautiful faces, smooth bodies, and tender flesh. If, as slave-girls for pleasure, they are imported while they are still young, they are saved from mutilation, for they are circumcised and all the flesh from the upper part of their pudenda is incised with a razor until the bone appears; they have become a byword. Similarly the nipples of men are cut off and a bone removed from the knee. . . . Bravery and thievery are innate and ingrained in them; they cannot therefore be trusted with money and are unsuitable for use as treasurer or custodian.

The Nubian women, of all the black races, have ease and grace and delicacy. Their bodies are dry, while their flesh is tender; they are strong and at the same time slender and firm. The climate of Egypt suits them, since they drink the water of the Nile, but if they are removed to some place other than Egypt, diseases of the blood and acute sicknesses overcome them and pain racks their bodies. Their characters are pure, their appearance attractive, and there is in them religion and goodness, virtue, chastity, and submissiveness to the master, as if they had a natural bent for slavery.

The women of Qandahār are like the Indian women. They have one merit above all other women, that the widow or divorcee again becomes like a virgin. . . .

The Turkish women combine beauty and whiteness and grace. Their faces tend to look sullen, but their eyes, though small, are sweet. They have a smooth brownness and their stature is between medium and short. There are very few tall ones among them. The beautiful ones are extremely beautiful and the ugly ones exceptional. They are treasure houses for children, gold mines for generation. It very rarely happens that their children are ugly or badly formed. They are clean and refined. Their pots are their stomachs on which they rely for preparing, cooking, and digesting food [?]. Bad breath is hardly ever found among them, nor any with large buttocks, but they have some nasty characteristics and are of little loyalty.

The Daylamī women are both outwardly and inherently beautiful, but they have the worst characters of all and the coarsest natures. They can endure hardship like the women of Ṭabaristān in every respect.

The women of Allān are reddish-white and well-fleshed. The cold humor predominates in their temperaments. They are better suited for service than for pleasure since they have good characters in that they are trustworthy and honest and are both reliant and compliant. Also, they are far from licentious.

The Greek women are blond, with straight hair and blue eyes. As slaves they are obedient, adaptable, serviceable, well-meaning, loyal, trustworthy, and reliable. They are good as treasurers because they are meticulous and not very generous. Sometimes they are skilled in some fine handicraft.

The Armenians would be beautiful were it not for their peculiarly ugly feet, though they are well-built, energetic, and strong. Chastity is rare or absent among them, and thievery widespread. Avarice is very rare among them, but they are coarse in nature and speech. Cleanliness is not in their language. They are slaves for hard work and service. If you leave a slave for an hour without work, his nature leads him to no good. Only fear and the stick make them behave properly, and their only merit is endurance of toil and heavy labor. If you see one of them idle, it is because of his bad character and not because of any lack of strength; therefore, use the stick. Be watchful in striking him and making him do what you want because this race is untrustworthy even when they are contented, not to speak of when they are angry. Their women are useless for pleasure. In fine, the Armenians are the worst of the whites as the Zanj are the worst of the blacks. And how much do they resemble one another in the strength of their bodies, their great wickedness, and their coarse natures!

Ibn Buṭlān, *Shirā al-Raqīq*, pp. 354–358, 371–378.

91. On Slaves, Slave-Girls, and Servants (Fourteenth–Fifteenth Centuries)

Section One: In Praise of Slaves and Slave-Girls and with Good Intentions toward Them

On the authority of 'Alī, May God be pleased with him, He said: The Prophet of God (God bless and save him) said: The first to enter Paradise are the martyr and the slave who has served God piously and his master loyally.

On the authority of Ibn 'Umar, may God be pleased with both father and son: The slave who has served his master loyally and served God piously will be rewarded twice.

Zayd ibn Ḥāritha was a servant of Khadīja (may God be pleased with her), bought for her in the market of 'Ukāẓ and given by her as a gift to the Prophet of God (may God bless and save him). Zayd's father came to the Prophet to redeem his son. "If your son desires it," said the Prophet, "I will do it." Zayd was asked, and replied, "The humiliation of servitude with the company of the Prophet of God is dearer to me than the honor of freedom apart from him." "Since he chooses us," said the Prophet, "we choose him." The Prophet freed him and married him to Umm Ayman and after her to Zaynab, daughter of Jaḥsh.

On the authority of 'Alī, may God be pleased with him, he said: The last words uttered by the Prophet of God were, "I advise you to pray and to act in a God-fearing way toward those whom your right hands possess [your slaves]."

On the authority of Abū Hurayra, may God be pleased with him, "Let none of you say 'My slave' or 'my slave-girl,' for you are all the slaves of God and all your women are God's slave-women, but let a man say 'my boy' [*ghulām*], 'my girl' [*jāriya*], 'my lad' [*fatā*], 'my lass' [*fatāt*]."

On the authority of Abū Mas'ūd al-Anṣārī, "I struck a boy who belonged to me, and I heard a voice behind me say 'Know, O Abū Mas'ūd, that God has more power over you than you have over this boy.' I turned round and I saw that it was the Prophet, may God bless and save him, 'O Prophet of God,' I said to him, 'for the sake of God my boy is free.' 'If you had not done this,' said the Prophet, 'Hell would have burned you.' "

It is related on the authority of Ibn 'Umar, may God be pleased with father and son, as follows: A man came to the Prophet of God, may God bless and save him, and said, "O Prophet of God, how many times do you forgive a servant?" The man repeated his question a second time and the Prophet remained silent. When he asked a third time, the Prophet replied, "I forgive him seventy times every day."

On the authority of Abū Hurayra, may God be pleased with Him. He said: Abu'l-Qāsim, the Prophet of repentance, may God bless and save him, told me: He who accuses his servant of something of which he is innocent will be given the legal penalty of flogging on the Day of Resurrection.

It is said that a man wished to sell his slave-girl and she wept. "What is the matter?" he asked. "If I owned you as you own me," she replied, "I would not part with you." He freed her and married her.

Abu'l-Yaqẓān said that Quraysh did not much care for slave-women as the mothers of their children until such women had given birth to three men who were the best of their time, namely, 'Alī ibn al-Ḥusayn, al-Qāsim ibn Muḥammad, and Sālim ibn 'Abdallāh. This happened because 'Umar, may God be pleased with him, brought as captives the daughters of Yazdajird, the son of Shahriyār, the son of Chosroes. Wishing to sell these women, he gave them to the crier to offer them for sale in the market. The crier uncovered the face of one of them, whereupon she gave him a vigorous slap in the face which made him cry out to 'Umar and complain. 'Umar called the girl and was about to whip her, but 'Alī, may God be pleased with him, said, "O Commander of the Faithful, the Prophet of God, may God bless and save him, has said, 'Give honor to the great who have been humbled and the rich who have become poor.' The daughters of kings should not be sold, but fix their price." He fixed their price, and it was paid, and he distributed the three of them to al-Ḥasan ibn 'Alī, Muḥammad ibn Abī Bakr, and 'Abdallāh ibn 'Umar. They gave birth to the three persons mentioned above.

It is said that the sons of 'Abd al-Malik competed among themselves in a horse-race and that they surpassed Maslama, who was the son of a slave-woman. Thereupon 'Abd al-Malik recited these verses of 'Amr al-'Abdī:

I forbid you to mount one of your baseborn half-breeds
on the day of the race, lest he be overtaken,
Lest his hands falter, his whip fall,
his legs grow numb and he not move.
Can two men be equal, of whom one the son of a free lady,
the other the son of a woman whose back is shared?

"May God forgive you, O Commander of the Faithful" said Maslama, "I am not like that, but rather as Ibn al-Mu'ammar said in these verses:

They did not willingly give us their daughters in marriage,
but we proposed with our lances, by force.
Captivity did not make us despise them;
they were never set to bake bread or to cook pots,
How often have you seen among us the son of a captive woman
who encounters heroes and strikes them right and left,
Who takes his battle-slaked lance in his hand,
drives it in white, and draws it out red?

'Abd al-Malik kissed Maslama's head and eyes and said, "Well spoken, my son! My God, that is indeed how you are." He gave him a gift of 100,000 dirhams as was given to the winner. But God knows best what really happened.

Section Two: In Dispraise of Slaves and Servants

On the authority of the Prophet of God, may God bless and save him, who said, "The worst property at the end of time is slaves [*mamlūk*]."

Mujāhid said, "Many servants, many devils."

Luqmān said to his son, "Do not entrust a secret to a woman, nor bed a maidservant whom you need for service."

Someone described a [black] slave [*'abd*] as follows: He eats with vigor, works with reluctance, hates people, and loves sleep.

When somebody was asked if he had a boy servant, he replied,

I have no servant on whom I can call, save only he whose
father is my uncle's brother."
Aktham said, "The free man is free, though evil befall him;
a slave though you dress him in pearls.

A man in Kūfa invited his friends, but his slave-girl failed to attend to them as she should have done. The man said,

If in a man's house there is no free lady, he will see defects
in what the girls do.
Let him not take one of them as a free wife, for they, by God,
are the worst of wives.

A man had a young slave who was very lazy. One day he sent him to buy grapes and figs. The slave took so long that the master lost patience. Finally he returned, but with only one of the two. His master struck him and said, "When I send you to do something, you should do both jobs and not just one." Later the man fell ill and sent his slave to fetch a doctor. The slave went away and came back with the doctor and another man. His master asked him who this was and he replied, "Did you not strike me and tell me to do both jobs and not just one? I brought you the doctor, and if God heals you, well and good; if not, this man will dig your grave. This one is a doctor, and that one, a grave digger."

It is said that while 'Amr al-'Ajamī was governor of Sind,

he wrote to Mūsā al-Hādī that a *sharīf* in India, one of the people of al-Muhallab ibn Abī Ṣurra, bought a black slave-boy whom he brought up and treated as his own son. When the boy grew up and became a young man, he conceived a passion for his owner's mistress. He seduced her, and she responded to him. One day his master arrived suddenly when he was not expected and found the slave in the arms of his mistress. The man attacked him, cut off his member, and left him weltering in his blood. Then he felt more kindly toward him, regretted what he had done, and tended him until he had recovered from his sickness. For a while after this, the slave waited, seeking to avenge himself on his master and devising a plot which would appease his rancor. His master had two sons, one a child and the other a boy, like the sun and the moon. One day the master left his house to attend to some business, and the black took the two boys and climbed with them to the top of a high roof, where he put them and then began to keep them occupied with food or with games until the master of the house returned. He raised his eyes and saw his two sons perched up there with the slave. "Woe to you!" cried the master. "You have exposed my two sons to death!" "Indeed so," replied the slave, "and I swear by God, than Whose there is no greater name by which a slave can swear, that if you do not cut off your own member as you cut off mine, I shall surely throw them down." "My God," cried the father, "you whom I brought up as my own child!" "Enough of that!" said the slave. "By God! It is only my life, and I would give it away like a drink of water." His master implored him again and again, but he would not respond. When the father tried to climb up, he held them over the edge. "Woe to you!" cried the father. "Have patience till I get a knife and do what you ask." So he hurried and got a knife and unmanned himself while the slave watched. When the black saw this, he threw the two children from the roof so that they were torn to pieces, and said, "Your self-mutilation is my revenge, and the death of your children is something extra." The black was arrested, and a letter sent to Mūsā al-Hādī to inform him of the matter. Mūsā wrote to the governor of Sind, 'Amr al-'Adjamī, ordering him to put the slave to death, and said, "I have never heard of anything like this." He ordered that all blacks should be expelled from his dominions. Is there anything more vile than black slaves, of less good and more evil than they? As for the *muwallad,* if you show kindness to one of them all your life and in every way, he will not be grateful, and it will be as if you had done nothing for him. The better you treat him, the more insolent he will be; the worse you treat him, the more humble and submissive. I have tried this many times, and how well the poet says:

If you honor the honorable you possess him
If you honor the ignoble, he will be insolent.

It is said that when the [black] slave is sated, he fornicates; when he is hungry, he steals. My grandfather on my mother's side used to say, "The worst use of money is bringing up slaves, and mulattoes are even worse and more wicked than Zanj, for the mulatto does not know his father, but the Zanjī often knows both parents. It is said of the mulatto that he is like a mule because he is a mongrel. The mule's mother is a mare and his father a donkey, or vice versa. Do not trust a mulatto, for there is rarely any good in him, and if there is, he is an exception, and exceptions do not make a rule.

I ask the pity of Almighty God. God suffices us and is the best of protectors. May God bless and save our lord Muḥammad, his family, and his Companions.

Al-Abshīhī, *Kitāb al-Mustaṭraf,* ii, pp. 75–77.

7 Social and Personal

13
Personal Documents

The following excerpts fall into three groups. The first consists of personal documents, one from Central Asia, the others—two epitaphs and two Geniza letters—from Egypt. The second contains three extracts from Arabic literary works, portraying social types or situations. The third consists of selections from three medieval Islamic collections of funny stories, one of them Persian, the others Arabic.

92. An Arabic Document from Central Asia (Probable Date: 718–719)

In the name of God, the Merciful and the Compassionate.

To the Amir al-Jarrāḥ ibn ʿAbdallāh, from his client Dīwāstī.

Peace be with you, O Amīr, and the mercy of God. I commend to you God, other than Whom there is no God. As follows . . . may God guide the Amir and prosper him; I . . . to the Amir my need and the need of the two sons of Tarkhūn, and that [or if] the Amir, may God prosper him, remember the two sons of Tarkhūn for good. And if the Amir thinks fit to [write] to Sulaymān ibn Abi'l-Sarī, to send them both [to the Amir], then let him do so, or let the Amir order me one of the horses of the postal service and I will send on it my servant to bring them both to the Amir. And may God make the [?] honor of the

Amir to the people of . . . succor and mercy. I pray God . . . and peace be with you, O Amir, and the mercy of God.

I. Y. Kračkovsky, ed. in *Sogdiyskiy Sbornik*, Leningrad, 1934. Reprinted in *Izbranniye Sočineniya*, i, 1955, p. 184.

93. Inscription on the Mausoleum of Sitt Kulthūm in Fusṭāṭ, Egypt (823)

In the name of God, the Merciful and the Compassionate. This is what Mākina, the daughter of Yaḥyā testifies. She testifies that there is no God but God alone, without partner, and that Muḥammad is his slave and Prophet [Qur'ān, ix, 33], that life and death are truth, that heaven and hell are truth, and that God will resurrect those who are in the grave. By this she lived, by this she died, and by this she will be resurrected, please God. May God forgive her sins, make her tomb spacious, and send her to join her Prophet Muḥammad, may God bless and save him. She died on 1 Muḥarram of the year 208 [May 16, 823].

RCEA, i, no. 154, pp. 122–123.

94. Inscription on a Tomb in Cairo (1089)

In the name of God, the Merciful and the Compassionate. Help from God and early victory for the slave and friend of God Ma'add Abū Tamīm, the Imam al-Mustanṣir Billāh, the Commander of the Faithful, may the blessings of God be upon him and on his pure ancestors and noble sons. The building of this gate was ordered by the illustrious Lord, the Commander of the Armies, the Sword of Islam, the Helper of the Imam, the Surety of the qāḍīs of the Muslims, the guide of the summoners [*dā'ī*] of the believers, may God strengthen the faith through him and let the Commander of the Faithful benefit by lengthening his life, and may He perpetuate his power and raise up his word and strengthen his arm by his illustrious son al-Afḍal, the Sword of the Imam, the glory of Islam, the honor of mankind, the defender of religion, the friend of the Commander of the Faithful, may God increase his greatness and let the Commander of the Faithful benefit by lengthening his life—in the month of Rabīʿ II in the year 482 [June 1089].

RCEA, vii, no. 2776, pp. 248–249.

95. A Letter from ʿAydhāb (1141)

Testimony submitted in our presence, of the witnesses whose signatures are appended.

We were present in ʿAydhāb, and on Tuesday, the 21st of the month of Tevet of the year [blank space], Abū Saʿīd ibn Maḥfūẓ, known as Ibn Jamāhir, entered the governors' audience and laid a complaint against Ṣāfī, the slave of Shaykh Abū Saʿīd ibn [Dosa], and asked for help against him. The governor summoned the slave Ṣāfī, and Abū Saʿīd himself summoned witnesses from among the Muslims of those with whom he sat, and they testified for Abū Saʿīd that this Ṣāfī had offended against him and that Ṣāfī had said to Abū Saʿīd something unrepeatable and [abused?] him and said to him: You had a slave-girl, and you got her with child, and when she bore you a son, you drove her away [while still suckling?] to Berbera. Abū Saʿīd appealed to the governor's audience and demanded justice against his adversary Ṣāfī. A messenger went out from the governor to collect the Jews who were in the city and to bring them to his audience. Some of them were absent, and some of them came, brought by the runners. When the governor heard Abū Saʿīd's appeal, he gave orders to beat Ṣāfī, and he shouted and appealed against this order, saying "I am the slave of the head of the Yeshiva," while Abū Saʿīd was saying, "I will not forego my right." And after the beating, the governor gave orders to imprison him and he was arrested in the presence of his adversary who had brought a complaint against him and in the presence of all those Jews who were at the governor's audience. Before the beating of the slave Ṣāfī, one of the Maghribī merchants went to the governor's house in order to release the slave, and when Abū Sa'īd ibn Jamāhir learned that he was seeking to release the slave, he began to incite some of the Muslims against this foreigner, and they caused him trouble and imposed punishment on him after threatening him. Ṣāfī was only released from imprisonment at some cost. This is what happened, and we wrote it in the last decade of the month of Tevet of the year [?] of the creation in the city of 'Aydhāb which lies on the shore of the Red Sea.

Geniza document, in Goitein, *Tarbitz*, xxi, pp. 186–187.

96. On Ransoming a Captive (ca. 1153–1187)

I wish to inform you, my dear and noble brother, may God lengthen your days and preserve you and give you life and not take you from me, that I was living in Askalon with 6,000 shares of well-being from the grace of God, when Musallam ibn Abī Sahl came to me, and I went with him to Nābulus and I bought his sister for him, and there remained a debt of 60 dinars. Then he urged me and said, "I beg you, by God, let me go with her to Egypt; perhaps she will be able to obtain part of her ransom money." And then he went and disappeared and left me, and now the payment of the 60 dinars has fallen due and the Frank has come to me. I tried to find someone who would lend me some money, and I did not succeed with anyone. I sent my son, offering him as collateral against the loan at interest and did not find anyone willing to accept him as pledge. There is no one left who thinks it licit to do good. What I desire, therefore, is that of your kindness you speak to him and ask him not to put me off any longer. Let him send me either the gold or the girl. Be urgent with him and summon him before the judges [three words missing], for you know that I have no [some words missing] greeting to you and to your children and request you to act for me urgently in this matter for I am [words missing] good terms [?] with the creditor.

To be sent to Bilbays, to my dear brother Shaykh Abu'l-Bahā ibn Ghanā'im, from his brother who kisses his hand, Abū Sa'd ibn Ghanā'im.

Geniza document, in Goitein, *Tarbitz*, xxxi, pp. 289–290.

14
Literary Portraits

97. Portrait of a Miser (Ninth Century)

There was a man who had attained the utmost limits of avarice and ranked as master. Whenever a dirham came into his hands, he spoke to it, whispered to it, pledged his devotion to it, and chided it for having tarried. He used to say, "Through how many parts have you passed; from how many purses have you parted; how many humble ones have you made great; how many great ones have you humbled! With me you may be sure that you will neither go naked nor be exposed to the sun" [Qur'ān, xx, 116–117]. Then he would put it in his purse and say to it, "Repose, in the name of God, in a place where you will not be slighted or humbled and from which you will never be disturbed."

Al-Jāḥiẓ, *Al-Bukhalā'*, pp. 207–208.

98. On Food and Love (Ninth Century)

Abu'l-Qumāqim ibn Baḥr al-Saqqā' was in love with a Medinan slave-girl. He sent a messenger to her saying, "My friends have visited me at home. Send me some heads so that we may dine and wine in your name." She did as he asked.

Next day he sent to her again saying, "My guests are still with me, and we have not parted. Send me a fried quarter of camel and a tasty side of beef so that we may lunch and drink in your name."

On the third day he sent her a message saying, "We have not yet parted. Send me a *sanbūsak* so that we may banquet in your name." She said to the messenger, "I know that love fills the heart and spreads to the liver and the bowels, but the love of our friend has never left his belly."

Abu'l-Ḥārith Jumayyiz was invited to the house of a woman whom he loved. She began to converse with him but made no mention of food. When he had enough of this, he said to her, "God make me your ransom! I hear no word about lunch." She said to him, "Are you not ashamed? Is there not enough in my face to turn your mind from such things?" He answered her, "God make me your ransom! If Jamīl and Buthayna[1] had sat together for an hour and eaten nothing at all, they would have spat in each other's faces and parted."

Al-Mubarrad, *Al-Kāmil*, pp. 419–420.

99. Portrait of a Parvenu

The Maḍīra (*Late Tenth Century*)

'Isā ibn Hishām told us the following: I was in Basra with Abu'l-Fatḥ al-Iskandarī, a master of language—when he summoned elegance, it responded; when he commanded eloquence, it obeyed. I was present with him at a reception given by some merchant, and we were served a *maḍīra*,[1] one that commended the civilization of cities. It quivered in the dish and gave promise of bliss and testified that Mu'āwiya, God have mercy on him, was Imam.[2] It was in a bowl such that looks glided off it and brilliance rippled in it. When it took its place on the table and its home in our hearts, Abu'l-Fatḥ al-Iskandarī started to curse it and him who offered it, to abuse it and him who ate it, to revile it and him who cooked it. We thought that he was jesting, but the fact was the reverse, for his jest was earnest, indeed. He withdrew from the table and left the company of brothers. We had the *maḍīra* removed, and our hearts were removed with it, our eyes followed behind it, our mouths watered after it, our lips smacked, and our livers were kindled. Nevertheless,

[1] A legendary pair of lovers.

[1] A dish of spiced meat, cooked in milk.
[2] The Caliph Mu'āwiya is said to have been a lover of *maḍīra*.

we joined with him in parting with it and inquired of him concerning it, and he said, "My story about the *maḍīra* is longer than the pain of my being deprived of it, and if I tell you about it, I am in danger of arousing aversion and wasting time."

We said, "Come on!" and he continued.

"When I was in Baghdad a certain merchant invited me to a *maḍīra* and stuck to me like a creditor and like the dog to the companions of al-Raqīm.[3] So I accepted his invitation, and we set out for his house. All the way he praised his wife, for whom, he said, he would give his life's blood. He described her skill in preparing the *maḍīra* and her refinement in cooking it, and he said, "O my master, if you could see her, with the apron round her middle, moving about the house, from the oven to the pots and from the pots to the oven, blowing on the fire with her mouth and pounding the spices with her hand; if you could see the smoke blacken that beautiful face and leave its marks on that smooth cheek, then you would see a sight which would dazzle the eyes! I love her because she loves me. It is bliss for a man to be vouchsafed the help of his wife and to be aided by his helpmate, especially if she is of his kin. She is my cousin on my father's side, her flesh is my flesh, her town is my town, her uncles are my uncles, her root is my root. She is however better natured and better looking than I."

"So he wearied me with his wife's qualities until we reached the quarter where he lived, and then he said, "O my master, look at this quarter! It is the noblest quarter of Baghdad. The worthy vie to settle here, and the great compete to dwell here. None but merchants live here, for a man can be judged by his neighbor. My house is the jewel in the middle of a necklace of houses, the center of their circle. How much, O my master, would you say was spent on each house? Make a rough guess, if you don't know exactly."

"I answered, 'A lot.'

"He said, 'Glory be to God, how great is your error! You just say "a lot." Then he sighed deeply and said, 'Glory to Him who knows all things.'

[3] Cf. Qur'ān, xvii, 8/9ff.

"Then we came to the door of his house, and he said, 'This is my house. How much, O my master, would you say I spent on this doorway? By God, I spent more than I could afford and enough to reduce me to poverty. What do you think of its workmanship and shape? By God, have you seen its like? Look at the fine points of craftsmanship in it, and observe the beauty of its lattice-work; it is as if it had been drawn with a compass. Look at the skill of the carpenter in making this door. From how many pieces did he make it? You may well say, "How should I know?" It is made of a single piece of teak, free from worm or rot. If it is moved, it moans, and if it is struck, it hums. Who made it, sir? Abū Isḥāq ibn Muḥammad al-Baṣrī made it, and he is, by God, of good repute, skillful in the craft of doors, dextrous with his hands in his work. God, what a capable man he is! By my life, I would never call on anyone but him for such a task.'

" 'And this door ring which you see, I bought it in the curio market from 'Imrān the curio dealer, for three Mu'izzī dinars. And how much yellow copper does it contain, sir? It contains six *raṭls!* It turns on a screw in the door. Turn it, by God! Then strike it and watch. By my life, one should not buy a door ring from anyone but 'Imrān, who sells nothing but treasures.'

"Then he rapped on the door, and we entered the hall, and he said, 'May God preserve you, O house! May God not destroy you, O walls! How strong are your buttresses, how sound your construction, how firm your foundation! By God, observe the steps and scrutinize the inside and the outside of the house, and ask me, "How did you obtain it, and by what devices did you acquire and gain possession of it?" I had a neighbor called Abū Sulaymān, who lived in this quarter. He had more wealth than he could store and more valuables than he could weigh. He died, may God have mercy on him, leaving an heir who squandered his inheritance on wine and song and dissipated it between backgammon and gambling. I feared lest the guide of necessity lead him to sell the house and he sell it in a moment of desperation or leave it exposed to ruination. Then I would see my chance of buying it slip away, and my grief would continue to the day of my death.'

" 'So I got some clothes of a kind difficult to sell and brought them and offered them to him and chaffered with him until he agreed to buy them on credit. The luckless regard credit as a gift, and the unsuccessful reckon it as a present. I asked him for a document for the amount, and he drew one up in my favor. Then I neglected to claim what was due until he was in the direst straits. And then I came and demanded what he owed. He asked for a delay, to which I agreed; he asked me for more clothes, which I brought him; and I asked him to give me his house as security and as a pledge in my hand. He did so, and then I induced him in successive negotiation to sell it to me so that it became mine by rising fortune, lucky chance, and a strong arm. Many a man works unwittingly for others, but I, praise be to God, am lucky and successful in matters such as these. Just think, O my master, that a few nights ago when I was sleeping in the house together with my household, there was a knock at the door. I asked, "Who is this untimely caller?" and there was a woman with a necklace of pearls, as clear as water and as delicate as a mirage, offering it for sale. I took it from her as if by theft, so low was the price for which I bought it. It will be of obvious value and abundant profit, with the help and favor of God. I have only told you this story so that you may know how lucky I am in business, for good luck can make water flow from stones. God is great! Nobody will inform you more truthfully than you yourself, and no day is nearer than yesterday. I bought this mat at an auction. It was brought out of the houses of the Ibn al-Furāt family when their assets were confiscated and seized. I had been looking for something like this for a long time and had not found it. "Fate is a pregnant woman;" no one knows what it will bear. It chanced that I was at Bāb al-Ṭāq, and this mat was displayed in the market. I weighed out so many dinars for it. By God, look at its fineness, its softness, its workmanship, its color, for it is of immense value. Its like occurs only rarely. If you have heard of Abū 'Imrān the mat maker, it is he who made it. He has a son who has now succeeded him in his shop, and only with him can the finest mats be found. By my life, never buy mats from any shop but his, for a true believer gives good advice to his brothers, especially those admitted to the sanctity of his table. But let us return to the *maḍīra,* for the hour of noon has come. Slave! Basin and water!'

"God is great, I thought, release draws nearer and escape becomes easier.

"The slave stepped forward, and the merchant said, 'Do you see this slave? He is of Greek origin and brought up in Iraq. Come here, slave! Uncover your head! Raise your leg! Bare your arm! Show your teeth! Walk up and down!'

"The slave did as he said, and the merchant said, 'By God, who bought him? By God, Abu'l-'Abbās bought him from the slave-dealer. Put down the basin and bring the jug!'

"The slave put it down and the merchant picked it up, turned it around, and looked it over; then he struck it and said, 'Look at this yellow copper—like a glowing coal or a piece of gold! It is Syrian copper, worked in Iraq. This is not one of those wornout valuables, though it has known the houses of kings and has circulated in them. Look at its beauty and ask me, "When did you buy it?" By God, I bought it in the year of the famine, and I put it aside for this moment. Slave! The jug!'

"He brought it, and the merchant took it and turned it around and said, 'Its spout is part of it, all one piece. This jug goes only with this basin, this basin goes only with this seat of honor, this seat of honor fits only in this house, and this house is beautiful only with this guest! Pour the water, slave, for it is time to eat! By God, do you see this water? How pure it is, as blue as a cat's eye, as clear as a crystal rod! It was drawn from the Euphrates and served after being kept overnight so that it comes as bright as the tongue of flame from a candle and clear as a tear. What counts is not the liquid, but the receptacle. Nothing will show you the cleanliness of the receptacles more clearly than the cleanliness of what you drink. And this kerchief! Ask me about its story! It was woven in Jurjān and worked in Arrajān. I came across it and I bought it. My wife made part of it into a pair of drawers and part of it into a kerchief. Twenty ells went into her drawers, and I snatched this amount away from her hand. I gave it to an embroiderer who worked it and embroidered it as you see.

Then I brought it home from the market and stored it in a casket and reserved it for the most refined of my guests. No Arab of the common people defiled it with his hands, nor any woman with the corners of her eyes. Every precious thing has its proper time, and every tool its proper user. Slave! Set the table, for it is growing late! Bring the dish, for the argument has been long! Serve the food, for the talk has been much!'

"The slave brought the table, and the merchant turned it in its place and struck it with his fingertips and tested it with his teeth and said, 'May God give prosperity to Baghdad! How excellent are its products, how refined its craftsmen! By God, observe this table, and look at the breadth of its surface, the slightness of its weight, the hardness of its wood, and the beauty of its shape.'

"I said, 'This is all fine, but when do we eat?'

" 'Now,' he said. 'Slave! Bring the food quickly. But please observe that the legs and the table are all of one piece.' "

Abu'l-Fatḥ said, "I was fuming, and I said to myself, 'There is still the baking and its utensils, the bread and its qualities, and where the wheat was originally bought, and how an animal was hired to transport it, in what mill it was ground, in what tub it was kneaded, in what oven it was baked, and what baker was hired to bake it. Then there is still the firewood, when it was cut, when it was brought, and how it was set out to dry; and then the baker and his description, the apprentice and his character, the flour and its praises, the yeast and its commentary, the salt and its saltiness. And then there are the plates, who got them, how he acquired them, who used them, and who made them; and the vinegar, how its grapes were selected or its fresh dates were bought, how the press was limed, how the juice was extracted, how the jars were tarred, and how much each cask was worth. And then there were the vegetables, by what devices they were picked, in what grocery they were packed, with what care they were cleaned. And then there is the *maḍīra,* how the meat was bought, the fat was paid for, the pot set up, the fire kindled, the spices pounded so that the cooking might excell and the gravy be thick. This is an affair that overflows and a business that has no end.'

"So I rose, and he asked, 'What do you want?'

"I said, 'A need that I must satisfy.'

"He said, 'O my master! You are going to a privy which shames the spring residence of the amir and the autumn residence of the vizier! Its upper part is plastered and its lower part is white-washed; its roof is terraced and its floor is paved with marble. Ants slip off its walls and cannot grip; flies walk on its floor and slither along. It has a door with panels of teak and ivory combined in the most perfect way. A guest could wish to eat there.'

" 'Eat there yourself,' I said. 'The privy is not part of the bargain.'

"Then I made for the door and hurried as I went. I began to run, and he followed me, shouting, 'O Abu'l-Fatḥ, the *maḍīra!*' The youngsters thought that *al-maḍīra* was my byname, and they began to shout it. I threw a stone at one of them, so angry was I, but the stone hit a man on his turban and pierced his head. I was seized and beaten with shoes, both old and new, and showered with blows, both worthy and vicious, and thrown into prison. I remained for two years in this misfortune, and I swore that I would never eat a *maḍīra* as long as I lived. Have I done wrong in this, O people of Hamadān?"

'Isā ibn Hishām said, "We accepted his excuse and joined in his vow, saying 'The *maḍīra* has brought misfortune on the noble and has exalted the unworthy over the worthy.' "

Badī' al-Zamān al-Hamadānī, *Maqāmāt,* pp. 104–117.

15
Humor

100. Some Anecdotes (Ninth Century)

A man once saw Muʻāwiya when he was a young boy, and said, "I think this boy will rule his people." Hind [Muʻāwiya's mother] said, "May I be bereaved of him if he only rules his own people."

i, p. 224.

A man had a dream in which he saw sheep being given to him, eight at a time. Then he opened his eyes and saw nothing. He closed his eyes again, stretched out his hand, and said, "All right, give them to me in fours."

ii, p. 38.

One of the fools of Quraysh was Muʻāwiya ibn Marwān, the brother of the Caliph ʻAbd al-Malik ibn Marwān. One day he was waiting for ʻAbd al-Malik at the Gate of Damascus, by the door of a miller's house. He looked at the miller's donkey and saw it turning the mill wheel with a bell round its neck. He asked the miller, "Why did you put a bell on the donkey's neck?" The miller answered, "Sometimes I doze or fall asleep, and if I don't hear the sound of the bell, I know that the donkey is standing still, and then I shout at it." Muʻāwiya asked, "And what if the donkey were to stand still and move its head? How would you know that it is standing still?" The miller replied, "And how should my donkey have the intelligence of the prince?"

ii, p. 42.

Muʻāwiya employed a man of the tribe of Kalb. He spoke of the Magians one day, and said, "God curse the Magians, who marry their mothers! By God, if I were given 10,000 I would not marry my mother!"

Word of this reached Mu'āwiya, who said, "God damn him, if they increased the price he would do it." And he dismissed him.

ii, p. 45.

Two men jointly owned a slave. One of them began to beat him. His partner asked him, "What are you doing?" The man answered, "I am beating my part."

ii, p. 52.

A Bedouin came to a money changer with a dirham. "This is counterfeit," said the money changer. "What is counterfeit?" asked the Bedouin. "It is copper inside and silver outside," said the money changer.

"It isn't," said the Bedouin.

"Break it," said the money changer, "and if it is as I say then I am absolved."

The Bedouin agreed and broke it. When he saw the copper, he said, "Hey you, tell me when I will die, for I see that you are one who knows hidden things."

ii, p. 58.

Someone said to Ash'ab;[1] "If you were to relate traditions [*ḥadīth*] and stop telling jokes, you would be doing a nobler thing."

"By God," answered Ash'ab. "I have heard traditions and related them."

"Then tell us," said the man.

"I heard from Nāfi'," said Ash'ab, "on the authority of Ibn 'Umar, that the Prophet of God, may God bless and save him, said, 'There are two qualities, such that whoever has them is among God's elect.'"

"That is a fine tradition," said the man. "What are these two qualities?"

"Nāfi' forgot one and I have forgotten the other," said Ash'ab.

ii, p. 55.

[1] A famous humorist of the early eighth century.

'Abd al-Malik ibn Hilāl al-Hīnābī had a basket full of pebbles, that he used as a rosary, taking them one by one as he uttered the praises of God. When he was bored, he took the pebbles two at a time or three at a time, and when he was very bored he took them in handfuls and said, "Praise be to God this much!" When he was thoroughly exasperated he seized the loops of the basket and said, "Praise be to God all this!"

ii, p. 59.

Some people came to al-Rustumī's house on some business, and the time came for the midday prayer. They asked him, "Which is the direction of Mecca in this house of yours?" He replied, "I only moved in a month ago."

ii, p. 59.

The daughter of al-Khuss was asked, "What would you say to a hundred goats?"
"Sufficiency!"
"To a hundred sheep?"
"Wealth."
"To a hundred camels?"
"Fulfillment."

ii, pp. 73–74.

Khalīl ibn Aḥmad said: There are four kinds of men: the man who knows and knows that he knows; learn from him; the man who knows and doesn't know that he knows; he is forgetful—remind him; the man who doesn't know and knows that he doesn't know; he seeks guidance—teach him; the man who doesn't know and doesn't know that he doesn't know; he is a fool—avoid him.

ii, p. 126.

Yaḥyā ibn Khālid said: People write the best of what they hear, remember the best of what they write, and speak the best of what they remember.

Al-Sha'bā said: If a man could remember what I have forgotten he would be wise.

A man said, describing another: His knowledge is at fault in four respects. What he hears is different from what he is told, what he remembers is different from what he hears, what he writes is different from what he remembers, and what he says is different from what he writes.

ii, p. 130.

A man of the Qadarī School[2] was traveling in the company of a Magian. The Qadarī asked him, "Why don't you become a Muslim, you Magian?" "When God wills it," replied the Magian. "God has already willed it," said the Qadarī, "but the devil won't let you." "I am with the stronger," said the Magian.

ii, p. 142.

Ibn Sīrīn said: I have seen nothing better in a man than eloquence, or in a woman than plumpness.

ii, p. 157.

Ibn Shubruma said: If it would please you to be great in the eyes of those in whose eyes you were small, and to see those who were great in your eyes become small in your eyes, then learn Arabic, for it will guide you to logic and bring you near to authority.

Maslama ibn 'Abd al-Malik said: A solecism in speech is worse than pockmarks on the face.

'Abd al-Malik said: A solecism in speech is worse than a tear in a fine garment.

ii, p. 158.

A Bedouin went to market and heard them speaking bad Arabic. "Praise be to God," he said. "They commit solecisms, and make profits. We commit no solecisms and make no profits!"

ii, p. 159.

Al-Ḥajjāj said to his children's tutor, "Teach them to swim before you teach them to write, for they can find someone else

[2] A group of theologians who believed in free will.

to write for them, but they will not find anyone to swim for them."

ii, p. 166.

The people gathered in the presence of Mu'āwiya, and the orators rose to proclaim Yazīd as heir to the Caliphate. Some of the people showed disapproval, whereupon a man of the tribe of 'Udhra, called Yazīd ibn al-Muqanna', rose to his feet. Drawing his sword a handspan from the scabbard, he said, "The Commander of the Faithful is that one!" and he pointed to Mu'āwiya. "And if he dies, then that one!" and he pointed to Yazīd. "And if anyone objects, then this one!" and he pointed to his sword.

Mu'āwiya said to him, "You are the prince of orators."

ii, p. 210.

A man said to Ibrāhīm ibn Adham, "O Abū Isḥāq, I would like you to accept this cloak from me to cover you." "If you are rich," he replied, "I will accept it, but if you are poor, I will not." "I am rich," said the man.

"How much have you?" asked Ibrāhīm. "I have 2,000," said the man. "Would you like to have 4,000?" asked Ibrāhīm. "Yes," said the man. "Then you are poor," said Ibrāhīm. "I will not take it."

ii, p. 362.

Abū 'Amr ibn al-'Alā' fell sick. His friends came to visit him, and one of them stayed late.

"Why have you stayed behind?" asked Abū 'Amr.

"I want to stay up with you," said the visitor.

"You are healthy," said Abū 'Amr, "and I am sick. Your health will not let you stay awake and my sickness will not let me sleep. Pray God to give gratitude to the healthy and patience and recompense to the sick."

iii, p. 47.

A Bedouin fell sick. People began to call on him and ask how he was and how he had been. When there were too many for him, he answered, "As I have told your friend."

iii, p. 47.

A man asked 'Ubaydallāh ibn Abī Bakra, "What do you say on the death of a parent?"

"More property."

"On the death of a spouse?"

"New nuptials."

"On the death of a brother?"

"A cropped wing."

"On the death of a child."

"An ache in the heart that cannot be overcome."

iii, p. 92.

A man was asked, "Which of your sons is dearest to you?" He replied, "The smallest till he grows up, the sick till he becomes well, the absent until he arrives."

iii, p. 92.

'Amr ibn al-'Aṣ called on Mu'āwiya when his daughter 'Ā'isha was with him. "Who is this, O Commander of the Faithful?" he asked.

"This is the delight of my heart," replied the Caliph.

"Send her away from you!" said 'Amr.

"Why?" asked the Caliph.

"Because women give birth to enemies, bring the distant near, and bequeath grudges," said 'Amr.

"Don't say that, 'Amr," said the Caliph, "for nobody can tend the sick, bewail the dead, and help in mourning as they do. You may also sometimes find an uncle to whom his sister's sons have rendered some service."

"How wise you are!," said 'Amr. "You have reconciled me to them."

iii, p. 99.

[The black poet] Nuṣayb said to [the Caliph] 'Umar ibn 'Abd al-'Azīz, "O Commander of the Faithful! My years have increased and my bones have become thin and I am afflicted with daughters. My color rubbed off on to them and they are left on my hands."

'Umar took pity on him and gave him a gift.

iii, p. 126.

A man came to Khālid ibn 'Abdallāh with a request, and said, "Shall I speak with the boldness of despair or the deference of hope?" "With the deference of hope," said Khālid. The man stated his request, and Khālid granted it.

iii, p. 127.

A man came to Yazīd ibn Abī Muslim with a petition and asked him to present it to al-Ḥajjāj. Yazīd looked at it and told the man that this was not the kind of request that could be put before the governor. "I ask you to put it before him all the same," said the man. "Perhaps it is predestined by fate, and he will grant it against his will."

Yazīd took the petition to al-Hajjāj and told him what the man had said. Al-Hajjāj looked at the petition and said to Yazīd, "Tell the man that it was predestined by fate and that I have granted it against my will."

iii, p. 130.

A man said to Mu'āwiya, "Assign Baḥrayn to me."

"I don't reach that far," replied Mu'āwiya.

"Then make me governor of Basra," said the man.

"I don't wish to dismiss the present governor," said Mu'āwiya.

"Then grant me 2,000 [dinars]," said the man.

"They are yours," said Mu'āwiya.

The man's friends said to him, "Woe to you! How could you be content with this, after your first two requests?"

"Be quiet!" he replied. "Were it not for the first two, I would not have been given this."

iii, p. 131.

A man said to Thumāma, "I want something from you."

"And I want something from you," said Thumāma.

"What is it?" asked the man.

"I will not tell you unless you promise to grant it," said Thumāma.

"I do so," said the man.

"What I want of you," said Thumāma, "is that you do not ask for what you want of me."

"I withdraw what I have given," said the man.

"But I do not return what I have taken," said Thumāma.

iii, p. 137.

Yazīd ibn 'Umayr al-Usayyidī said to his sons, "My sons, learn to refuse, for it is more powerful than to give. If the Banū Tamīm know that one of you has a 100,000 dirhams, they will respect him more for having it than they would for sharing it out among them. It is better for you if they say, 'He is miserly and rich, rather than 'He is generous but poor.' "

iii, p. 138.

Ḥubba al-Madīniyya was asked, "What is the wound that does not heal?"

"When the generous has need of the mean and is refused," she said.

"What is humiliation?" she was asked.

"When the noble stands by the door of the ignoble and is not admitted," she said.

"What is nobility?" she was asked.

"A necklace of virtues round the neck of man" she said.

iii, p. 139.

The Caliph Hishām ibn 'Abd al-Malik said to Sālim ibn 'Abdallāh as they entered the Ka'ba together, "Ask me for whatever you need."

Sālim replied, "In God's house I would not ask of any but God."

iii, p. 186.

Al-Aṣma'ī quoted Dhu'l-Rumma as saying, "If you ask a man what milk is best, and he says sour milk, then ask him whose slave he is; if he says fresh milk, ask him whose son he is."

A man of Quraysh met a woman of the desert Arabs and asked her, "Is there any milk for sale?"

"You must be mean," she said, "or closely connected with people who are mean."

iii, p. 207.

A fat man was asked what made him fat. He replied, "Eating hot, drinking cold, leaning to my left, and eating at others' cost."

Another fat man replied to the same question, "Little thinking, much relaxing, sleep after gorging."

iii, p. 324.

Three things cause emaciation: drinking water on an empty stomach in the morning, going to sleep without making a bed, and much talking in a loud voice.

It is said that four things are injurious to life and often kill: to go into the bath in gluttony, to have intercourse after repletion, to eat dried jerked meat, and to drink cold water on an empty stomach in the morning. Some add: to have intercourse with an old woman.

iii, p. 271.

'Umar ibn al-Khaṭṭāb mentioned three kinds of misfortune: a neighbor who when he sees good, conceals it, when he sees evil, broadcasts it; a wife who abuses you at home and whom you cannot trust when you are away; a ruler who does not praise you when you do right, but kills you when you do wrong.

iv, p. 4.

Al-Aṣma'ī said: A Bedouin said to his cousin, "I want a woman who is white, tall, and slender, with long, curly hair; when she stands her shift only touches the tips of her shoulders, the nipples of her breasts, the contours of her buttocks and her kneecaps; when she lies down, if you were to throw a large citron under her, it would come out on the other side."

"Where will you find such a one," said his cousin, "except in Paradise?"

iv, pp. 5–6.

One day Khālid ibn Ṣafwān's wife said to him, "How beautiful you are!" "Do not say that," he said, "for I have not the pillar of beauty, nor the garment of beauty, nor the burnus of beauty." "And what," she asked, "are the pillar and garment and burnus of beauty?" "The pillar of beauty," he said, "is height—and I am short; its garment is whiteness—and I am not white; its burnus is black hair—and I am bald. Now if you said, 'How sweet you are and how handsome you are,' that would be better."

iv, p. 23.
Ibn Qutayba, *'Uyūn al-akhbār.*

101. From a Thirteenth-Century Persian Joke Book

Sultan Maḥmūd[1] was attending a sermon in the Mosque. Talhak went there after him. When he arrived, the preacher stood up and said that if anyone had committed pederasty, then on the Day of Judgment the youth whom he had abused would be placed on his neck, and he would have to carry him over the Bridge of Doom. Sultan Maḥmūd wept. Talhak said, "O Sultan, do not weep but be of good cheer. On that day you won't have to go on foot either."

The Caliph al-Mahdī once got separated from his party during a hunt. In the night he came to a Bedouin's house. The Bedouin was sitting at a meal and had a jug of wine in front of him. When they had drunk a glass, al-Mahdī said, "I am one of al-Mahdī's courtiers." They drank another glass, and al-Mahdī said, "I am one of al-Mahdī's amirs." When they had drunk a third glass, he said, "I am al-Mahdī." The Bedouin took the jug away and said, "You drank the first glass and claimed to be a courtier. With the second glass you claimed to be an amir, and with the third, to be Caliph. If you drink another glass, you will surely claim to be God Almighty." The next day when the Caliph's party arrived, the Bedouin fled in fear. Al-Mahdī commanded that he should be found and brought before him, whereupon he gave him some gold pieces. The Bedouin said, "I bear witness that you speak truth, even if you make the fourth claim."

A man announced that he was God. He was brought before the Caliph who said to him, "Last year there was someone here

[1] Sultan Maḥmūd of Ghazna, reigned 998–1030.

who claimed to be a prophet. He was executed." "That was well done," said the man, "for I had not sent him."

A Qazvīnī[2] went to war against the heretics with a huge shield. From the fortress they threw a stone which hit him on the head and wounded him. The Qazvīnī was furious and said, "Are you blind, man? Can't you see a shield as big as this that you have to throw a stone straight on to my head?"

A number of Qazvīnīs went to war against the heretics. When they came back from the battle, each of them was carrying the head of a heretic on a pole. One of them had a foot on his pole. They asked him, "Who killed this one?" He answered, "I did." They asked him, "Why didn't you bring his head?" He answered, "They took his head away before I got there."

Someone asked Mawlānā 'Aḍud al-Dīn, "How is it that in the time of the Caliphs many men claimed to be God or Prophet, and now they do not?" He replied, "The men of our time are so beset by oppression and hunger that they reck nothing of God or Prophet."

A Rāzī, Gīlānī, and a Qazvīnī went together on pilgrimage. The Qazvīnī was bankrupt, the Rāzī and the Gīlānī were rich. When the Rāzī put his hand on the curtain ring of the Ka'ba, he said, "O God, in thanksgiving to Thee for bringing me here safely I set free my slaves Balban and Banafsha." When the Gīlānī grasped the curtain ring, he said, "In thanksgiving for this I set free my slaves Mubārak and Sunqur." When the Qazvīnī grasped the curtain ring he said, "O God, Thou knowest I have neither Balban nor Sunqur, neither Banafsha nor Mubārak. In thanksgiving for this, therefore, I set free my old Fāṭima with a triple divorce."

In the time of the Caliph Wāthiq a woman laid claim to prophethood. The Caliph asked her, "Was Muḥammad a Prophet?"

[2] Qazvīn, where 'Ubayd-i Zākānī was born, was the main base for campaigns against the Ismā'īlī stronghold at Alamūt.

"Certainly," she replied. "Then," said the Caliph, "since Muḥammad said, 'There will be no Prophet after me,' your claim is false." The woman replied, "He said, 'There will be no Prophet after me.' He did not say, 'There will be no Prophetess after me.' "

One day when Sultan Maḥmūd was hungry, they brought him a dish of eggplant. He liked it very much and said, "Eggplant is an excellent food." A courtier began to praise the eggplant with great eloquence. When the sultan grew tired of the dish he said, "Eggplant is a very harmful thing," whereupon the courtier began to speak in hyperbole of the harmful qualities of the eggplant. "Man alive," said the sultan, "have you not just now uttered the praises of the eggplant?" "Yes," said the courtier, "but I am your courtier and not the eggplant's courtier. I have to say what pleases you, not what pleases the eggplant."

A tumbler scolded his son and said, "You do no work and you waste your life in idleness. How often must I tell you to practice somersaults and to learn how to dance on a rope and to make a dog jump through a hoop so that you can achieve something with your life. If you don't listen to me, I swear by God I shall abandon you to the *madrasa* to learn their dead and useless science and to become a scholar so as to live in contempt and misery and adversity and never be able to earn a penny wherever you go."

Shaykh Sharaf al-Dīn Darguzīnī asked Mawlānā 'Aḍud al-Dīn, "Where in the Qur'ān has God spoken of shaykhs?" He answered, "At the side of the learned in this verse, 'Shall the learned and the ignorant be treated in the same manner?' " [xxxix, 12].

Mawlānā Sharaf al-Dīn Dāmghānī was passing by the door of a mosque just as the mosque servant got hold of a dog and beat him inside the mosque. The dog howled. Mawlānā opened the mosque door, and the dog fled. The mosque servant abused Mawlānā. "My friend," said Mawlānā, "excuse the dog. He has no understanding; that is why he went into the mosque.

We others, who have understanding, you will never see us in the mosque."

A Khurāsānī went to a physician and said, "My wife is ill. What should I do?" The physician said, "Bring me a specimen in a bottle tomorrow. Then I will look and tell you." By chance the Khurāsānī himself felt ill later that day. Next day he came to the physician with a bottle with a piece of string tied round the middle. The physician asked, "Why did you tie on this string?" The man said, "I also felt sick. The upper half is my water and the lower half is my wife's." Next day the physician repeated this story to everybody. A Qazvīnī was present and said, "Master, please excuse him, for the Khurāsānī has no sense. Was the string tied inside or outside the bottle?"

They asked a wise man, "Why do the nomads never need a physician?" He answered, "As the wild ass needs no vet."

Shams-i Muzaffar said one day to his disciples, "One should learn when one is young. What one learns in youth one never forgets in age. It is now fifty years since I learned the first verse of the Qur'ān and I can still remember it, though I never read it since."

A man said, "I have pain in my eyes and as a cure I use Qur'ān verses and prayers." Talhak said to him, "But you should use a little eye-salve too."

The devil was asked, "Which group of people do you love best?" He replied, "The market brokers [*dallāl*]." They asked him why. He answered, "Not only do they speak falsehood, which in itself delights me, but they swear to it as well."

A king had three wives, one Persian, one Arab, and one Coptic. One night he lay beside the Persian woman and asked her, "What time is it?" She answered, "It is the hour of dawn." He asked her, "How do you know?" She answered, "Because the scent of the roses and basil is rising and the birds are beginning to sing."

The next night he lay with the Arab woman and asked her the same question. She answered, "It is the hour of dawn. I know it because the pearls of my necklace feel cold against my breast." On the third night he lay with the Coptic woman and he asked her the same question and she answered, "It is the hour of dawn. I know because I have to go to stool."[3]

In the month of Ramaḍān someone said to a dealer, "In this month there is no business." He answered "God give long life to the Jews and the Christians."

A man met another man who was riding on a wretched donkey. "Where are you going?" he asked. "I am going to the Friday prayer," answered the other. "Woe betide you, it's only Tuesday," said the first. "Yes," said the rider, "but I shall be lucky if this donkey can bring me to the mosque by Saturday."

Abū Dulaf became a Shi'ite and used to say that whoever did not declare himself a Shi'ite was a child of fornication. His son said to him, "I am not of your sect." Abū Dulaf answered, "Yes, indeed, by God. I bedded your mother before I bought her."

A man said to a woman, "I would like to taste you, to know which has a better flavor, you or my wife." She answered, "Ask my husband, he has tasted us both."

Abū Nuwās saw a drunken man and looked at him in wonderment. He was asked, "Why do you find this funny? You yourself are in the same state every day." Abū Nuwās replied, "I have never seen a drunken man before." "How is that?" they asked him. "Because," he replied, "I am always the first to get drunk and the last to recover so I don't know what happens to those who get drunk after I do."

One day Abū Nuwās was seen with a glass of wine in his hand, a bunch of grapes on his right, and a dish of raisins on

[3] The first two answers contain well-known literary themes used in dawn poetry.

his left, and every time he drank from the glass he took a grape and a raisin. "What does this mean?" they asked him, and he replied, "This is the Father, the Son, and the Holy Ghost."

A Bedouin was eating with all five fingers. He was asked, "Why do you behave like this?" "If I were to eat with only three," he replied, "the other fingers would be angry." They said to another Bedouin, "You are eating with five fingers." "Yes," he said, "what can I do? I have no more."

Abu'l-Ḥārith was asked, "Can a man of eighty have a child?" He answered them, "Yes, if he has a neighbor of twenty."

A man with bad breath came to a physician and complained of a toothache. When the physician opened his mouth, a terrible smell came out. The physician said, "This is not my job. Go to the sweepers."

A bore visited a sick man and stayed with him too long. The sick man said, "I am plagued with too many visitors." The bore said, "I will go and shut the door." "Yes," said the sick man, "but from the outside."

A man who claimed to be a prophet was brought before the Caliph al-Muʿtaṣim. Al-Muʿtasim said, "I bear witness that you are a stupid prophet." The man replied, "I have only come to people like you."

A man said to Ḥajjāj, "I saw you yesterday in a dream, and it seemed that you were in Paradise!" Ḥajjāj replied, "If your dream is true, then the injustice in the hereafter is even greater than in this world."

They said to a Ṣūfī, "Sell your cloak." He replied, "If a fisherman sells his net, with what shall he fish?"

A Bedouin went on pilgrimage and reached Mecca ahead of the others. He grasped the curtains of the Kaʿba and said, "O God, forgive me before the crowd gets to You."

A man married a woman, and on the fifth day after the wedding she bore a child. The man went to the market and bought tablets and ink. They asked him, "What is this?" He answered, "A child that can come into the world after five days can go to school after another three."

The mark of the fool is that he comes at the wrong time and stays too long.

'Ubayd-i Zākānī, *Kulliyyat*, pp. 241–308 (extracts).

102. From a Fourteenth-Century Arabic Joke Book

A man claimed to be a prophet. They asked him, "What are the proofs of your being a prophet?" He said, "I shall tell you what is in your mind." They asked him, "What is in our minds?" He said, "You are thinking that I am a liar and not a prophet."

Another man claimed to be a prophet in the days of the Caliph al-Ma'mūn. He asked him, "What is your miracle?" The man said, "Ask what you wish." The Caliph had in his hand a lock. "Take this and open it," he said. "God preserve you," the man replied. "I did not say that I was a blacksmith." The Caliph laughed, called on him to repent, and let him off.

A man said, "I said to a slave-girl whom I wanted to buy, 'Don't be misled by my gray hair, for I still have strength." She replied, 'Would you be pleased to have a randy old woman?' "

Two slave-girls were brought to al-Mu'taṣim, one a virgin, the other not. He preferred the virgin, and the other said, "There is nothing between us but one day." The virgin said, "One day with thy Lord is as a thousand years of your reckoning" [Qur'ān xxii, 47].

An elegant lady was asked, "Are you a virgin?" "God preserve me from being left on the shelf," she replied.

The Caliph al-Mutawakkil asked a slave-girl whom he was inspecting, "Are you a virgin or what?" "I am what, O Commander of the Faithful," she replied.

A man wrote to his beloved, "Send me a vision of you in my dreams." She wrote back, "Send me two dinars and I will come in person."

A man sued a woman marriage-broker. He said to the judge, "May God preserve you, this old woman got me a wife, and when I came to her, I found her lame."

The old woman replied, "May God preserve the judge. I found him a wife to take to bed. I did not know that he wanted to ride her on pilgrimage, enter her for the races, or play polo on her back."

When 'Ā'isha the daughter of Ṭalḥa was given in marriage to Muṣ'ab, he said, "By God, this night I shall kill her with passion." He took her once and then fell asleep and did not awaken till dawn when she shook him and said, "Wake up, killer."

A blind man married a black woman and she said to him, "If you could see my beauty and my loveliness and my whiteness you would love me even more." He replied, "If you were as you say, the sighted ones would not have left you to me."

One day Ash'ab was sitting next to the prince Marwān ibn Abān ibn 'Uthmān, and Marwān let fly a loud smell. Ash'ab got up and went away so that people should think that he was the one who had emitted it. When Marwān went home, Ash'ab called upon him and said, "My compensation." "Compensation?" asked Marwān, "For what?" 'Compensation for the wind for which I relieved you of responsibility," said Ash'ab. "If not, I will blacken your name." He did not leave him alone until he bought him off.

Ash'ab heard Ḥubbā the woman of Medina say, "O please God, do not let me die until you have forgiven me for my sins!"

Ash'ab said to her, "Wicked woman! You are not asking God for forgiveness, you are asking Him for immortality." He meant that God would never forgive her.

Al-Nuwayrī, *Nihāyat al-Arab*, iv, pp. 15–30.

Glossary

Abbreviations

Dozy R. Dozy, *Dictionnaire détaillé des noms des vêtements chez les arabes*, Amsterdam (Müller), 1845.

EI[1] *Encyclopaedia of Islam*, first edition, Leiden (Brill), 1908–1938.

EI[2] *Encyclopaedia of Islam*, second edition, Leiden (Brill), 1954– in progress.

IMG W. Hinz, *Islamische Masse und Gewichte*, Leiden (Brill), 1955.

Schacht J. Schacht, *An Introduction to Islamic Law*, Oxford (Clarendon), 1964.

'Abd: the commonest Arabic term for slave, often combined with one or another of the divine names or attributes to form personal names, for example, 'Abd Allāh, slave of God; 'Abd al-Raḥmān, slave of the Merciful; 'Abd al-Karīm, slave of the Generous. In most Arabic-speaking countries the word *'abd* was in time specialized to mean "black slave," later simply "black." Male white slaves, usually military, were called *mamlūk*, a passive participle meaning "owned." Other terms for slaves included *ghulām* and *khādim* [q.v.] (*EI*[2], s.v.).

'Adāla: rectitude, good morals. A legal term denoting certain qualities, possession of which is a condition for public and juridical functions and offices. The possessor of *'adāla* is called *'adl*. A witness in proceedings before a qāḍī must be an *'adl*. In time groups of recognized, irreproachable witnesses, called *shāhid* or *'adl*, came to form a branch of the legal profession and acted as notaries or scriveners (*EI*[2], " 'Adl").

'Adl: see *'Adāla*.

'Ahd: covenant or pact, usually used for political treaties and arrangements such as the appointment of an heir apparent, the

safeguards conceded in a surrender on terms, and the limited rights granted to non-Muslims, whether inside the Islamic state (see *dhimma*); or outside it (see *amān*). The person or group granted *ʿahd* is called *muʿāhad* (*EI*², "ʿAhd").

Ahl: people, family, or kin (Arabic—cf. Hebrew *ohel,* tent). *Ahl al-Bayt,* people of the house, normally refers to the family and descendants of the Prophet. *Ahl al-dhimma,* people of the pact, is a common term for the protected non-Muslim subjects (see *dhimma*); *ahl al-ḥarb,* people of war, denotes non-Muslims beyond the Islamic frontier (see *Dār al-Ḥarb*).

Amān: safety, protection, or, in battle, quarter; sometimes also the pardon given to a rebel or similar offender. It is used technically for the safe-conduct or pledge of security given to a non-Muslim from outside the Islamic state (see *ḥarbī*). It may be given at the termination of hostilities or, more commonly, to an outsider visiting the Muslim lands for a limited period. The recipient of *amān* is called *mustaʾmin* (*EI*², s.v.).

Amīr: an Arabic title literally meaning "commander," often translated "prince." *Amīr al-Muʾminīn,* Commander or Prince of the Believers, was one of the earliest and most distinctive titles of the Caliphs. The title "amir" was variously used of high military officers, governors of provinces, and increasingly, of the virtually independent rulers who emerged in many parts of the Islamic Empire under the nominal suzerainty of the Caliph. In the tenth century the title *Amīr al-Umarāʾ,* amir of amirs, was adopted by the military rulers of the capital to indicate their primacy over the other amirs in the provinces (*EI*², s.v.).

Amṣār: plural of *miṣr,* the term applied to the fortress cities established or maintained by the Arabs in the early days of their empire. The most important *amṣār* were Kūfa and Basra in Iraq, Qumm in Persia, Fusṭāṭ in Egypt, and Qayrawān in North Africa. As a proper name Miṣr means Egypt or its capital city.

Anṣār: literally helpers, the designation applied to the Medinans who joined the Prophet Muḥammad after his migration to Medina from Mecca (*EI*², s.v.).

Ardabb or *Irdabb:* a measure of capacity of varying value, in medieval times usually about 90 liters (*IMG,* pp. 39–40).

'Arrāda: a medieval siege weapon, in which a projectile is propelled by a shaft driven forward by the release of a rope (*EI*[2], s.v.).

Atabeg, Atabek: a Turkish title, meaning literally "father-prince," given to the tutors or guardians of Seljuq and other Turkish princes. In time the *atabegs* became powerful officers of state, even governors and founders of dynasties. In Mamlūk Egypt the Atabeg was the commander-in-chief of the army (*EI*[2], s.v.).

Banū: sons of; commonly used in the names of Arab tribes.

Barīd: from the Latin *veredus,* Greek *beredos,* a post-horse (cf. German *Pferd*), the term commonly applied to the post and intelligence services of Islamic states and also to the couriers, mounts, and stages. The head of the organization was called *Ṣāḥib al-Barīd*—postmaster (*EI*[2], s.v.).

Bay'a: recognition of authority, especially the act by which a new Caliph or heir apparent is proclaimed and recognized (*EI*[2], s.v.).

Beg, Bey: a Turkish title, roughly "lord" or "prince," often used as equivalent of the Arabic "amir" (*EI*[2], s.v.).

Bid'a: innovation; a belief or practice for which there is no authority in tht *Sunna.* In Islamic usage it is used in a sense approximate to heresy (*EI*[2], s.v.).

Caliph: see *Khalīfa.*

Dā'ī: summoner; a religious propagandist or missionary, especially among the Ismā'īlīs and similar dissenting groups. The mission is called *da'wa* (*EI*[2], s.vv.).

Dāniq: a coin or weight, one-sixth of a dirham or, more frequently, of a dinar.

Dār al-Ḥarb: House of War; the non-Muslim world beyond the Islamic frontier. Between the House of War and the House of Islam (*Dār al-Islām*) there must be, according to legal theory, a perpetual state of war until all the world accepts the rule of Islam (see *jihād*). Until then the state of war may be suspended by truces but cannot be ended by a peace. A person coming from the House of War is called *ḥarbī* (*EI*[2], s.v.).

Da'wa: see *dā'ī*

Devshirme: the Ottoman Turkish term for the periodic levy of

Christian boys, collected for training and recruitment into the Janissaries, the Imperial Household, and the administration (*EI*,[2] s.v.).

Dhimma: the pact or covenant accorded by the Muslim state and community to the followers of other revealed religions living under their rule, according them protection and certain limited rights on the condition of their recognition of the supremacy of Islam. Members of religious communities benefiting from the *dhimma* are called *dhimmī* (*EI*[2], s.v.).

Dhirāʿ: the cubit, or arm's length, subdivided into 24 digits (*aṣbaʿ*). The length of the cubit varies in different regions and for different purposes. It is usually in the neighborhood of 50 to 60 centimeters (*EI*[2], s.v.; *IMG*, pp. 55–62).

Dihqān: the country gentry of pre-Islamic Persia. Under the early Caliphate they retained for a while their fiscal functions and social privileges but later sank gradually to the level of the peasantry (*EI*[2], "Dihḳān").

Dīnār: from the Greek *dênarion*, Latin *denarius*, the unit of gold currency under the Caliphate. The term went out of use between the twelfth and fourteenth centuries but has been revived in modern times (*EI*[2], s.v.).

Dirham: from the Greek *drakhmê*, the unit of silver currency used in the Islamic states from the beginning to the Mongol conquests. The term is also used to designate a weight, which varied greatly at different times and places and for different commodities (*EI*[2], s.v.; *IMG*, pp. 1–2).

Dīwān: an Arabic word of Persian origin, probably from a root meaning "to write." In early Islamic times the term was used of the central register of Muslim warriors and pensioners; later it denoted government departments in general. In the Ottoman Empire the *dīwān* was a kind of state council, presided over by the Sultan and later by the Grand Vizier. The collected poems of a poet are known as his *dīwān* (*EI*[2], s.v.).

Emir: see amir.

Faqīh: see *fiqh*.

Farsakh: a measure of distance, based on the ancient Persian parasang and used in the eastern provinces of the Caliphate. It was regarded as the equivalent of three miles, as used in the western (ex-Byzantine) provinces. The mile, of 4000 cubits (*dhirā'*), is estimated at about 2 kilometers (*EI*², s.v.; *IMG*, pp. 62–63).

Fatwā: a ruling or opinion on a point of holy law issued by a muftī (*q.v.*) and corresponding to the Roman *Responsa prudentium*. The Turkish form is *fetva* (*EI*², s.v.).

Fetva: see *Fatwā*.

Fiqh: the technical term for the science of Islamic law. The doctors of the law are called *faqīh*. Of the various schools of *fiqh* that arose among Sunnī Muslims, four are regarded as orthodox. They are named after the jurists whose teachings they follow: Ḥanafī (after Abū Ḥanīfa, d. 767); Mālikī (after Mālik ibn Anas, d. 795); Shāfi'ī (after al-Shāfi'ī, d. 820); and Ḥanbalī (after Aḥmad ibn Ḥanbal, d. 855). The Shī'a, Khārijites, and other sects have their own schools of jurisprudence, differing in some particulars from those of the Sunnīs (*EI*², "Fiḳh").

Fitna: a word originally meaning "testing" or "temptation," commonly used in the sense of sedition and upheaval (*EI*², s.v.).

Ghāzī: an Arabic term originally meaning "one who took part in a *ghazwa*," razzia; later used to designate those who took part in the Holy War against the unbelievers. The name was also adopted by associations of march warriors, notably in Anatolia (*EI*², s.v.).

Ghiyār: the compulsory mark or sign worn by the *dhimmīs* (see *dhimma*) to distinguish them from Muslims. It usually consisted of a patch of cloth of a prescribed color and sometimes also of other items of clothing (*EI*², s.v.).

Ghulām: a young, male slave. The term is variously used of a servant or bodyguard, a palace guard or attendant, a young mamlūk (q.v.), or an artisan bound to a master. The term, the root meaning of which is "young man," is sometimes also used of freedmen bound by certain ties to their former masters (see *mawlā*) and even of free servants and attendants (*EI*², s.v.).

Ḥadd (plural *Ḥudūd*): impediment, limit, frontier, and hence the restrictive commandments contained in the Qur'ān. In the technical vocabulary of Islamic law, *ḥadd* denotes the punishments for certain offenses specified in the Qur'ān. The offenses are fornication, false accusation of fornication, drinking wine, theft, and highway robbery. The punishments are execution, amputation of the hand and/or foot, and flogging (*EI*², s.v.).

Ḥadīth: a tradition relating an action, utterance, or decision of the Prophet. The corpus of *ḥadīth* constitutes one of the major sources of Islamic law (*EI*², s.v.).

Ḥajj: the pilgrimage to Mecca, 'Arafāt and Minā, required of a Muslim at least once in his lifetime. One who has performed the pilgrimage is called *Ḥājj* in Arabic and *Ḥajjī* in Persian and Turkish (*EI*², s.v.).

Ḥanafī: see *fiqh.*

Ḥanbalī: see *fiqh.*

Ḥaram: an Arabic term conveying the meaning of forbidden, sacrosanct, or taboo. It is used especially for the holy places in Mecca and Medina and for sanctuaries in Jerusalem, Karbalā', Meshed, and elsewhere. The word is also used at times to designate the women's quarters of a house.

Hijra: often misspelled *Hegira;* the migration of the Prophet Muḥammad from Mecca to Medina in A.D. 622, according to most accounts on September 20. The Muslim calendar dates, not, as is commonly supposed, from the *Hijra,* but from the beginning of the Arab year in which the *Hijra* took place, that is, from July 16, 622. The Muslim year is purely lunar and has 354 days. The months do not therefore correspond to seasons, and there are approximately 103 Hijrī years to one hundred solar years according to the Gregorian calendar (*EI*², s.v.).

Ḥisba: see *muḥtasib.*

Ichoghlanï: a Turkish term, literally "inside boy," meaning "page of the inner (palace) service." It was applied in Ottoman usage to the boys recruited through the *devshirme* (*q.v.*) and also to other recruits—slaves, hostages, and later even free-born Muslims—selected and trained for the palace and imperial services (*EI*², "'Ič-oghlanï").

'Īd: festival. There are two major religious festivals in the Muslim year: the festival of sacrifices (*'Īd al-aḍḥā*), which is connected with the Pilgrimage to Mecca, and the festival of breaking the fast (*'Īd al-fiṭr*) after the end of Ramaḍān (*EI*², s.v.).

Ijāza: license, that is, to teach; the document given by a Muslim teacher to a disciple certifying that he has satisfactorily attended a course and is therefore able to teach it. The certificate is often appended to the disciple's transcript of his master's lectures (*EI*[2], s.v.).

Ijmā‘: consensus (that is, of the *‘ulema’*), one of the major sources of Islamic law. Technically it is defined as "the unanimous doctrine and opinion of the recognized religious authorities at any given time." In the absence of any constituted ecclesiastical authority in medieval Islam, it comes to mean something like the climate of opinion among the learned and the powerful (*EI*[2], s.v.).

Ijtihād: literally, "exerting onself"; in the technical language of Islamic law, "the use of individual reasoning," later restricted to "reasoning by analogy." In the late ninth century it came to be accepted that only the great masters of early Islam had had the right to use individual reasoning and that, since all important questions had been considered and resolved by them, "the gate of *ijtihād* was closed." One who exercised *ijtihād* was called *mujtahid* (*EI*[2], s.v. "‘Idjtihād").

Il-Khan: see khan.

Imām: a leader, especially in prayer, and hence by extension the sovereign head of the universal Islamic state and community. *Imām* is one of the titles of the Caliph and that most commonly used by the jurists when discussing the laws relating to the Caliphate. The term is also used by the Shī‘a for their own claimants to the headship of Islam and in this sense connotes an extensive spiritual authority absent from Sunnī usage. The office of Imam is called *Imāma* (*EI*[2], s.v. "‘Imāma’").

Iqṭā‘: an administrative grant, often misleadingly translated "fief." The term is used generically for a number of different types of grant, each with its own designation. An early form was a cession, in practice irrevocable, of public lands to an individual who collected all taxes on these lands and paid only the tithe to the state (see *‘ushr*). This was in time replaced by another type, the *iqṭā‘* proper, whereby the state granted all its fiscal rights over lands that remained juridically the property of their previous owners. The grantee paid no tax to the state but held his grant in lieu of payment from the public treasury for service. His grant was thus in principle limited, functional, and revocable, and carried only fiscal rights over the land and its inhabitants. At times such *iqṭā'* became long-term or even hereditary. A third type was a form of fiscal autonomy whereby the taxes for a region or group were commuted for a fixed annual payment (*EI*², "Ḍay'a," "Ighār," "Iḳṭā'").

Jāhiliyya: (the time of) ignorance, that is, pre-Islamic Arabia.

Jarīb: a measure of capacity, variously assessed at about 16, 26, 29.5 liters and in Mongol Persia at about 130 liters (*IMG*, p. 38). *Jarīb* was also used of a square measure, fixed for canonical purposes at 1592 square meters but with local variants (*IMG*, pp. 65–66).

Jihād: literally effort or striving; the name commonly given to the Holy War for Islam against the unbelievers. Jihād, in medieval times usually understood in a military sense, was a collective duty imposed on the Muslim community by the Holy Law. A fighter in *jihād* is called *mujāhid* (*EI*², "Djihād").

Jizya: the poll tax paid by protected non-Muslim subjects of the Muslim state (see *dhimma*). The rate was in time fixed by Holy Law at one, two, or four gold pieces per annum for each adult male, according to his wealth (*EI*², "Djizya").

Jund: an Arabic word of Iranian origin denoting troops or an army. In the early Caliphate it was used especially for the army corps quartered in the various districts of Syria and Palestine and hence to the districts themselves. The term was not used in this sense for the military districts of Iraq or Egypt, but it reappeared in Spain with the settlement of the eastern *junds* from 742 A.D. (*EI*², "Djund").

Ka'ba: a cubelike building, almost in the center of the great mosque in Mecca. The Black Stone, venerated as a sacred object, is inside the building, built into the wall at the eastern corner. The four inside walls are covered with black curtains (*kiswa*), fastened to the ground with copper rings. The Ka'ba is regarded as the palladium of Islam and forms the focal point of the ceremonies of pilgrimage (*EI*¹, s.v.).

Kāfir: an unbeliever, that is, one who does not accept Islam. Sometimes this term is applied to a heretical Muslim whose beliefs or practices go beyond the limits of permitted variation. The condition or doctrines of the *kāfir* are called *kufr.* To denounce a person or group as *kāfirs,* or a doctrine as *kufr,* is called *takfīr* (*EI*[1], s.v.).

Khādim: a servant or attendant, whether slave or free, male or female. At certain times and places the term connoted a eunuch; at others, a black slave or slavewoman (*EI*[2], "'Abd"; *EI*[1], s.v.).

Khalīfa: an Arabic term combining the notions of deputy and successor; adopted as title by the successors of Muḥammad in the headship of the Islamic state and community. With the rapid growth of that state into a vast empire, the term came to connote imperial sovereignty, combining both religious and political authority. With the rise of the military power of the amirs and the Sultans, the status of the Caliphs declined, and they became little more than figureheads with some religious prestige as titular heads of Sunnī Islam but no real power. In the forty years after the death of the Prophet, the period known as the patriarchal Caliphate, four Caliphs held office by a form of election. Thereafter the Caliphate became in practice, though not in theory, dynastic and was held by two successive dynasties, the Umayyads based on Syria and the 'Abbasids based on Iraq. The 'Abbasid Caliphate was extinguished by the Mongol conquest in 1258, but a line of puppet Caliphs, sired by a refugee from Baghdad, survived at the Court of the Mamlūk Sultans in Cairo until 1517. Rival Caliphates were maintained for a while by the Umayyads in Cordova and, with an Ismā' īlī religious basis, by the Fatimids in Tunisia and then in Egypt.

Khan: (a) a large building for the accommodation of travelers, merchants, and their wares. In Persia the usual term was *karvānsarāy.* (b) a Turkish title, originally a contraction of *khāqān* which, as a title of sovereignty, usually denoted supremacy over a group of tribes or territories. The title *khan* was used by Turkish Muslim rulers in central Asia from the tenth century onward; in the Mongol period it was at first used exclusively by members of the house of Jenghiz and later, by abuse, by other rulers. The Mongols at first distinguished between *khān* and *khāqān,* reserving the latter for their supreme ruler in East Asia.

The Mongol rulers of Persia were known as *Il-Khāns*, a term indicating subordination to a superior authority (*EI*[2], "Il;" *EI*[1], "Khāḳān," "Khān").

Kharāj: at first a generic term for taxes and tribute, then specialized to mean land tax as opposed to poll tax (*EI*[2], "Ḍarība," "Djizya;" *EI*[1], "Kharadj").

Kharijites: from Arabic *Khārijī*, plural *Khawārij;* the name of the earliest body of sectaries to secede from the main body of Muslims. They differed from others on two main points: in their theory of the Caliphate, which was strictly elective and consensual, and in their rejection of the doctrine of justification by faith without works (*EI*[1], "Kharidjites").

Khāṣṣ, Khāṣṣa: special, particular, as opposed to *'āmm, 'āmma,* general. This pair of words is used in various contexts, especially to denote the contrast between the common people (*'āmma*) and the privileged (*khāṣṣa*), that is, those who have power, wealth, position, descent, and education. The term *khāṣṣ* is also applied to military and other personnel attached to the person of the sovereign, and, later, to crown lands and revenues.

Khaṭīb: see *khuṭba.*

Khil'a: a robe bestowed by a sovereign as a mark of favor or honor (*EI*[1], s.v.).

Khuṭba: an address or sermon given during the public prayers in the mosque on Friday. In early times this was often a pronouncement by the sovereign or governor, dealing with political, military, and similar matters. Later it came to be a kind of sermon delivered by a preacher known as the *khaṭīb* and normally included the bidding-prayer for the sovereign. Mention in the *khuṭba* was one of the recognized tokens of sovereignty or suzerainty in Islam; omission from it was a signal of revolt (*EI*[1], s.v. and "Masdjid," pp. 346–349.

Kunya: part of the Arab personal name. The *kunya* was an appellation consisting of *Abū* (father of) or *Umm* (mother of) and followed by a name, usually that of the bearer's eldest son (*EI*[1], "Ism").

Madhhab: school of religious doctrine or law; usually applied to the four main schools of Sunnī jurisprudence (see *fiqh*).

Madrasa: a college or seminary for Muslim learning, frequently but not necessarily attached to a mosque. The Turkish form is *medrese* (*EI*[1], "Masdjid," pp. 350 ff.).

Mahdī: divinely guided; a messianic figure of the kin of the Prophet who according to popular belief, will return to earth and inaugurate an era of justice and plenty. His coming will be preceded and accompanied by various signs and portents. Many pretenders to this office have appeared in the course of the centuries. For the Twelver Shī'a (q.v.), the Mahdī is the twelfth Imam in the line of 'Alī ibn Abī Ṭālib, the cousin and son-in-law of the Prophet (*EI*[1], s.v.).

Makrūh: disapproved, deplored. Islamic law classifies actions in five categories: mandatory, recommended, permitted, disapproved, and forbidden (*EI*[1], "Sharī'a," p. 322).

Mālikī: see *Fiqh.*

Mamlūk: owned, hence a slave. The term mamlūk was in practice restricted to male white slaves, in particular those serving in the army and in government. This form of slavery came to be the usual path to military and political preferment and power. Many dynasties were founded by mamlūks, the most notable being the Egyptian regime known to scholarship but not to contemporaries as the Mamlūk Sultanate, which lasted from about 1250 to 1517.

Maqṣūra: a box or compartment erected in the mosque for the ruler, usually near the prayer niche (*EI*[1], "Masdjid," p. 336).

Mawālī: see *mawlā.*

Mawlā (plural *mawālī*): an Arabic term, the commonest meaning of which is "freed slave," "freedman," or "client." After liberation, the *mawlā* retains certain ties with his former master and becomes a client member of his master's tribe. The same term was used by adoptive or client members of a tribe who were not necessarily former slaves. In the early Islamic centuries the term *mawālī* was applied generally to the non-Arab converts to Islam.

Maẓālim: plural of *maẓlama* (grievance). *Al-Naẓar fi'l-maẓālim* (the investigation of grievances) was a court of inquiry, conducted at first by the Caliph in person and later by an official appointed for the purpose, to examine complaints of miscarriage or denial of justice brought against agents of the government, powerful individuals, or the qāḍīs themselves. It became a regular judicial institution with its own rules and procedure (*EI*², "Nāẓir al-Maẓālim"; Schacht, p. 51).

Milk (in Ottoman usage *mülk*): a form of ownership in Islamic law, corresponding approximately to the modern freehold. A grant of *milk* was called *tamlīk* (*EI*², s.v.; Schacht, p. 136).

Mithqāl: a unit of weight, particularly for precious metals, based on the Byzantine *solidus*. The dinar weighed one *mithqāl* of an average standard weight of 4.231 grams (*EI*¹, "Mithḳāl"; *IMG*, pp. 1–2).

Muʿāhad: see *ʿahd.*

Mudd: a canonical measure of capacity in early Islam, probably a little over a liter (*IMG*, pp. 45–46).

Muftī: an authoritative specialist in Islamic law, competent to issue a *fatwā* (*q.v.*). Unlike the qāḍī (q.v.), the muftī was not at first an official appointee. His status was private, his function advisory and voluntary, and his authority derived from his personal scholarly reputation. Later some rulers appointed official muftīs from among recognized scholars, without thereby increasing their authority or eliminating the private practitioners (Schacht, pp. 73–75).

Muḥtasib: an officer entrusted with the maintenance of public morals and standards in the city, especially in the markets. His task is defined as "to promote good and prevent evil," that is, detect and punish immorality, the use of false weights and measures, the adulteration of wares and similar offenses, and generally to enforce the rules of honesty, propriety, and hygiene. He was appointed by the state but was usually a jurist (*faqīh*) by training. The function of the *Muḥtasib* is called *ḥisba* (*EI*¹, s.v.; *EI*², "Ḥisba").

Mujāwir: a sojourner, especially in or near a mosque or holy place, whose purpose was study or religious meditation.

Mujāhid: see *jihād.*

Mujtahid: see *ijtihād.*

Muqāṭaʿa: a term used in a variety of technical senses, mostly connected with the collection of taxes in the form of a global, agreed sum instead of by variable, separate assessment. It often, but not always, connotes some form of tax farming.

Murābiṭ: see *ribāṭ*.
Musta'min: see *amān*.
Muwallad: literally begotten, born; originally a person, usually a slave, of non-Arab origin brought up among the Arabs. The term was later applied to the children of non-Arab converts to Islam to distinguish them from first-generation converts (see *mawlā*). Later the term was applied to the children of mixed marriages, Arab and non-Arab, slave and free, black and white. At some stage it seems to have acquired the meaning of mulatto (*EI*[1], s.v.).
Nā'ib: a deputy or substitute, especially of a qāḍī. In the Mamlūk Sultanate the *Nā'ib al-Salṭana* was a sort of deputy Sultan (*EI*[1], s.v.).
Pādishāh: a Persian title of sovereignty, often understood to connote imperial supremacy. It was used chiefly by Persian and Turkish-speaking dynasties.
Qāḍī: a judge administering the Holy Law of Islam (*EI*[2], "Ḳāḍī;" Schacht, pp. 34 ff; 50 ff; 188 ff).
Qā'id: leader, especially a military leader or senior officer. In Muslim Spain it connoted a general, an admiral, or even a commander-in-chief. In North Africa it was also used for tribal or regional chiefs recognized or appointed by the government (*EI*[2], "Ḳā'id").
Qalansuwa: a high, often conical cap worn by men, either under the turban or by itself (Dozy, pp. 365–371; *EI*[1], "Ḳalansuwa").
Qayṣariyya: From Greek *kaisareia*, imperial, belonging to Caesar; a public building or group of buildings with markets, shops, workshops, warehouses, and sometimes living quarters (*EI*[1], "Ḳaiṣarīya").
Qibla: The direction of Mecca, toward which Muslims turn in prayer. In mosques it is indicated by the prayer niche (*miḥrāb*) (*EI*[1], "Ḳibla").
Qīrāṭ: from the Greek *keration*, a grain or seed; one twenty-fourth part of a *mithqāl* and, by extension, one twenty-fourth part of any whole. As a unit of weight for commodities, the *qīrāṭ* shows some variation (*EI*[1], "Ḳīrāṭ"; *IMG*, p. 27).
Qisṭ: a measure of capacity, variously assessed at from 1.2 to 2.5 liters (*IMG*, p. 50).

Qurrā': readers, especially of the Qur'ān.
Raṭl: a unit of weight, varying greatly with time, place, and the material weighed and ranging from under a pound to more than 4 pounds (*EI*[1], s.v.; *IMG*, pp. 27–33).
Ra'īs: head or chief; a title given to certain functionaries in medieval Islamic administration. The *ra'īs* might be the head of a government department (see *dīwān*). Under the Seljuqs and their successors the term was most commonly used for the officer in charge of civil affairs in a city, whose duties included police duties. He might be either a notable of the city, recognized and appointed by the royal authority, or a royal officer.
Ribāṭ: a fortified Muslim monastery, usually in the border areas between the Islamic world and its non-Muslim neighbors. Its inhabitants, called *Murābiṭ* (plural *Murābiṭūn*), were pious volunteers, dedicated to the Holy War for Islam (*EI*[1], s.v.).
Rūm: the Arabic word for Rome. In medieval times this was the normal Islamic term for the Byzantine Empire and was sometimes extended to European Christians in general. After the Turkish invasion of Anatolia, the term was commonly used for the former Byzantine territories under Turkish rule and sometimes even for the Turks themselves.
Ṣadaqa: alms, probably from the Hebrew *ṣedāqā;* sometimes used in the general sense of almsgiving and sometimes, more technically, as a synonym of *zakāt* (q.v.) (*EI*[1], "Ṣadaḳa").
Sayyid: lord, master. At first this title was applied to the chief of an Arabian tribe; later it was used as an honorific appellation for other men of authority, including Sufi saints and teachers. *Sayyidī* or *Sīdī* ("my master"), was a usual form of respectful address to such persons. The term *Sayyid* was also used extensively, but not exclusively, for the descendants of the Prophet (*EI*[1], "Sharīf," pp. 325–326).
Shāfi'ī: see *fiqh*.
Shāhid: a witness, more specifically one whose name appears on the list of trustworthy witnesses drawn up under the qāḍī's authority (see *'adāla*).
Sharī'a: the Holy Law of Islam (*EI*[1], s.v.).
Sharīf (plural *Ashrāf*): noble, well-born; at first used generally

of the leading families, then more particularly of the descendants of the Prophet (*EI*[1], s.v.).

Shaykh: an Arabic word meaning "old man," "elder"; used in a wide variety of contexts: for the chiefs of tribes, religious dignitaries, for the heads of religious fraternities or of craft guilds and generally as a term of respect for men of position, authority, or advancing years.

Shīʿa: party or faction, hence specifically the party of ʿAlī, the kinsman and son-in-law of the Prophet. The *Shīʿa* began as a group of Muslims who advocated the claims of ʿAlī, and later of his descendants, to the Caliphate. It developed rapidly into a religious movement differing on a number of points of doctrine and law from Sunnī Islam. The Shīʿa split into many subsects the most important of which are the *Ithnāʿasharī* (Twelver) Shīʿa (so called because of their acceptance of twelve Imams), the Ismāʿīlīs, and the Zaydīs (*EI*[1], s.v.).

Sipāhī: a Persian word meaning "soldier" and later specialized to mean a horse soldier. In the Ottoman Empire the *sipāhī* was a quasi-feudal cavalryman who received a grant known as *timar* (*EI*[1], "Timar"; *EI*[2], "ʿAskarī").

Sulṭān: an abstract noun meaning ruler or power, particularly that of the government. At first informally, then, from the eleventh century, officially, it was applied to the person of the ruler and came to designate the supreme political and military authority, as contrasted with the religious authority to which the Caliphs were increasingly restricted (*EI*[1], s.v.).

Sunna: see Sunnī.

Sunnī: a Muslim belonging to the dominant majority group in Islam, sometimes loosely translated "orthodox." A Sunnī is a follower of the *Sunna,* the accepted practice and beliefs of the Islamic community, based on the precedents of the Prophet, his Companions, and his accredited successors, as established and interpreted by the consensus (see *ijmāʿ*) of the learned (*EI*[1], s.v.).

Tamlīk: see *milk.*

Takbīr: to pronounce the formula *Allahu Akbar,* God is very great (*EI*[1], s.v.).

Tarāwīḥ: special prayers recited during the night in Ramaḍān (*EI*[1], s.v.).
Ṭaylasān: A kind of hood or scarf, worn over the head and shoulders or the shoulders only. In earlier times it was regarded as the distinguishing mark of the doctors of the Holy Law (Dozy, pp. 254 ff., 272 ff.).
Timar: see *sipāhī.*
Ṭirāz: a word of Persian origin meaning embroidery, hence embroidered or brocaded robes, and then the workshop, usually state-controlled, in which these were manufactured. *Ṭirāz* was often embroidered with suitable inscriptions. The wearing of *ṭirāz* and the granting of *ṭirāz* to other persons were royal prerogatives (*EI*[1], s.v.).
'Ulamā': plural of *'ālim,* a scholar, specifically in religious subjects. The term *'ulamā'* is used to describe the class of professional men of religious learning who form the nearest Muslim entity to a clergy (*EI*[1], s.v.).
Ulema: an Anglicized Turkish form of the Arabic *'ulamā'* (q.v.).
Umm walad: literally mother of a child; a slave-women who has born her master a child and thereby acquired certain legal rights (*EI*[1], s.v.).
Umma: an Arabic term meaning approximately "community," used of both religious and ethnic entities. The two were not clearly differentiated, although the religious meaning usually predominated. The term was commonly used for the religio-political community of Islam as a whole; it was also used for non-Muslim entities, both religious (for example, the Christians) and, less commonly, ethnic (for example, the Franks). It was not normally used in medieval times for ethnic groups within Islam.
'Ushr: tithe; a tax imposed by the Holy Law on Muslim-owned property for charitable and other purposes (*EI*[1], s.v.).
Vizier: see *wazīr.*
Walī: a term with several distinct meanings, derived from the Arabic root *waliya,* to be near, to be friends, to rule, to take charge, or to control. In the religious sense it means something like saint or holy man, that is, a friend of God. In law it denotes a guardian or legal tutor. In political and administrative usage

it means the authorized holder or executant of an office, a function, a duty, or a privilege.

Waqf: a form of endowment or trust, of land or other income-producing property, the proceeds of which are assigned by the founder to a specific purpose. The endowment, which is irrevocable and permanent, may be either for some pious object, such as a mosque, school, or charity, or for the benefit of named persons, normally the founder's family (*EI*[1], "Waḳf").

Wāsiṭa: an officer of state under the Fatimid Caliphs, corresponding approximately to the *wazīr* (q.v.).

Wazīr: A high officer of state, usually a civilian. The power and status of the office varied greatly. In some periods, as under the early 'Abbasids, the *wazīr* was the head of the bureaucracy and virtually in charge of the day-to-day conduct of government. Under the Seljuq Sultans he was effectively head of the administration. At other times he was a relatively minor official. The Ottoman Sultans had several *wazīrs,* the chief of whom came to be known as the Grand Vizier (*EI*[1], s.v.).

Zakāt: the alms tax, one of the five basic duties of a Muslim. According to Islamic law it is collected from certain categories of property and assigned to certain specified purposes (*EI*[1], s.v.).

Zanj, Zanjī: a word of uncertain origin, used to designate the people of East Africa, and hence more loosely, blacks in general.

Zindīq: a word of uncertain, probably Iranian origin. At first it was applied to the Manicheans but was later used extensively to denote the holders of unpopular or heretical beliefs, particularly those regarded as dangerous to the state and society (*EI*[1], s.v.).

Zunnār: from the Aramaic *zunnārā* and ultimately from the Greek *zōnē,* a belt. In medieval Islam the name was used in particular for the distinctive belt or sash which non-Muslims were required to wear (*EI*[1], s.v.).

Index